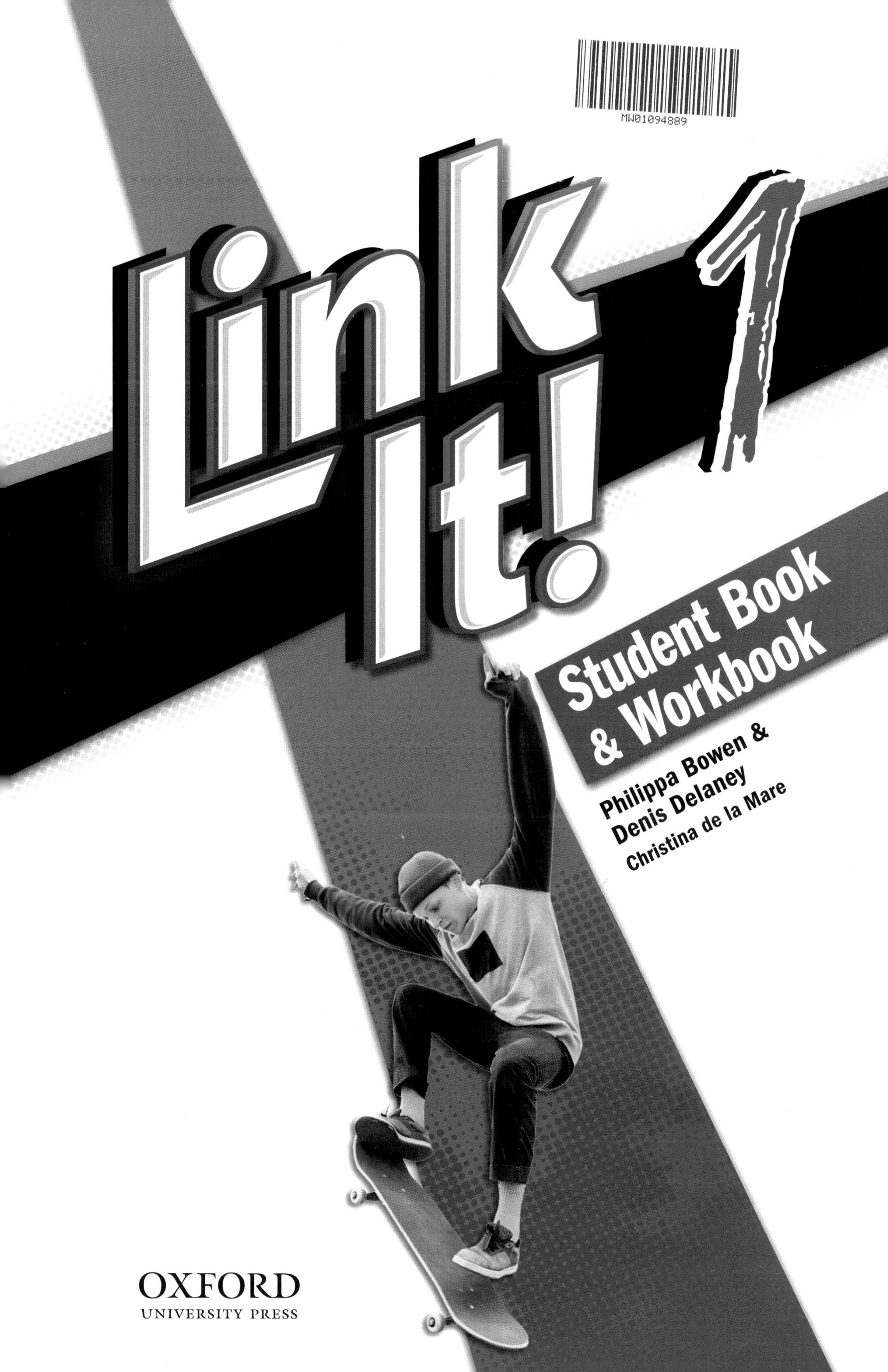
MW01094889
Link It! 1
Student Book & Workbook
Philippa Bowen & Denis Delaney
Christina de la Mare
OXFORD
UNIVERSITY PRESS

Contents

W Welcome to Link It! 1

Classroom language

1 **Match the sentences in the box with the pictures 1–7.**

~~Open your books!~~ Read! Look! Listen! Sit down! Don't write! Close your books! Don't talk!

Open your books!

1 ____________

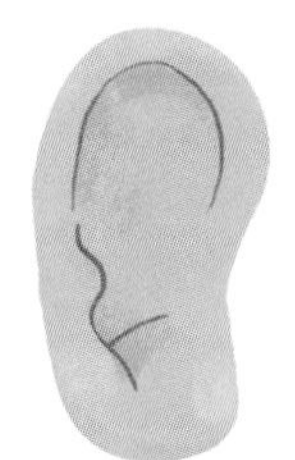

2 ____________

3 ____________

4 ____________

5 ____________

6 ____________

7 ____________

2 **Match the sentence halves.**

1 Write — c
2 Open
3 Look
4 Talk
5 Read
6 Listen

a to the song.
b at the picture.
c your name.
d your books to page 11.
e the email on page 6.
f to your partner.

3 **Complete the questions with the words in the box. How do you say the questions in your language?**

~~restroom~~ book board the dictionary

Can I go to the *restroom*, please?

1 Can I use ____________, please?
2 Can I go to the ____________, please?
3 Can I write in the ____________?

Look!

Use these expressions to say *yes* or *no* to questions with *Can I ...?*

✓ *Yes, of course.*

✗ *No, I'm sorry. You can't.*

4 002 **Listen. Does the teacher say *yes* or *no* to the questions? Put a check (✓) or an ✗.**

1 [✗] 2 [ ] 3 [ ] 4 [ ]

5 **Pairwork** **Use the prompts to ask and answer questions.**

use a dictionary? (✓)

Can I use a dictionary?

Yes, of course.

1 talk to my partner? (✓)
2 go to the board? (✗)
3 use a red pen? (✗)
4 go to the restroom? (✓)

The alphabet

6 003 **Listen. Then listen again and repeat.**

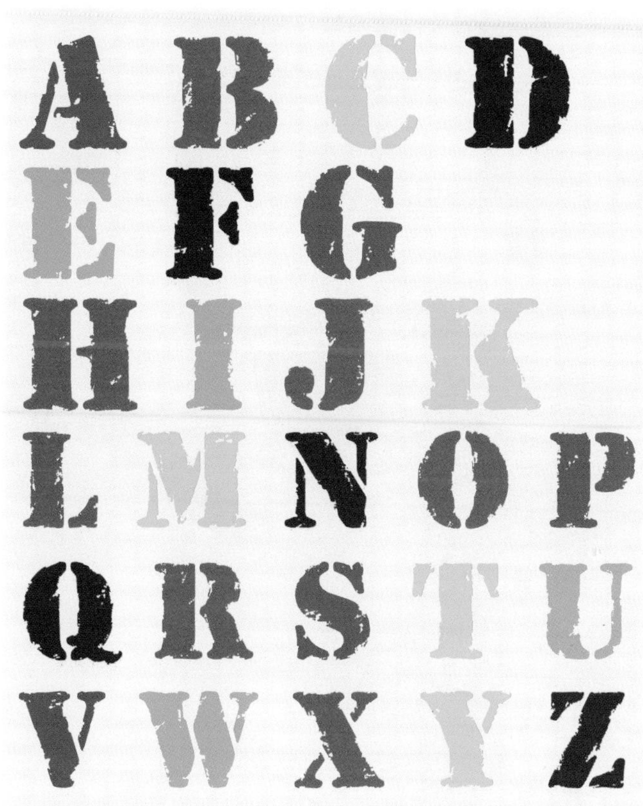

7 004 **Listen and sing the alphabet song.**

8 005 **Listen and choose the letters you hear.**

	U	(W)	3	J	Y	6	I	Y
1	A	E	4	A	H	7	S	C
2	E	I	5	G	J	8	O	U

9 006 **Listen and write the names you hear. Then compare your answers with your partner.**

Vanessa 3 ______
1 ______ 4 ______
2 ______ 5 ______

10 007 **Real English** **Listen. Then listen again and repeat. Practice the dialogue with a partner. Then, in pairs, write a similar dialogue with information about you.**

1
A What's your name?
B My name's Clara.
A How do you spell that?
B C-L-A-R-A.

2
A What's your last name, Clara?
B My last name's Espinosa.
A How do you spell that?
B E-S-P-I-N-O-S-A.

Numbers (0–100)

11 **Complete the chart with the numbers in the box.**

~~two~~ twelve twenty-seven seventeen five twenty eight thirteen twenty-two three

0	zero	16	sixteen
1	one	17	______
2	*two*	18	eighteen
3	______	19	nineteen
4	four	20	______
5	______	21	twenty-one
6	six	22	______
7	seven	23	twenty-three
8	______	24	twenty-four
9	nine	25	twenty-five
10	ten	26	twenty-six
11	eleven	27	______
12	______	28	twenty-eight
13	______	29	twenty-nine
14	fourteen	30	thirty
15	fifteen	31	thirty-one

12 008 **Listen and choose the numbers you hear.**

	(13)	30	2	15	50	4	17	70
1	14	40	3	16	60	5	18	80

13 009 **Listen and complete the sentences.**

How old are you?

1 Lisa — I'm ____.
2 Mr. Davis — I'm ____.
3 Sam — I'm ____.
4 Mom — I'm ____.

14 **Pairwork** **Complete the chart with eight numbers from 1–100. Listen to your teacher and play *Bingo!***

Bingo!

8		13	
	27		
			99

School things

15 Look at the picture of the classroom. Match the words in the box with the objects a–f in the picture.

clock <u>b</u>	board ____	laptop ____	desk ____	door ____	chair ____

16 Match the words (a–l) with the objects 1–12 on the desk.

a pen <u>7</u>
b ruler ____
c backpack ____
d notebook ____
e pencil sharpener ____
f pencil ____
g magic marker ____
h calculator ____
i colored pencils ____
j pencil case ____
k textbook ____
l eraser ____

17 Find ten more school things in the wordsearch.

M N O T E B O O K S T S
A T Y P J A L L H H R M
G E P E N C I L C A S E
I X O N M K A R T R K A
C T N B N P R U Y P A G
M B F E R A S E R E Y Z
A O I O A C U A N N P A
R O L E R K B R O E L W
K K N I O D K U V R N B
E A C A L C U L A T O R
R P E N C I L E V X R Y
A C K C R O A R L N D E

Telling the time

18 Complete the sentences with the numbers.

~~five~~	forty	fifty	ten	fifty-five	twenty-five

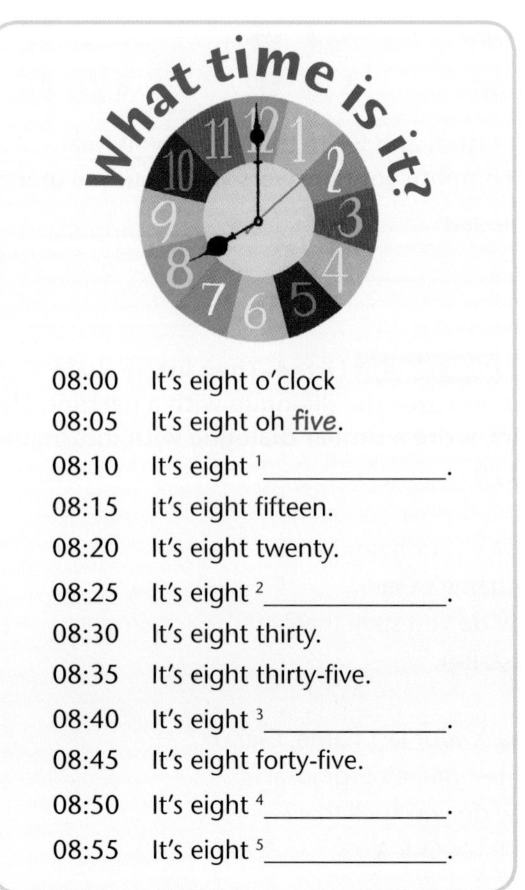

08:00 It's eight o'clock
08:05 It's eight oh <u>five</u>.
08:10 It's eight [1]______________.
08:15 It's eight fifteen.
08:20 It's eight twenty.
08:25 It's eight [2]______________.
08:30 It's eight thirty.
08:35 It's eight thirty-five.
08:40 It's eight [3]______________.
08:45 It's eight forty-five.
08:50 It's eight [4]______________.
08:55 It's eight [5]______________.

19 010 **Look at the clocks. Write the time. Then listen and repeat.**

It's six o'clock.

1 It's ______________.

2 It's ______________.

3 It's ______________.

4 It's ______________.

5 It's ______________.

20 **Pairwork** **Write three times in your notebook. Ask and answer questions about the times.**

6:45

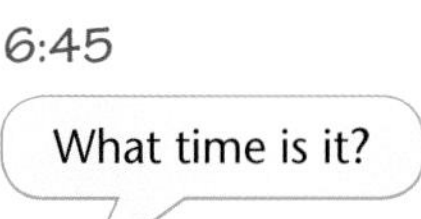

It's six forty-five.

Days and months

21 **Find the days of the week in the wordsearch.**

~~Saturday~~ Thursday Friday Monday Sunday Wednesday Tuesday

S	A	T	U	R	D	A	Y	S
H	O	H	R	D	W	J	C	U
F	T	U	E	S	D	A	Y	N
E	F	R	I	D	A	Y	O	D
R	L	S	U	R	H	N	M	A
W	E	D	N	E	S	D	A	Y
Y	S	A	L	C	A	Y	W	L
N	H	Y	M	O	N	D	A	Y

Look!

In English, we write the days of the week and the months with a capital letter.

Monday, Tuesday, ... January, February, ...

Look!

In American English, we write dates like this:
September 19th

We write dates with numbers like this:
September 19th = 09/19

month day

22 **Look at Alessa's notebook. Complete the sentences with the correct month. Which month is missing?**

Veronica: 12/30	Renzo: 11/13
Sandra: 01/24	David: 07/20
Cisca: 10/31	Jack: 08/06
Alexander: 05/29	Omar: 03/09
Eva: 04/14	Pablo: 02/26
Ruth: 09/01	

Veronica's birthday is in December.

1 Cisca's birthday is in ______________.
2 Jack's birthday is in ______________.
3 Renzo's birthday is in ______________.
4 Sandra's birthday is in ______________.
5 Alexander's birthday is in ______________.
6 David's birthday is in ______________.
7 Eva's birthday is in ______________.
8 Ruth's birthday is in ______________.
9 Pablo's birthday is in ______________.
10 Omar's birthday is in ______________.

Missing month: ______________

23 **Match the words in the box with the pictures.**

winter summer spring fall

1 __________

2 __________

3 __________

4 __________

24 **Pairwork** **Ask and answer questions about your favorite day, month, and season.**

What is your favorite day / month / season?

My favorite day / month / season is ...

Pets and colors

25 **Match the words in the box with the pictures.**

mouse ~~cat~~ fish bird rabbit horse dog snake hamster guinea pig

cat

1 ____________

2 ____________

3 ____________

4 ____________

5 ____________

6 ____________

7 ____________

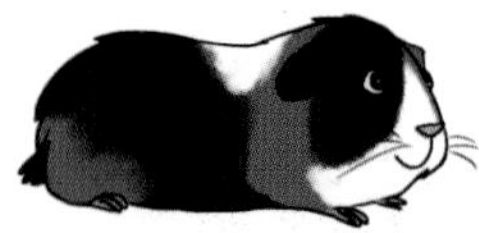

8 ____________

9 ____________

26 011 **Listen and complete the chart with the names in the box.**

Inma	a *dog* and a [1]__________
John	a [2]__________ and a hamster
Emilio	two [3]__________
Kevin	three [4]________ and a [5]________________
Jazmin	a [6]________

27 **Pairwork** **Ask and answer about your pets.**

Do you have pets?

Yes, I have ... / No, I don't have any pets.

28 **Match the words in the box with the colors in the pictures.**

~~black~~ white red blue yellow green brown orange purple pink gray

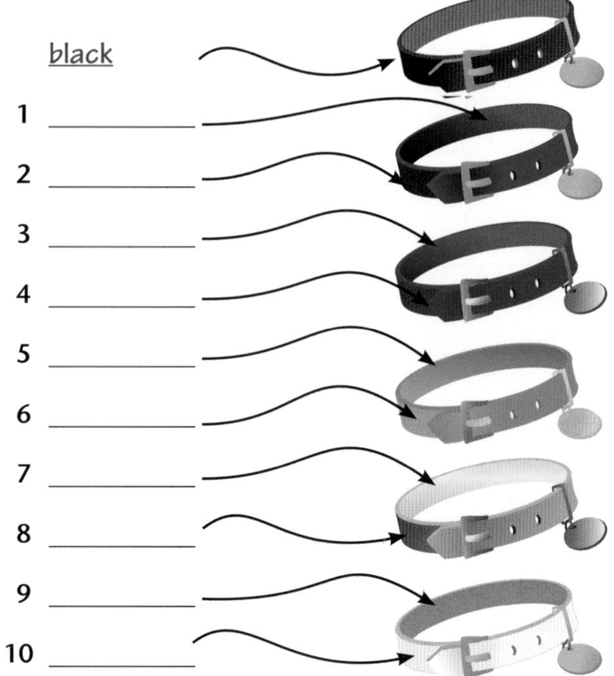

black

1 ____________

2 ____________

3 ____________

4 ____________

5 ____________

6 ____________

7 ____________

8 ____________

9 ____________

10 ____________

29 **Read and color the animals.**

I have a bird. He's green, red, and yellow. His name is Kiko.

I love my dog! She's brown and white. She's 4, and her name is Mel.

This is my cat, Jacqui. She's orange and black.

My sister has a blue and pink fish. It's very beautiful.

Parts of the body

0 Look at the selfie. Match the words in the box with the correct parts of the body.

leg hand ~~hair~~ finger eye arm toe nose shoulder mouth foot ear

1 hair
2 ________
3 ________
4 ________
5 ________
6 ________
7 ________
8 ________
9 ________
10 ________
11 ________
12 ________

31 Copy the letters with the same color. Put the letters in the correct order to make parts of the body words.

A	I	E		A	S	A		O	Y	U
E	R	G		O	H	R		F	T	T
R	F	N		D	N	N		O	E	H
M	A	R		E	I	H		E	M	O

finger

1 ________
2 ________
3 ________
4 ________
5 ________
6 ________
7 ________
8 ________

32 Read the descriptions. Look at the picture and complete the sentences with the correct name.

Charlie
Max
Sam

1 Hi! I'm ________.
I have blond hair and blue eyes.

2 Hello! I'm ________.
I have black hair and brown eyes.

3 Hi! I'm ________.
I have red hair and green eyes.

33 012 **Real English** **Listen and repeat. In pairs, practice introducing yourself. Use information that is true for you.**

Hi, I'm Rosanna and I'm 12.
I have brown hair and blue eyes.

1 It's your big day!

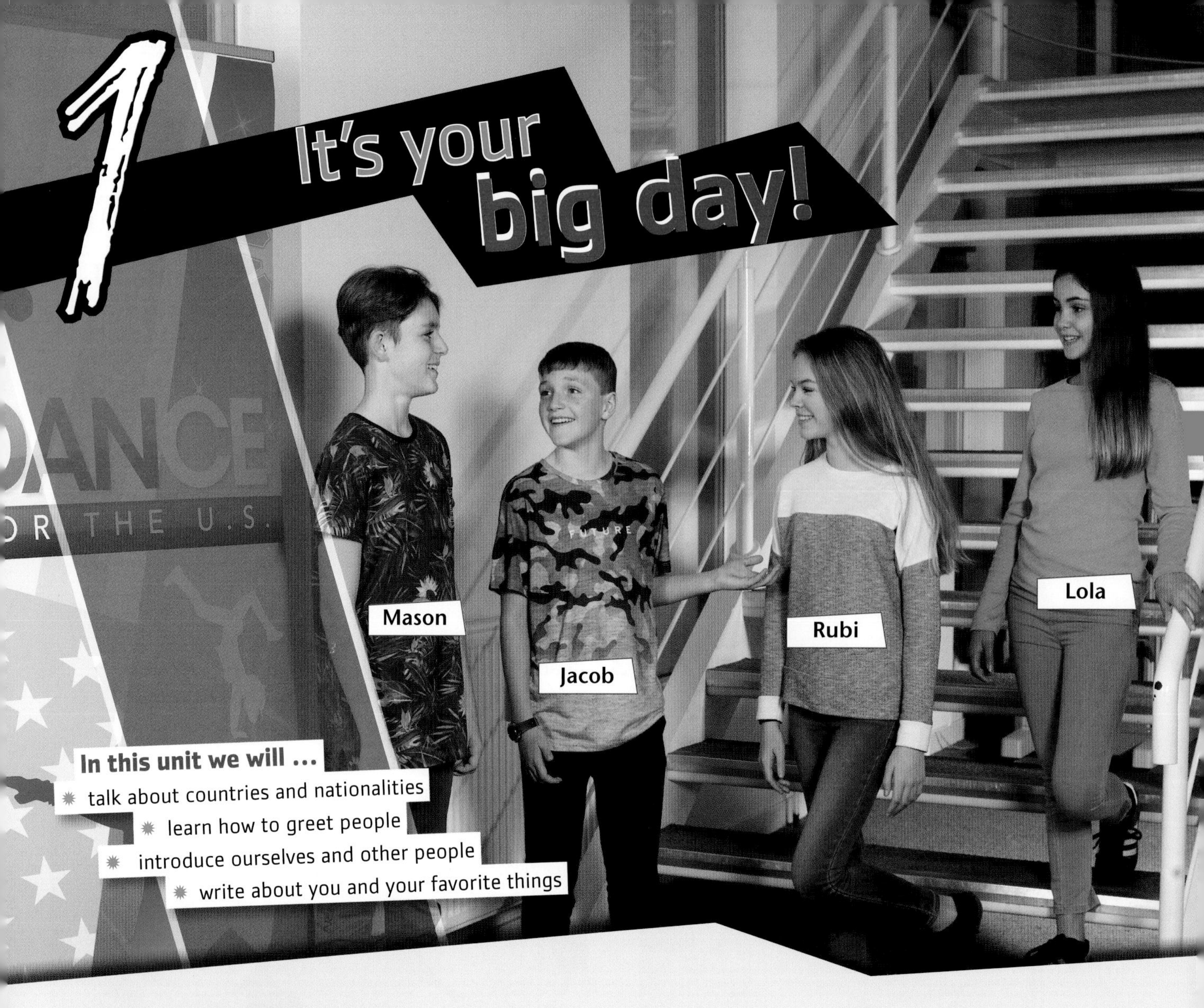

In this unit we will ...

- talk about countries and nationalities
- learn how to greet people
- introduce ourselves and other people
- write about you and your favorite things

1 013 **Read and listen** **Who is nervous: Mason or Jacob?** ___________

It's a big day for Mason and Jacob. They're at the auditions for the *Dance for the U.S.* competition, but Mason is late ...

Jacob You're late!
Mason Chill out, Jacob. I'm here now.
Jacob I'm nervous.
Mason Don't worry, we're a great team.
Jacob Oh no, the judges are here!
Mason Look, it's Simon Jackson.
Jacob He's a great dancer. His dance schools are in Australia, the U.K., Japan, and Turkey. They're very famous!
Mason Yes, he's my hero!
Jacob Oh, here's Rubi ...
Mason With a friend. She's nice!
Rubi Hi, guys.
Lola Hello, I'm Lola.
Mason Hi, I'm Mason. And he's Jacob.
Rubi It's your big day!
Mason We're ready, bring it on!

Later ...

Man Mason and Jacob, you're next.

2 **Comprehension** **Match the sentence halves.**

1 I'm	a hero!
2 We're	b big day!
3 He's my	c nervous.
4 She's	d a great team.
5 It's your	e nice!

Check it out!

Find these words and phrases and check their meaning.

competition	I'm nervous.
You're late!	Don't worry
Chill out	bring it on

Link to life **Do you think it's rude to be late? Are you normally late to meet friends, for school, or if you go to the doctor?**

Step 1

3 Find and underline the phrases in the dialogue in exercise 1.

~~You're late!~~ **She's** nice! **I'm** Lola. **It's** your big day! **We're** ready **They're** very famous! **he's** Jacob

Step 2

4 014 **Complete the dialogues with the phrases in the box. Then listen and check.**

They're very famous we're a great team I'm nervous it's Simon Jackson he's Jacob ~~I'm here now~~ I'm Lola

1

Jacob You're late!
Mason Chill out, Jacob. I'm here now.
Jacob [1] ______________________.
Mason Don't worry, [2] ______________________.

2

Mason Look, [3] ______________________.
Jacob He's a great dancer. His dance schools are in Australia, the U.K., Japan, and Turkey. [4] ______________________!

3

Lola Hello, [5] ______________________.
Mason Hi, I'm Mason. And [6] ______________________.
Rubi It's your big day!
Mason We're ready, bring it on!

014 **Now listen again and repeat.**

Step 3

5 **Read the dialogues in exercise 4. Then write similar dialogues. Use the names in the box.**

Boys: Danny Ramon Luis Samuel Gabriel **Girls:** Natalia Lily Catalina Sofia Camila

Hi, I'm Danny.

Hello, Danny. I'm Natalia, and he's Luis.

Hi, Luis!

6 **Pairwork** **Practice your dialogues from exercise 5.**

Workbook p.W4

Countries and nationalities

1 015 **Look at the map and complete the chart with the countries in the box. Then listen and check.**

China Australia Brazil ~~Canada~~ Chile Japan Portugal Turkey Mexico Spain the U.K. the U.S.

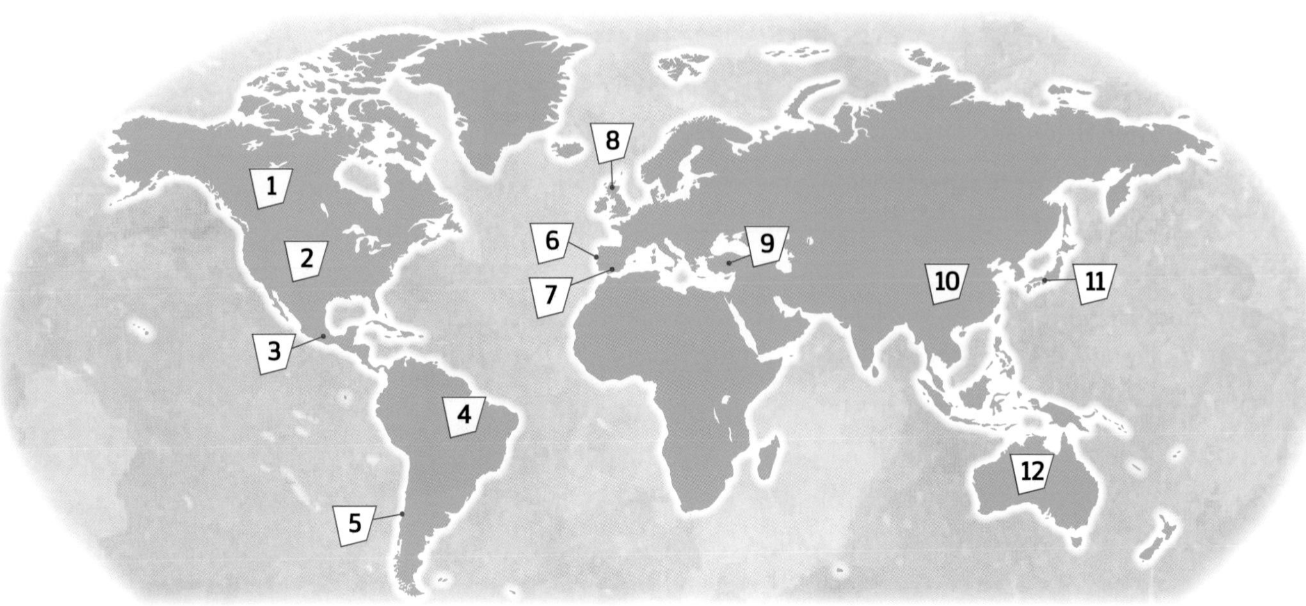

Look!

In English, we use capital letters for countries and nationalities.

She's from Japan. She's Japanese.

		Country	Nationality
1		*Canada*	*Canadian*
2			
3			
4			
5			
6			
7			
8			
9			
10			
11			
12			

2 016 **Complete the chart in exercise 1 with the nationalities. Then listen, check, and repeat.**

Chilean Portuguese Chinese American British Japanese Brazilian ~~Canadian~~ Turkish Spanish Australian Mexican

Vocabulary strategy

Looking for patterns

When you learn new words, look for patterns or similarities. For example, look at the endings of these words:

Japan**ese** – Portugu**ese** – Chin**ese**

Canad**ian** – Austral**ian** – Brazil**ian**

Brit**ish** – Turk**ish** – Span**ish**

3 **Pairwork** **Look at the example. Take turns to choose a city and ask and answer questions.**

Tokyo New York City Beijing London Moscow Sydney Mexico City Brasilia

Where are you from?

I'm from Beijing, in China. I'm Chinese.

Workbook p.W4

Subject pronouns

He's a great dancer.
We're ready.

Singular	Plural
I you he she it	we you they

Rules p.W2

1 Match 1–6 with the subject pronouns a–f.

1 Melissa — c she
2 the city of Lima
3 Jack and I
4 the men
5 David
6 you and Dad

a we
b he
c she
d it
e you
f they

2 Complete the sentences with subject pronouns.

Haru is from Kyoto. He's Japanese.

1 Amy and Ellie are friends. ________'re students.
2 I'm from Natal. ________'s a city in Brazil.
3 Diego Luna is famous. ________'s a great actor.
4 Liam and I are Australian. ________'re from Sydney.
5 Ellie Goulding is British. ________'s a fantastic singer.

Possessive adjectives

His dance schools are in Australia.
It's **your** big day.

Subject pronouns	Possessive adjectives
I	my
you	your
he	his
she	her
it	its
we	our
you	your
they	their

Rules p.W2

Think!

Complete the sentences with the words in the box.

same its his her

Possessive adjectives are the [1]________ for singular and plural.

Leo is my friend. *Leo and Sara are my friends.*

We use [2]________ when we talk about a girl's possession.
We use [3]________ for a boy's possession. When we talk about the possession of a thing, place, animal, etc., we use [4]________.

He's David. It's his pencil.
She's Eva. It's her cell phone.
That's my dog and that's its ball.

3 Choose the correct alternatives.

London is famous for **her** / **(its)** monuments.

1 She's in my class. **Her** / **Your** name's Martha.
2 He's Chilean. **His** / **Its** name's Santiago.
3 We're students at Wood Green High School. **Our** / **Their** school is in Canberra.
4 I'm Brazilian. **Your** / **My** name's Larissa.
5 They're Joe and Helen. **Our** / **Their** mom is my History teacher.
6 "Hi, I'm Maddie."
"Wow, **my** / **your** name is cool!"
7 Jin is Chinese, but **his** / **their** mom is American.
8 "Here are **your** / **their** books." "Thanks."

4 Complete the sentences with a possessive adjective.

I'm Spanish. My name's Daniel.

1 She's Yessica. ________ dad is a teacher.
2 "Hi, I'm Jason. What's ________ name?"
"My name is Lina."
3 We're from Texas. ________ address is 2652 Montana Drive.
4 It's ________ birthday. I'm 13 years old today.
5 You're very good students. ________ grades are excellent.
6 He's my friend. ________ name's Peter.
7 Max and Julieta are in 11th grade. Mrs. Hall is ________ Art teacher.
8 The dance school is in Chicago. ________ name is The Dance Academy.

Challenge

Write a description of a boy and a girl in your class. Include information about:

name age nationality favorite subject

His name's Samuel. He's 12 years old and he's Mexican. His favorite subject is Math.

Puzzles p.118

Grammar link

Workbook p.W4

Greetings

1 017 **Watch, listen, or read** **Complete the dialogues with the words in the box. Then listen again and check.**

1

Not bad	~~Hi~~	And you?	See you later!

Dominic Hey, Arianna!
Arianna Hi, Dominic.
Dominic How are you, Arianna?
Arianna I'm good, thanks. [1] ____________
Dominic [2] ____________, thanks.
Later ...
Dominic Bye then. [3] ____________
Arianna Bye. See you!

2

I'm very well	How are you?	Goodbye
See you on Monday.	Good morning	

Mrs. Bauer [4] ____________, Arianna.
Arianna Hello, Mrs. Bauer.
Mrs. Bauer [5] ____________
Arianna I'm fine, thanks. And you?
Mrs. Bauer [6] ____________, thank you.
Later ...
Mrs. Bauer [7] ____________, Arianna. Have a good day.
Arianna Thanks. Goodbye. [8] ____________

Speaking strategy

Speaking in formal and informal situations

In informal situations, we normally use the person's first name.
Hi, Dominic.

In formal situations, we normally use a title and the person's last name.
Good morning, Mr. Rogers.

For men, we always use *Mr.* (/ˈmɪstər/).

For women with no husband, we use *Miss* (/mɪs/).

For married women, we use *Mrs.* (/ˈmɪsəz/).

If we don't know if a woman is married or not, we can use *Ms.* (/mɪz/).

2 018 **Real English** **Listen and repeat.**

Hey. (informal)
Hello / Hi!
Good morning / afternoon / evening.
How are you?
I'm very well / fine / good / not bad, thanks.
Goodbye / Goodnight.
Bye / Bye then.
See you later!
See you on Monday.
Have a good day / nice weekend.

3 019 Listen to the conversations. Decide if the people are meeting each other (*M*) or leaving each other (*L*).

1 L 2 ____ 3 ____ 4 ____ 5 ____

Beat the clock

In two minutes, create a word map of ways to say hello and goodbye. Then compare with your partner.

Meeting someone

Hello

Leaving someone

Goodbye

4 Pairwork Put the sentences in the correct order to make a dialogue. Then, practice the dialogue.

____ You, too! Bye. ____ Goodbye. ____ Have a good weekend. ____ Hey! How are you?
__1__ Hi, Simon. ____ I'm fine, thanks. And you? ____ Not bad, thanks.

5 Pairwork Write a dialogue between you and your teacher. Use the dialogues in exercise 1 to help you. Practice the dialogue with your partner.

Link it!

Pairwork Look at the pictures. Choose one of the people. Write a dialogue between you and that person.

your aunt

the president of your country

a famous actor

your little cousin

Workbook p.W6 Extra communication p.31

be: Simple present

Affirmative

You**'re** late.
He**'s** my hero.

Full form	Short form
I **am**	I**'m**
you **are**	you**'re**
he **is**	he**'s**
she **is**	she**'s**
it **is**	it**'s**
we **are**	we**'re**
you **are**	you**'re**
they **are**	they**'re**

Rules p.W3

1 Choose the correct alternatives.

I (am) / **is** Portuguese.

1 You **are** / **am** a good dancer.
2 It **is** / **are** my birthday today.
3 We **is** / **are** in 8th grade.
4 They **are** / **am** nice.
5 I **is** / **am** from Paraguay.
6 She **is** / **am** British.

2 Rewrite the sentences in exercise 1 with the short form of the verb *be*.

I'm Portuguese.

1 ______________________.
2 ______________________.
3 ______________________.
4 ______________________.
5 ______________________.
6 ______________________.

3 Complete the sentences with the short form of the verb *be*.

It's a red pen.

1 This is Jen–she____ 14 years old today!
2 I ____ from Istanbul, in Turkey.
3 Messi–he____ my hero.
4 You ____ intelligent!
5 It ____ a pencil case.

Challenge

Write a sentence for each subject pronoun.

I you he she it we you they

I'm from Cali, in Colombia. You're …

4 Complete the texts with the missing subject pronouns and the short form of the verb *be*.

Hi, I'm Charlie. My hometown is Ontario. [1]_______ in Canada. My brother, Max, is 16, and [2]_______ at the same school together. [3]_______ a big school.

This is Josh and Ava. [4]__________ American and [5]__________ students at Edison High School in Miami. Ava is 11, but [6]_______ her birthday next week. Josh is 12 and [7]_______ a fan of rock music.

Think!

Look at the sentences and check (✓) the correct alternative. Then complete the rule.

I'm 13 years old. ☐

I have 13 years old. ☐

In English, we use the verb ______ to talk about our age.

Rules p.W3

5 Complete the chart with information about yourself. Then write a short description of yourself.

Name	
Age	
Nationality	
Town / City	
School	

I'm Juan. I'm 12 years old, and …

Challenge

Write a short description of your best friend. Use the texts in exercise 4 to help you.

He's Alex. He's 11 years old, and he's …

She's Shinhye. She's 12 years old, and she's …

Puzzles p.118

Listening and speaking

Step 1

1 020 **Listen and check (✓) the correct answers.**

Listening strategy

Listening twice

If you don't hear the answer to a question in a listening exercise, leave it, and go to the next question. You will probably listen to the audio twice.

Name	Flor ☑	Vanessa ☐
Age	13 ☐	14 ☐
Town	Lima ☐	Cartago ☐
Nationality	Peruvian ☐	Costa Rican ☐
Favorite singer	Rihanna ☐	Adele ☐
Favorite actor	Ashton Kutcher ☐	Ryan Reynolds ☐

Step 2

2 021 **Listen and complete the paragraphs.**

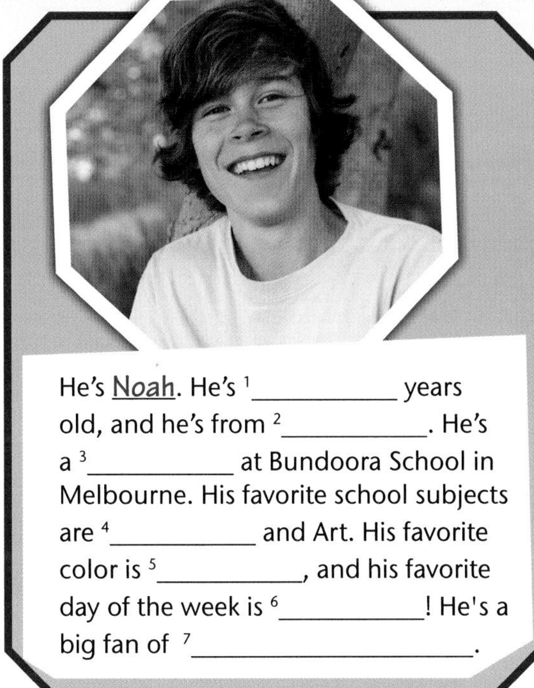

He's Noah. He's [1]__________ years old, and he's from [2]__________. He's a [3]__________ at Bundoora School in Melbourne. His favorite school subjects are [4]__________ and Art. His favorite color is [5]__________, and his favorite day of the week is [6]__________! He's a big fan of [7]____________________.

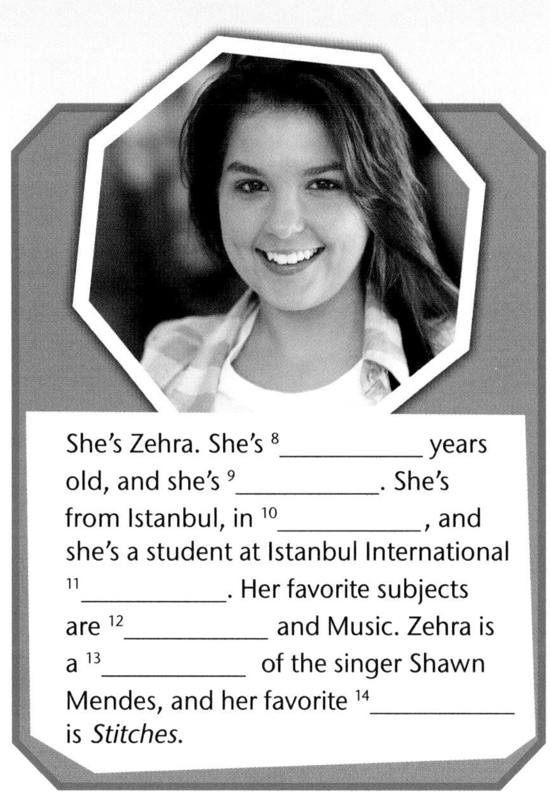

She's Zehra. She's [8]__________ years old, and she's [9]__________. She's from Istanbul, in [10]__________, and she's a student at Istanbul International [11]__________. Her favorite subjects are [12]__________ and Music. Zehra is a [13]__________ of the singer Shawn Mendes, and her favorite [14]__________ is *Stitches*.

Step 3

3 Look at the topics in the list. Write notes about yourself.

- name
- age
- nationality
- school
- favorite subjects
- favorite singer or band
- favorite color
- favorite animals

4 Presentation **Write a presentation about yourself. Use your answers from exercise 3. Look at the texts in exercise 2 to help you.**

My name's … I'm … and …

5 Groupwork **In small groups, take turns to give your presentation. Take notes about the other people in your group.**

Workbook p.W6

The Next Step

Hi, my name's Lara. I'm 13, and I'm from San Francisco, California, in the U.S. My sister Megan and I are dancers. My favorite dance is hip-hop, and Megan's favorite dance is contemporary.

At home, our favorite hobby is watching TV, and one of our favorite TV shows is *The Next Step*. It's on TV every night, and it's awesome!

The Next Step is a reality drama. It's about a group of young Canadian dancers at *The Next Step* dance studio in Toronto, in Canada. The stories on the show are very interesting, with competitions, great dances, and arguments between the dancers, too!

All the dancers are amazing. And all the dance styles on the show–from ballet to street dance–are fantastic.

My two favorite dancers on the show are Richelle and LaTroy. In real life, their names are Briar Nolet and Akiel Julien. Briar is also a gymnast–she's very talented! Akiel is from Grenada, but now his home is in Toronto.

Is *The Next Step* on TV in your country? Are you a fan of dance? If the answers to these questions are *yes*, then *The Next Step* is the show for you!

Check it out!

Find these words and phrases and check their meaning.

TV show	in real life
reality drama	gymnast
arguments	talented

Reading

1 022 **Read and listen** **Choose the correct answers.**

1 Lara's favorite dance style is
 a contemporary. **b** hip-hop. **c** ballet. **d** street dance.

2 *The Next Step* is a
 a TV show. **b** type of hobby. **c** dance competition. **d** dance style.

3 The dance studio is in
 a the U.S. **b** the U.K. **c** Canada. **d** Grenada.

2 **There is incorrect information in each sentence. Rewrite the sentences with true information.**

Megan is Lara's friend. Megan is Lara's sister.

1 At home, Lara's favorite hobby is dancing.

____

____

2 *The Next Step* is about singers.

____

3 The TV show is only on Monday and Tuesday.

____

4 Richelle and LaTroy are teachers.

____

5 Akiel is from China.

____

6 His home is in Louisiana.

____

7 *The Next Step* is for fans of music.

____

3 **Match the nationalities (A–D) with the countries (1–4). Then match the countries with the cities (a–d).**

Nationality	Country	City
A American	**1** Grenada	**a** Toronto
B Grenadian	**2** Canada	**b** St. George's
C Russian	**3** the U.S.	**c** Moscow
D Canadian	**4** Russia	**d** San Francisco

Culture focus

Biggest countries in the world–top three!

1 Russia
2 Canada
3 the U.S.

Canada is a very big country, but the population isn't very big.

Japan is smaller than Canada, but there are more peop

Writing

Step 1

4 **Ethan and Chloe are dancers. Complete the paragraphs about them. Use the information in the fact files.**

FACT FILE

Name	Ethan	Chloe
Age	13	14
From	New Orleans, U.S.	London, U.K.
Dance style	ballet dancer	contemporary dancer
Favorite TV show	*So You Think You Can Dance*	*The Next Step*
Favorite dancer	Isaac Hernández	Maddie Ziegler

Ethan is 13 years old. He's from [1]__________, in the U.S. He's a ballet [2]__________. His favorite TV show is [3]__________, and his favorite dancer is the ballet dancer [4]__________.

Chloe is [5]______ years old. She's from [6]__________, in England. She's a [7]__________ dancer. Her favorite TV show is [8]__________, and her favorite dancer is [9]__________.

Writing strategy

Using capital letters

In English, we always use capital letters for:

- the first word of a sentence
- the subject pronoun
- names of people, TV shows, books, etc.
- cities, countries, and nationalities

Hi, I'm Ivan. I'm Russian. I'm from Volgograd, in Russia.

Step 2

5 **Use the information in the fact file to write a paragraph about Lara's sister, Megan.**

FACT FILE

Name	Megan
Age	12
From	San Francisco, U.S.
Dance style	contemporary
Favorite TV show	*The Next Step*
Favorite dancer	Lamar Johnson

Megan is 12 years old. She's __________

____

____

____

____

Step 3

6 **Write a paragraph about yourself. Use the texts in exercise 4 to help you.**

Challenge

Write sentences about the following things:

- your favorite movie
- your favorite actor
- your favorite food
- your three favorite songs
- your favorite book
- your two favorite countries
- your two favorite towns or cities

Culture p.106

2 Are you ready?

In this unit we will ...

- talk about family
- talk about dates and special days
- ask and answer questions about personal details
- write about people and their interests

1 023 **Read and listen** Who has to make a decision: Mason or Jacob? ___________

Mason and Jacob dance, but then something strange happens ...

Judge	Hello, what are your names?
Mason	I'm Mason, and this is Jacob.
Judge	Is he your friend?
Mason	No, he isn't. He's my little brother. We're Bro-Beat!
Judge	Where are you from?
Mason	We're from New York City.
Judge	And how old are you?
Mason	I'm 14, and he's 12.
Jacob	I'm not 12! I'm 13.
Judge	Who's here with you today?
Mason	Our friends and our mom and dad.
Judge	OK, boys. Are you ready? This is your moment! Good luck.

Later ...

Judge	Jacob, you're great! You're a star, but your brother isn't very good.
Mason	No way! Are you serious?
Judge	Yes, we are. It's a "no" for you, Mason. Jacob, it's your brother or the competition. Yes or no?
Jacob	Sorry, Mason ... my answer is "yes."
Mason	What?!

2 **Comprehension** Choose the correct alternatives.

Mason and Jacob are **friends** / **brothers**.

1. They're from **the U.S.** / **the U.K.**
2. Jacob is **12** / **13** years old.
3. They're at the competition with their **friends** / **friends and family**.
4. The judge says that **Jacob** / **Mason** is great.
5. Jacob's answer is **yes** / **no**.

Link to life **What do you say to a friend who is upset about bad grades or losing in a competition?**

Check it out!

Find these phrases and check their meaning.

Good luck.
You're a star
No way!
Are you serious?
Sorry

Step 1

3 **Find and underline the phrases in the dialogue in exercise 1.**

Are you serious? **And how old** are you? **Is he** your friend? **No,** he **isn't.** **Where** are you from? **Yes,** we **are.** your brother **isn't** very good

Step 2

4 024 **Reorder the words to complete the dialogues. Then listen and check.**

1

Judge Hello, / are / names? / your / what
Hello, what are your names?
Mason I'm Mason, and this is Jacob.
Judge your / he / friend? / Is
1 ______________________________
Mason No, he isn't. He's my little brother.

2

Judge And / are / how / you? / old
2 ______________________________
Mason I'm 14, and he's 12.
Jacob I'm not 12! I'm 13.
Judge with / you / today? / Who's / here
3 ______________________________
Mason Our friends and our mom and dad.

3

Judge star, / a / good. / You're / very / but / your / brother / isn't
4 ______________________________
____
Mason way! / No / you / serious? / Are
5 ______________________________
Judge are. / Yes, / we
6 ______________________________

024 **Now listen again and repeat.**

Step 3

5 **Imagine you are in the *Dance for the U.S.* competition. Answer the judge's questions.**

Judge What's your name?
You *My name is…*
Judge Where are you from?
You ______________________________
Judge How old are you?
You ______________________________
Judge Who's here with you today?
You ______________________________
Judge OK! Are you ready? This is your moment! Good luck.

6 **Pairwork** **Practice your dialogues from exercise 5.**

Family

1 025 **Look at Lola's family scrapbook. Complete the sentences with the words in the box. Then listen and check.**

uncle	dad	cousin	~~grandparents~~	sister	mom	parents	grandma	brother	aunt	grandpa

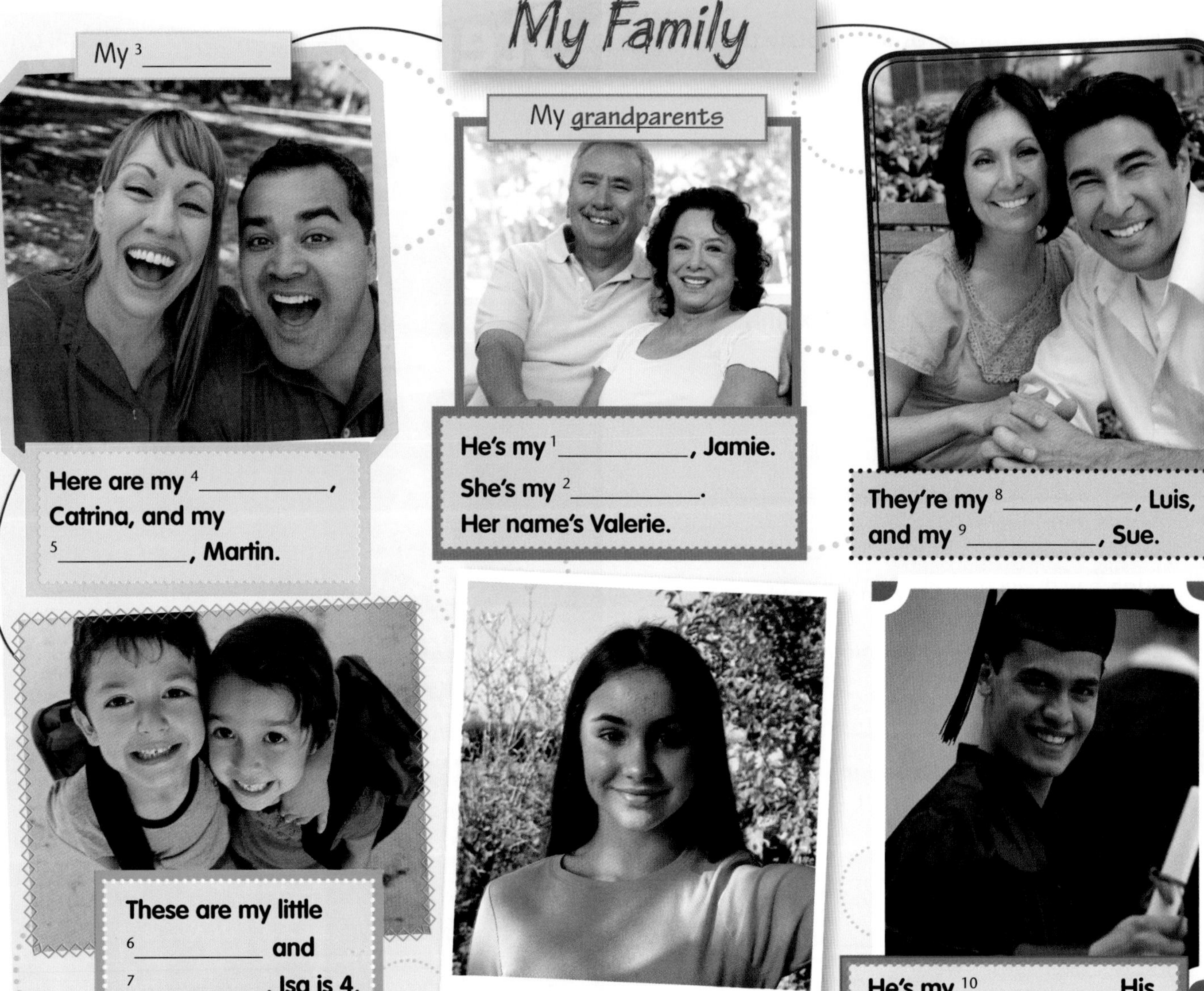

My Family
My grandparents
He's my 1 ________, Jamie.
She's my 2 ________.
Her name's Valerie.
My 3 ________
Here are my 4 ________, Catrina, and my 5 ________, Martin.
They're my 8 ________, Luis, and my 9 ________, Sue.
These are my little 6 ________ and 7 ________. Isa is 4, and Oliver is 6.
This is me.
He's my 10 ________. His name is Luis, like his dad.

2 026 **Now listen and repeat the family words.**

3 027 **Lola's cousin, Luis, is describing his family. Complete the sentences with family words. Use Lola's family tree to help you. Then listen and check.**

Catrina is my aunt.

1 Oliver, Lola, and Isa are my ________.

2 My ________'s name is Luis.

3 Jamie is my ________.

4 Martin is my ________.

5 Sue is my ________.

6 Valerie is my ________.

4 Pairwork **Draw your family tree. Don't show your partner. Then describe it to your partner and ask him / her to draw it. Compare your pictures. Is your partner's picture correct?**

Mauricio is my grandpa. Agustina is my grandma …

Workbook p.W10

be: Simple present

Negative

I'm **not** 12!
Your brother **isn't** very good.

Full form	Short form
I **am not**	I**'m not**
you **are not**	you **aren't**
he **is not**	he **isn't**
she **is not**	she **isn't**
it **is not**	it **isn't**
we **are not**	we **aren't**
you **are not**	you **aren't**
they **are not**	they **aren't**

Think!

Complete the rule.

When we make negative sentences with the verb *be*, we put ______ after the verb.

Rules p.W8

1 Reorder the words to make negative sentences. Then rewrite the sentences using short forms.

serious. / not / She / is
She is not serious. She isn't serious.

1 15 years old. / I / not / am

2 is / red. / The / pen / not

3 Australia. / He / not / is / from

4 not / are / cousins. / Walter and Rafael

5 not / funny. / You / are

6 sisters. / not / are / We

2 Write sentences with the affirmative (✓) or negative (✗) form of the verb *be*. Use short forms.

I / at school (✓) — I'm at school.
You / late (✗) — You aren't late.

1 Ella / in my class (✗)
2 It / 5p.m. (✓)
3 The students / at school (✗)
4 I / Japanese (✗)
5 You / very intelligent (✓)
6 They / my parents (✓)

Interrogative and short answers

Is he your friend? No, **he isn't**.
Are you serious? Yes, **we are**.

Interrogative	Short answers	
	Affirmative	Negative
Am I happy?	**Yes**, you **are**.	**No**, you **aren't**.
Are you happy?	**Yes**, I **am**.	**No**, I**'m not**.
Is he happy?	**Yes**, he **is**.	**No**, he **isn't**.
Is she happy?	**Yes**, she **is**.	**No**, she **isn't**.
Is it happy?	**Yes**, it **is**.	**No**, it **isn't**.
Are we happy?	**Yes**, you **are**.	**No**, you **aren't**.
Are you happy?	**Yes**, we **are**.	**No**, we **aren't**.
Are they happy?	**Yes**, they **are**.	**No**, they **aren't**.

Think!

Choose the correct alternative.

To make questions, we put the verb *be* **before** / **after** the subject.

Rules p.W8

3 Complete the questions and answers.

Is soccer your favorite sport?
Yes, it is.

1 ______ they in the computer lab? No, ____________.
2 ______ Mark your uncle? Yes, ____________.
3 ______ we on your team? No, ____________.
4 ______ you American, Nathan? Yes, ____________.
5 ______ it 8.00? No, ____________.

4 Use the prompts to write questions. Then answer the questions with short answers that are true for you.

your teacher / American?
Is your teacher American?
Yes, she is. / No, she isn't.

1 you / 11 years old?
2 it / Monday today?
3 you / from London?
4 you / at school?
5 your birthday / in August?

Challenge

Look at Lola's family scrapbook on page 22. Write six questions about her family, and answer them. Write three questions with affirmative answers and three with negative answers.

Is Jamie her dad? No, he isn't.
Are Martin and Catrina her parents?
Yes, they are.

Puzzles p.118

Dates and special days

1 028 **Complete the chart with the ordinal numbers in the box. Then listen and check.**

~~second~~ fifth twenty-second sixteenth thirty-first third twenty-seventh twelfth twentieth eighth

1st	first	9th	ninth	17th	seventeenth	25th	twenty-fifth
2nd	*second*	10th	tenth	18th	eighteenth	26th	twenty-sixth
3rd	1 ______	11th	eleventh	19th	nineteenth	27th	8 ______
4th	fourth	12th	4 ______	20th	6 ______	28th	twenty-eighth
5th	2 ______	13th	thirteenth	21st	twenty-first	29th	twenty-ninth
6th	sixth	14th	fourteenth	22nd	7 ______	30th	thirtieth
7th	seventh	15th	fifteenth	23rd	twenty-third	31st	9 ______
8th	3 ______	16th	5 ______	24th	twenty-fourth		

028 **Now listen again and repeat.**

2 029 **Watch, listen, or read Choose the correct alternatives. Then listen again and check.**

1

Dominic Hey, Arianna!
Arianna Hey!
Dominic It's February (2nd) / 7th. Happy Groundhog Day!
Arianna It's not Groundhog Day today!
Dominic What?!
Arianna Look! It's February 1st / 3rd today!

2

Dominic What's the date today?
Arianna It's August 13th / 14th. My birthday's in August.
Dominic Oh! When's your birthday?
Arianna It's on August 21st / 23rd.

Speaking strategy

Talking about dates

When we talk about a month, we say *in*. *It's* ***in*** *August.*

When we talk about a specific day, we say *on*. *It's* ***on*** *August 14th.*

When we want to say the date today, we don't use prepositions. *Today, it's July 11th.*

3 030 **Real English Listen and repeat.**

What's the date today?
It's May 2nd.
When's your birthday?
It's on March 28th.

4 031 Listen and complete the dates.

June 10th

1 December __________
2 __________ 6th
3 November __________
4 __________

Culture focus

Important dates in the U.S.

Groundhog Day	February 2nd
(Saint) Valentine's Day	February 14th
Independence Day	July 4th
Christmas Eve	December 24th
Christmas Day	December 25th
New Year's Eve	December 31st
New Year's Day	January 1st

Thanksgiving Day is also an important holiday in the U.S. It is on the fourth Thursday of November.

Beat the clock

In two minutes, write six dates that are important in your country. Try to find dates in six different months. Compare your list with your partner. Can you find more than six?

5 Pairwork Look at the Culture focus on *Important dates in the U.S.* Ask and answer questions like this:

When's Valentine's Day?

It's on February 14th.

Link it!

Groupwork Do a survey. Ask six people in your class about their birthday. Complete the chart with their name and the date of their birthday.

Name	Birthday
Evandro	May 17th

Pairwork Ask and answer the questions.

When's (Evandro's) birthday?

It's on (May 17th).

Workbook p.W12 Extra communication p.31

Question words + *be*

Where are you from?
Who's here with you today?

Question word	Verb	Subject
Who	is	your Art teacher?
What	is	your name?
Where	are	the boys?
When	is	your Music class?
Which	is	your book?
How old	are	you?

Rules p.W8

1 Choose the correct question words.

"(What) / **Where** is it?" "It's a pencil case."
1 "**Who** / **How old** are they?" "They're my brothers."
2 "**When** / **Where** is the concert?" "It's at 7 p.m."
3 "**Where** / **How old** is your sister?" "She's 9."
4 "**Who** / **Which** is your pen?" "It's the blue pen."

Look!

We use *Which ...?* to choose between a small number.
***Which** is your bag? The red or the brown bag?*
We use *What ...?* when there is a wider choice.
***What**'s your favorite color?*

2 Complete the questions.

"Where is your book?" "It's in my school bag."
1 "__________ is he?" "He's my dad."
2 "__________ is your dog?" "He's 5 years old."
3 "__________ is your ball?" "It's the yellow ball."
4 "__________ is the English test?" "It's today!"

3 Write questions. Then answer them so they are true for you.

What / your name? What's your name? It's Mia.
1 How old / you?
2 Where / your school?
3 Who / your best friend?
4 When / your birthday?

4 Write questions to complete the mini-dialogues.

A What's your name?
B My name's Zachary.
1 A __________________________?
B I'm from Johannesburg, in South Africa.
2 A __________________________?
B I'm 14 years old.
3 A __________________________?
B My favorite music is pop music.
4 A __________________________?
B My favorite singer is Drake.

Demonstratives

this, that, these, those

I'm Mason, and **this** is Jacob.

Singular	Plural
This is a blue pen.	**These** are red pens.
That's my teacher.	**Those** are my teachers.

Think!

Complete the rules with *this, that, these,* and *those*.

We use [1]________ and [2]________ to refer to nearby people or things.

We use [3]________ and [4]________ to refer to distant people or things.

Rules p.W9

5 Look at the pictures and complete the sentences with *this, that, these,* or *those*.

These are my pets.

1 ________ 's my bike!

2 ________ are my favorite books.

3 Oh no! ________ are my DVDs!

4 ________ is my new school bag.

5 Wow! ________'s a fantastic car!

Challenge

Draw a picture of your classroom with different classroom objects in it. Write about the things in your classroom using *this, that, these,* and *those*.

This is a picture of my classroom. These are my books. That's the whiteboard ...

Puzzles p.118

Listening and speaking

Step 1

1 032 **Listen to the questions and choose the correct answers. Then listen again and check.**

	(a) Sophie	b 11 years old	c yellow
1	a January	b address	c London
2	a a student	b Foster	c 13 years old
3	a Jenny	b March 20th	c 15 years old
4	a No, he isn't.	b Yes, they are.	c Yes, she is.
5	a a pen	b blue	c New York City
6	a No, it isn't.	b Yes, they are.	c Yes, I am.
7	a dogs	b books	c Saturday

Listening strategy

Reading before you listen

Before you listen, read the exercise. It will tell you the general areas that you need to listen out for.

Step 2

2 033 **Listen to an interview with a singer. Complete the profile with the missing information.**

Name: *Jamie Fernandez*

Age: 1 ________

Birthday: 2 ________

Family: 3 ________

____

Favorite color: 4 ________

Favorite singer: 5 ________

Favorite sport: 6 ________

Celebrity facts

Name: Edward Christopher Sheeran
Nationality: British
Birthday: February 17th
Favorite color: orange
Favorite book: all Harry Potter books
Favorite singers: Stevie Wonder, Eminem
Favorite TV show: *The Fresh Prince of Bel-Air*
Favorite sport: soccer
Favorite movie: *Goodfellas*

Step 3

3 Pairwork **Look at the fact file about Ed Sheeran. Ask and answer questions. Use the prompts in the box.**

What / full name? Where / from? When / birthday?
What / favorite color? What / favorite books?
Who / favorite singers? What / favorite TV show?
What / favorite sport? What / favorite movie?

What's his full name?

His name's Edward Christopher Sheeran.

Where's he from?

He's from …

4 Pairwork **Use the prompts in exercise 3 to ask and answer questions about you and your partner.**

What's your name?

My name is …

Workbook p.W12

West High School News

A student from West High School is in the final of a TV quiz show! Jordan Davis is in 10th grade at our school. He and his family are in the final of the popular TV quiz show, *In the Family*. It's on channel 3 at 7 p.m. on May 22nd. The questions are in five categories: music, movies, sports, history, and geography. They aren't easy! The first prize is a family vacation in Hawaii.

Meet the team!

Grandpa

Lucas Davis is 64 years old. His passion is history. He loves British history. His favorite historical figure is Henry VIII. His favorite TV show is *The Crown*.

Mom

Mary-Kate Davis is 40 years old. She's the team's movie expert. Her favorite actor is Leonardo di Caprio, and her favorite movie is *The Revenant*.

Son

Jordan Davis is 16 years old. He's in 10th grade at our school. He's a baseball fan. His favorite team is the Boston Red Sox, and his favorite player is Mookie Betts. He's the sports expert.

Uncle

Michael Davis is 45 years old. He's into traveling. His favorite countries are Australia and Brazil. Michael is the geography expert.

Cousin

Abigail Davis is 17 years old. She's crazy about music. Her favorite band is Imagine Dragons, and her favorite song is *On Top of the World*. She's the team's music expert.

Good luck to Jordan and his family!

Check it out!

Find these words and phrases and check their meaning.

prize historical figure traveling vacation He's into She's crazy about team

Reading

1 034 **Read and listen** **Choose the correct answers.**

In the Family is a
a song. (c) TV quiz.
b movie. d pop band.

1 Lucas Davis is an expert in
a movies. c sports.
b history. d geography.

2 Mookie Betts is
a a singer. c a baseball player.
b an actor. d a student.

2 Answer the questions.

1 What grade is Jordan Davis in?
2 What are the five categories for the questions in the quiz show?
3 What is the first prize?
4 How old is Lucas Davis?
5 Who is the movie expert?
6 Where is Jordan a student?
7 Who is the music expert?
8 What is Abigail's favorite song?

Reading strategy

Using visuals

Texts often use pictures to help you understand. Sometimes pictures give you information about the text. You can also use pictures to help you find the section of a text you need to answer a question.

Culture focus

Top 5 names in the U.S.

	Last names	Girls?	Boys?
1	Smith	Emma	Liam
2	Johnson	Olivia	Noah
3	Williams	Ava	William
4	Jones	Isabella	James
5	Brown	Sophia	Logan

What first names and last names are common in your country?

Writing

Step 1

3 Imagine you are interviewing Jordan Davis for the school website. Complete the questions.

You What's your name?
Jordan My name's Jordan.
You 1 ______________________________?
Jordan I'm 16.
You 2 ______________________________?
Jordan My favorite sport is baseball.
You 3 ______________________________?
Jordan My favorite baseball player is Mookie Betts.
You 4 ______________________________?
Jordan The final of *In the Family* is on May 22nd.
You Who 5 ______________________________?
Jordan The people on my team are my grandpa, my mom, my uncle, my cousin, and me.
You What 6 ______________________________?
Jordan The prize is a family vacation in Hawaii.

Writing strategy

Using apostrophes

Remember to include apostrophes when you write short forms of the verb *be*. We can only use the short form of *is* with question words.

I'm in 10th grade.

What's your favorite TV show?

We're the Vega family.

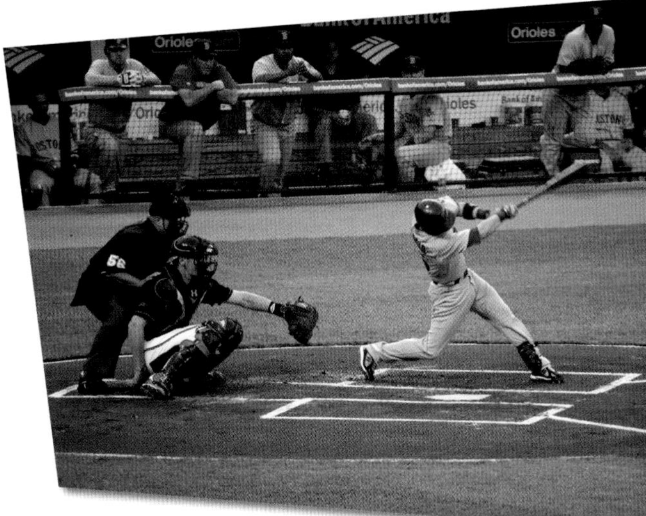

Step 2

4 Imagine you and four members of your family are in the final of *In the Family*. Complete the chart with the people on your team (mom, dad, aunt, cousin, etc.).

Categories	My team
music	
movies	
sports	
history	
geography	

5 Now imagine a journalist comes to interview you. Write the interview questions and answers. Use the prompts and the dialogue in exercise 3 to help you.

- What / name?
- Where / from?
- How / old?
- What / name of your school?
- What / your passion?
- Who / the people on your team?
- What / they experts in?

Step 3

6 Write three short paragraphs introducing three people on your team.

Brother

Fernando Lopes is 15 years old. He's crazy about music.

His favorite ...

Challenge

nationality good at free time favorite sports music food movies TV shows favorite day of the week

You are a journalist. You want to find out more information about a contestant on the show *In the Family*. Write all the questions you can think of. Use the ideas in the box to help you. Add your own ideas, too.

Culture p.107

Vocabulary

1 Write the nationalities of the countries in the box in the correct columns.

Japan Canada Portugal Mexico ~~Brazil~~ Spain the U.K. Chile

-an	-ese	-ish
Brazilian	4 ______	6 ______
1 ______	5 ______	7 ______
2 ______		
3 ______		

2 Complete the nationalities, countries, and family words with the missing letters.

My family is very international. My g r a n d p a, Azmi, is [1]T __ __ k __ s h. He's from Istanbul. My [2]__ r a n __ m a, Banu, is from [3]T __ __ k e __, too, but she's from the city of Bodrum.

My [4]u n __ __ e, Chen, is from Beijing, in [5]C __ i __ a. My [6]a __ n t, Alexa, is from the [7]__. S., so my [8]c o __ s i __ s, Lucia and Danny, are half [9]C h __ __ e __ e, half [10]A __ e r __ __ a n!

My [11]m __ __, Sara, is from the U.S., too, but my [12]__ __ d, Al, is from Sydney, in [13]A __ s __ r __ __ i a. So my [14]s __ __ t __ r, [15]b r __ __ h __ r, and I are half [16]__ u __ t r __ l __ a n!

Grammar

3 Complete the sentences with the affirmative (✓) or negative (✗) form of *be* in the simple present.

My name is Suzie. I [1]______ (✓) 13 years old. My sisters, Jenna and Katie, [2]______ (✓) 15 and 11. We [3]______ (✓) American, but our parents [4]______ (✗) from the U.S. They [5]______ (✓) Canadian.

I [6]_____ (✓) into music and dance. Jenna [7]______ (✗) interested in those things. She [8]_____ (✓) crazy about art. I [9]______ (✗) good at art. My pictures [10]______ (✓) terrible! Katie [11]____ (✓) interested in sports. She [12]____ (✓) an expert on tennis!

4 Choose the correct alternatives.

Shelley (What) / Where's your name?
Caleb It's Caleb.
Shelley [1]**How old** / **Who** are you?
Caleb I'm 14.
Shelley [2]**When** / **Where** are you from?
Caleb I'm from Detroit, in the U.S.
Shelley [3]**Are** / **Is** you into sports?
Caleb No, I [4]**am** / **'m not**. I'm into music.
Shelley [5]**Which** / **Who** is your favorite singer?
Caleb Dua Lipa.
Shelley Dua Lipa? [6]**Am** / **Is** she from the U.S.?
Caleb No, she [7]**aren't** / **isn't**. She's British.
Shelley [8]**Are** / **Is** *One Kiss* one of her songs?
Caleb Yes, [9]**it is** / **they are**. It's my favorite song!

5 Look at the pictures. Match the sentences in the box with the pictures.

That's my sister. These are my grandparents. This is my brother. ~~This is my sister.~~ Those are my brothers. Those are my grandparents.

This is my sister.

1 ______________

2 ______________

3 ______________

4 ______________

5 ______________

Communication

1 035 **Complete the dialogues with the words in the box. Then listen and check.**

are bad day good morning goodbye ~~hi~~ how later see thanks well

1

James Hey, Sophia!
Sophia Hi, James.
James 1________ are you, Sophia?
Sophia I'm fine. And you?
James Not 2________, thanks.

Later ...

James Bye. See you 3________!
Sophia Bye. 4________ you!

2

Mr. Jackson 5________, Thea.
Thea Hello, Mr. Jackson.
Mr. Jackson How 6________ you?
Thea I'm fine, 7________. And you?
Mr. Jackson I'm very 8________, thank you.

Later ...

Mr. Jackson Goodbye, Thea. Have a good 9________.
Thea Thanks. 10________. See you on Thursday.

Pronunciation

2 036 **Listen to the intonation in the questions. Then listen again and repeat.**

1 Are you a student?
2 Is today April 24th?
3 Are your grandparents Brazilian?
4 Is this your book?
5 How old are you?
6 What's the name of your school?
7 Who's your best friend?
8 When's your birthday?

Video link

3 037 **Watch or listen**

Choose the correct answers.

Ludmila is
a 14.
(b) 13.
c 12.

1 Her birthday is on
a June 9th.
b June 19th.
c July 9th.

2 Ludmila's mom is
a Russian.
b American.
c Australian.

3 Mario is
a 20.
b 11.
c 12.

4 His birthday is on
a November 6th.
b November 5th.
c November 16th.

5 His mom is
a Italian.
b Korean.
c Mexican.

6 Clara's birthday is on
a May 23rd.
b May 3rd.
c March 23rd.

7 Clara's sister's name is
a Erin.
b Alex.
c Kath.

Make a time capsule

We will ...
- use initiative
- think creatively
- work well with a partner

What's up?

1 Match the pictures with the words in the box.

letter pictures toy ~~magazine~~ book

magazine

1 ___________

2 ___________

3 ___________

4 ___________

Get thinking

2 Read the letter. Find the other objects from exercise 1.

Hi!

I'm in my house in Dallas. This is my family time capsule. It's a plastic box with special things in it from my mom, dad, sister, and grandparents. My favorite things are in it, too!

So, what's inside the time capsule? Inside is a poster of my favorite singer, Rita Ora; a magazine from today, July 4th; some pictures of my grandparents; a book from Mom and Dad; and a fluffy cat! That's from my sister–don't worry, it isn't real: it's only a toy! In ten years we can open it again. OK! Let's bury it!

From Mike (12 years old)

Check it out!

Find these words and phrases and check their meaning.

plastic box — don't worry!
fluffy — Let's bury it!

Get involved

3 Write five things from your home that you could put in a time capsule.

The project

4 Groupwork In groups, talk about your ideas from exercise 3. Agree what to put in your group's time capsule.

1 What is inside the time capsule? (*Let's put a .... inside*)
2 Who are the objects from? (*This .... is from my brother.*)
3 When can you open the time capsule again? (*In five / ten years*)

Real English

How about a ...? — Great idea!
This is perfect! — I'm not sure.
What about this?

5 Write a letter to put in your time capsule. Say what the date is and how old you are. Include your answers from exercise 4, too. Finally, bury your time capsule!

How did you do?

Write the statements into your notebook and score yourself from 1 to 5.

I can ... talk about different objects for a time capsule.

1 2 3 4 5
not very well — very well

I can ... say who the things are from.

1 2 3 4 5
not very well — very well

Speaking competences

I can identify different countries and nationalities. (p.12)

1 Complete the sentences with the words in the box.

~~Japanese~~ Chile Australia American Brazilian Colombian

I'm *Japanese*. I live in Kyoto.

1 I am from Recife. I'm ____________.
2 Thanksgiving Day is an important ____________ celebration.
3 The capital of ____________ is Santiago.
4 Gabriel García Márquez is a famous ____________ writer.
5 There are lots of koalas and kangaroos in ____________.

/5

I can greet people. (p.14)

2 Complete the dialogue with the questions and sentences.

And you? ~~Good morning, Joe.~~ Goodbye, Joe. Hello, Mrs. Elton. See you soon. Thanks.

Mrs. Elton *Good morning, Joe.*
Joe 1____________
Mrs. Elton How are you?
Joe I'm fine, thanks. 2____________
Mrs. Elton I'm very well, thank you.

Later …

Mrs. Elton 3____________ Have a good day.
Joe 4____________ Goodbye.
5____________

/5

I can introduce myself. (p.17)

3 Complete the text with the words in the box. Then practice.

their Music student I'm ~~13~~ my

My name's Belén. I'm *13* years old, and 1____________ from Medellín, in Colombia. I'm a 2____________ at the Medellín International School. 3____________ favorite subjects at school are English and 4____________. My favorite band is Clean Bandit. 5____________ song *Solo* is fantastic!

/5

I can talk about family. (p.22)

4 Complete the family words in the questions.

"Who's your b*rother*?" "It's Sam."

1 "Which one is your s____________?" "The girl with the blue bag."
2 "Where's your m____________?" "She's at work."
3 "Is he your d____________?" "Yes, he is."
4 "Are they your a____________ and u____________?" "No, they aren't. They're my parents."

/5

I can talk about dates and special days. (p.24)

5 Write the dates as you say them.

Today is 2/24.
Today is February twenty-fourth.

1 Tomorrow is 11/5.
2 My birthday is on 1/7.
3 Independence Day is 7/4.
4 Christmas Eve is 12/24.
5 My mom's birthday is 3/3.

/5

I can talk about people and their favorite things. (p.27)

6 Look at the chart and write 5 more sentences.

Gabriela and her interests	
Age	14
Birthday	April 9th
Favorite color	yellow
Favorite animal	horse
Favorite movie	*Interstellar*
Favorite singer	Ariana Grande
Favorite sport	soccer

Gabriela is 14. Her birthday is April 9th. Her favorite …

/5

Listening, reading, and writing competences

	Yes	I'm not sure	No
I can understand someone introducing themselves. (p.17)	◯	◯	◯
I can read and answer questions about a TV show. (p.18)	◯	◯	◯
I can write a paragraph about myself and my favorite things. (p.19)	◯	◯	◯
I can understand someone talking about people and their interests. (p.27)	◯	◯	◯
I can read and answer questions about a family and its interests. (p.28)	◯	◯	◯
I can write three paragraphs about people and their interests. (p.29)	◯	◯	◯

3 Are there any movie channels on your TV?

In this unit we will ...

- talk about where we live
- talk about quantities
- ask and answer questions about our homes
- write about our ideal bedroom

1 038 **Read and listen** **Who tries to make Mason feel better?** ___________

Rubi and Lola are at Jacob and Mason's house, but they soon see that all is not well between the brothers ...

Rubi Are there any movie channels on your TV?
Jacob Yes, there are.
Rubi Great!
Lola Where's the remote control?
Jacob Good question. It isn't on the armchair.
Lola There are some things on those shelves. Is it there?
Jacob No, it isn't. Look under the cushions on the couch.
Rubi Oh yes! Here it is!

Mom arrives.

Mom Hi, I'm home!
Jacob Hi, Mom. We're in the living room.
Mom Hi, kids. Where's Mason? Is he at basketball?
Jacob No, he isn't. He's upstairs.
Mom Oh, no! Again? Mason!
Mason What?
Mom Oh, Mason. Your bedroom is a mess. Look, there's a sandwich on the bed and there are some clothes on the floor ...
Mason Leave me alone, Mom!
Mom Come on, Mason. Cheer up–it's only a dance competition.
Mason It isn't the competition, Mom. It's Jacob. He's horrible.

2 **Comprehension** **Are the sentences true (T) or false (F)? Correct the false sentences.**

There are some movie channels on the TV. T

1 The remote control is on the armchair. ____
2 Mason is at basketball. ____
3 There's a sandwich on the floor. ____
4 Mason is upset with Jacob. ____
5 Mason and Jacob are in the final of the dance competition. ____

Check it out!

Find these words and phrases and check their meaning.

Here it is!	Come on
a mess	Cheer up
Leave me alone	

Link to life **Do your parents often ask you to clean your room? Do you think an organized bedroom makes your life easier? Why / Why not?**

Step 1

3 **Find and underline the phrases in the dialogue in exercise 1.**

Yes, there are. Are there any movie channels on your TV? There are some things on those shelves. Look under the cushions there's a sandwich on the bed We're in the living room.

Step 2

4 039 **Complete the dialogues with the phrases in the box. Then listen and check.**

~~Are there any~~ There are some and there are some there's a Yes, there are

1

Rubi *Are there any* movie channels on your TV?
Jacob [1]________________.

2

Lola Where's the remote control?
Jacob Good question. It isn't on the armchair.
Lola [2]________________ things on those shelves. Is it there?
Jacob No, it isn't. Look under the cushions on the couch.

3

Mom Look, [3]________________ sandwich on the bed [4]________________ clothes on the floor …
Mason Leave me alone, Mom!

039 **Now listen again and repeat.**

Step 3

5 **Imagine your bedroom is a mess. Complete the sentences with the words in the box.**

~~a laptop~~ some clothes a pizza some books a backpack some DVDs

There's *a laptop* under the bed.

1 There are ________________ on the bed.
2 There's ________________ under the bed.
3 There are ________________ on the floor.
4 There's ________________ on the bed.
5 There are ________________ under the bed.

6 **Pairwork** **Use the sentences from exercise 5 to describe your messy bedroom to your partner. Your partner draws the objects (DVDs, laptop, pizza, etc.) in the correct place in the room.**

My bedroom is a mess. There's a …

Workbook p.W16

Vocabulary

House and furniture

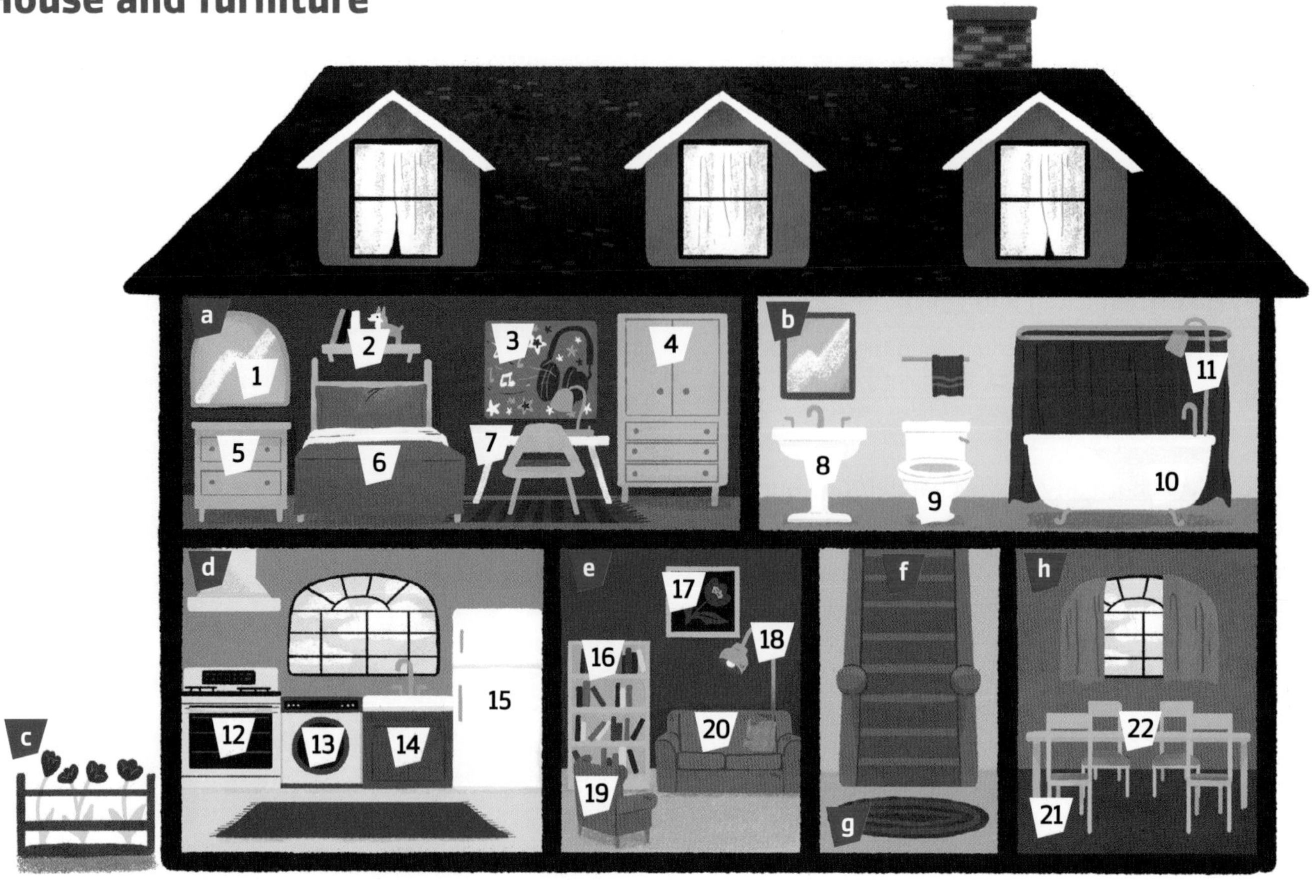

1 040 **Match the words with the letters (a–h) in the picture. Now listen and check. Then listen again and repeat.**

__b__ bathroom
____ bedroom
____ dining room
____ hallway
____ kitchen
____ living room
____ stairs
____ backyard

Look!

When we talk about a floor above us, we say **upstairs**.
"Where's the bathroom?"
*"It's **upstairs**."*

When we talk about a floor below us, we say **downstairs**.
"Where is your bag?"
*"It's **downstairs** in the hallway.*

2 041 **Match the words with the numbers (1–22) in the picture. Now listen and check. Then listen again and repeat.**

__10__ bathtub
____ sink
____ chair
____ armchair
____ fridge
____ bookcase
____ painting
____ cabinet
____ bed
____ shelf
____ stove
____ toilet
____ lamp
____ dresser
____ poster
____ couch
____ wardrobe
____ table
____ mirror
____ shower
____ desk
____ washing machine

3 **Pairwork** **Play the guessing game. Choose an object in the picture, but don't tell your partner. Your partner asks questions and guesses what the object is.**

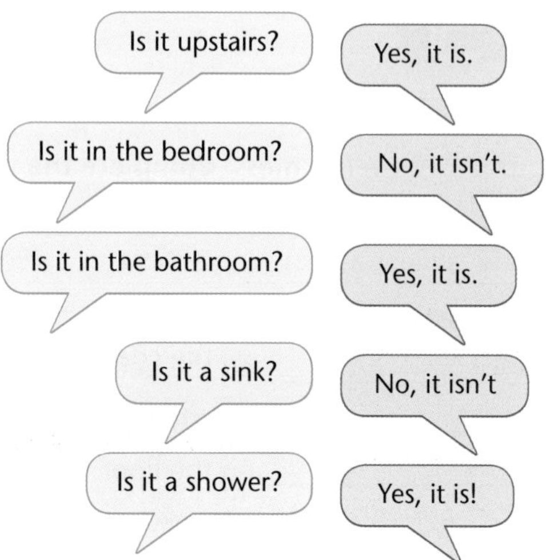

Is it upstairs?
Yes, it is.
Is it in the bedroom?
No, it isn't.
Is it in the bathroom?
Yes, it is.
Is it a sink?
No, it isn't
Is it a shower?
Yes, it is!

Workbook p.W16

Prepositions of place

Look **under** the cushions **on** the couch.

1 in

2 on

3 under

4 near

5 between

6 behind

7 across from

8 next to

9 in front of

Think!

Look at the picture in exercise 1 on page 36. Complete the sentences with *in front of* and *across from*.

The armchair is [1] _______________ the bookcase.

The table is [2] _______________ the window.

Rules p.W14

1 Look at the picture. Complete the sentences with the correct prepositions.

The chair is near the desk.

1 The laptop is _______________ the desk.
2 The bookcase is _______________ the door.
3 The lamp is _______________ the desk and the couch.
4 The backpack is _______________ the chair.
5 The mirror is _______________ the armchair.
6 The table is _______________ the couch.
7 The cat is _______________ the couch.
8 The books are _______________ the backpack.

Plural nouns

Regular plurals

Singular	Plural
table + -*s*	table**s**
chair + -*s*	chair**s**
vacation + -*s*	vacation**s**

Spelling variations

Singular	Plural
sandwich + -*es*	sandwich**es**
bus + -*es*	bus**es**
box + -*es*	box**es**
hero + -*es*	hero**es**
family + -*ies*	famil**ies**
shelf + -*ves*	shel**ves**

Irregular plurals

Singular	Plural
child	**children**
man	**men**
woman	**women**
person	**people**
mouse	**mice**
fish	**fish**
foot	**feet**

Rules p.W14

2 Write the plural forms of the words in the box.

nationality book day table person baby class

3 Rewrite the sentences with the plural of the words in bold. Remember to use the plural form of the verbs.

His **foot** is on the couch.
His feet are on the couch.

1 The **bus** is red.
2 The **shelf** is across from the door.
3 The **mouse** is in the kitchen.
4 The **box** is next to the desk.
5 The **child** is in the backyard.
6 The **fish** is green and blue.

Challenge

Look at the picture of the living room in exercise 1. Write five sentences that are false.

The laptop is on the armchair.

Puzzles p.119

Quantity

1 042 **Complete the numbers with the words in the box. Then listen and check.**

~~one hundred seven~~	nine hundred thirty	three hundred ninety-nine	seven hundred twelve	two hundred ten

100 one hundred
107 *one hundred seven*
124 one hundred twenty-four
210 [1] ______________________
345 three hundred forty-five
399 [2] ______________________
672 six hundred seventy-two
712 [3] ______________________
930 [4] ______________________
1,000 one thousand

2 043 **Listen and choose the numbers you hear. Then listen and repeat.**

(a) 108 b 180
1 a 289 b 298
2 a 333 b 330
3 a 976 b 576
4 a 750 b 715
5 a 417 b 470

Speaking strategy

Saying numbers

Some numbers sound very similar, so try to pronounce them carefully: *13* and *30*; *14* and *40*; *15* and *50*; *16* and *60*; *17* and *70*; *18* and *80*; *19* and *90*.

3 044 **Watch, listen, or read Choose the correct alternatives.**

Quizmaster Welcome, Dominic. Your topic is the Empire State Building, right? Are you ready for your first question?
Dominic Hi! Yes, I'm ready!
Quizmaster How many floors are there in the Empire State Building?
Dominic There are (**103**) / **115** floors.
Quizmaster Correct. How tall is the building?
Dominic It is [1] **443** / **414** meters tall.
Quizmaster How many windows are in the building?
Dominic There are [2] **6,540** / **6,514** windows.
Quizmaster How many hotels are there?
Dominic [3] **There's one hotel** / **There are five hotels.**
Quizmaster Sorry, that isn't correct. There aren't any hotels. OK, next question: how many steps are there?
Dominic There are [4] **1,872** / **1,822** steps.
Quizmaster How many elevators are there?
Dominic There are [5] **17** / **73** elevators.
Quizmaster Our time is up! Thanks for joining us, Dominic ...

4 045 **Real English** Listen and repeat.

How many hotels are there?
How many elevators are there?

There's one hotel.
There are 73 elevators.

Beat the clock

In two minutes, create a word map of rooms in the house and furniture that goes in the rooms.

Then compare with your partner.

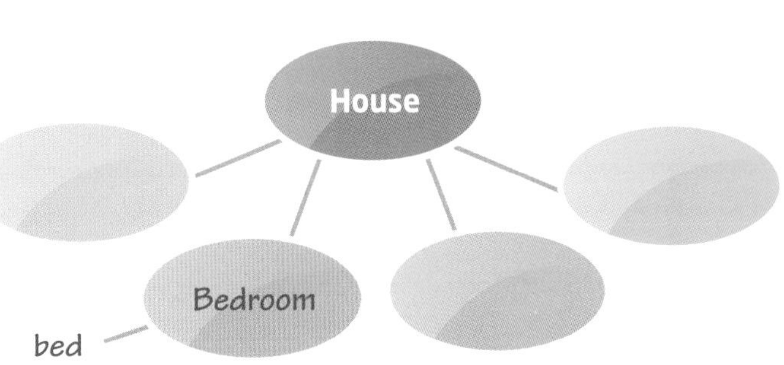
House
Bedroom
bed

5 **Pairwork** Take turns to ask and answer questions with *How many …?* Use the prompts in the box.

pages / in this book? days / in a year? students / in your school? girls / in your class? boys / in your class? seconds / in five minutes? people / in your family? days / in February? windows / in your house / apartment? letters / in the English alphabet?

How many pages are there in this book?

There are …

Link it!

Research a famous building in your country (or choose one below). Write questions and answers for a quiz show about the rooms and furniture in the building.

1

Buckingham Palace, U.K.

2

the White House, U.S.

3

Burj Al Arab, Dubai

4

the Costanera Center, Chile

Workbook p.W18 Extra communication p.55

there is / isn't, there are / aren't

Affirmative and negative

There's a sandwich on the bed.
There aren't any hotels.

	Singular	Plural
Affirmative	**There's** a desk. **There is** a desk.	**There are** five desks.
Negative	**There isn't** a bed.	**There aren't** two beds.

Rules p.W14

1 **Correct the sentences with the information in parentheses.**

There's one shelf on the wall. (two shelves)
There isn't one shelf on the wall.
There are two shelves on the wall.

1 There's one bed in the room. (two beds)
2 There are three posters on the wall. (one poster)
3 There's one lamp on the desk. (two lamps)

Is there ...? / Are there ...?

Interrogative and short answers

Are there any good movies on TV tonight?
No, there **aren't**.
Is there a sandwich on the bed? **Yes**, there **is**.

	Singular	Plural
Interrogative	**Is there** a TV in the living room?	**Are there** two beds in the bedroom?
Short answers	✓ Yes, **there is**. ✗ No, **there isn't**.	✓ Yes, **there are**. ✗ No, **there aren't**.

Rules p.W15

2 **Are the statements true for you? Complete the chart with true (T) or false (F).**

four people in your family ____
a TV in your living room ____
a desk in your bedroom ____
six letters in your name ____
good apps on your cell phone ____

3 **Now write questions and short answers with the information in the chart.**

Are there four people in your family?
No, there aren't.

some / any

There are **some** things on those shelves.
Are there **any** movie channels on your TV?

Affirmative	There are **some** chairs.
Negative	There aren't **any** DVDs.
Interrogative	Are there **any** sandwiches?

Think!

Choose the correct alternatives.

We use **some** and **any** with plural nouns when we don't want to say the exact quantity.

- We use [1]**some** / **any** in affirmative sentences.
- We use [2]**some** / **any** in negative sentences and questions.

Rules p.W15

4 **Complete the sentences with *some* or *any*.**

There aren't *any* difficult exercises on this page.

1 Are there ________ clothes on the shelf?
2 There aren't ________ mirrors in the hallway.
3 There are ________ cool songs on your cell phone.
4 Are there ________ games on your laptop?
5 There are ________ photos of my dog on my cell phone.

they're / their / there

They're my cousins.
Their dad is Spanish.
There are some books on the shelf.

Rules p.W15

5 **Choose the correct alternatives.**

"**They're** / **Their** in the backyard." *(They're circled)*

1 **There's** / **Their's** a lamp on the desk.
2 Are **there** / **their** any chairs in the dining room?
3 **Their** / **They're** names are Clara and Denise.
4 "Where are the boys?" "**They're** / **There** at school."
5 Amy and Mia aren't sisters. **They're** / **Their** cousins.

Challenge

Pairwork **Write all the questions you can with *Is there ...? / Are there ...?* Then, ask and answer the questions.**

Puzzles p.119

Step 1

1 046 **Listen to the conversation. Choose the correct answers.**

Chloe's address is
(a) 176 Lakeside Avenue. b 167 Lakeside Avenue. c 767 Lakeside Avenue.

1 It's a
a big house. b big apartment. c small house.

2 In Chloe's house, there are
a five rooms. b four rooms. c six rooms.

3 There are
a two bedrooms. b two bathrooms. c three bedrooms.

4 In the living room, there are
a two armchairs. b two couches. c two tables.

5 Chloe's favorite room is
a the living room. b her bedroom. c the bathroom.

Step 2

2 046 **Listen to the conversation again. Complete the questions.**

What's your address?

1 Is it an apartment or ___________ ___________?

2 ___________ ___________ ___________ are there in your house?

3 How many ___________ ___________ ___________?

4 And ___________ ___________ ___________ are there?

5 What's in ___________ ___________ ___________?

6 ___________ ___________ ___________ ___________?

Listening strategy

Listening for unstressed words

When we speak, we don't normally stress articles (*a*, *the*), prepositions (*for*, *to*), and possessive adjectives (*your*, *her*). They are sometimes difficult to hear. Unstressed words often come before key words.

Step 3

3 **Pairwork** **Ask your partner about his / her ideal house and complete the questionnaire. Use the questions in exercise 2 to help you.**

4 **Presentation** **Tell the class about your partner's ideal house or apartment. Use the answers to the questionnaire from exercise 3.**

His / Her address is …
It's an apartment / a house.
There are … rooms.

Address: ______________________
____

Apartment ☐ **House** ☐

Total number of rooms: _____

Number of bedrooms: _____

Number of bathrooms: _____

What's in the rooms?

Living room: ______________________

Kitchen: ______________________

Bathroom: ______________________

Bedroom: ______________________

Favorite room: ______________________

Workbook p.W18

Welcome to my bedroom

Is your bedroom big or small? Is it neat, or is it a mess? What color is it? Are there any posters on the walls? Is your bedroom your favorite room in the house? The *Welcome to my bedroom* website is about you and your bedroom. Bedrooms are a space for you! They are for homework, music, art, fun, friends, and sleep! Why is your bedroom important to you?

Amelia, 13

My bedroom is small, but it's bright. There's a big window–my bed is across from the window. There are some pictures of my friends and family on the wall behind my bed. My favorite picture is of my best friends, Emi and Leah.

In the picture, we're at a Small Pools concert. They're my favorite band. There are some shelves across from my bed, next to the window. They're for my books, games, and other things.

I love the ocean, so my favorite thing in my bedroom is my collection of seashells.

Liam, 14

I share my bedroom with my brother, and it's a mess! There are two big wardrobes in the room, but there aren't any clothes in the wardrobes–they're on the floor, under the bed, or on the chairs! There are two beds in the room. My bed is between the door and the window. There's a TV in our room, and a game console.

I'm a big fan of comic books. My favorite characters are Wolverine and Iron Man. My comics are under my bed, in two big, plastic boxes.

But my favorite thing in my room is a boomerang. It's from my cousin, Lucas. He's from Australia.

Reading strategy

Finding and checking answers

Before you read a text for the first time, look at the questions. Look for the sentence(s) in the text that give you the answer to the question. Underline the sentence(s). This can help you to check your answers when you finish.

Check it out!

Find these words and check their meaning.

neat	sleep	share
space	bright	characters

Reading

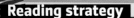

1 047 **Read and listen** Choose the correct answers.

1 On the wall behind Amelia's bed, there are
- a pictures.
- b posters.
- c a mirror.
- d shelves.

2 Amelia's favorite thing is
- a her books.
- b her collection of seashells.
- c Small Pools.
- d her picture with her friends.

3 Liam's bed is
- a across from the door.
- b between the door and the wardrobe.
- c near the bed.
- d between the door and the window.

4 Liam's cousin is from
- a the U.S.
- b the U.K.
- c Australia.
- d Canada.

2 Answer the questions.

1 Where is Amelia's bed?
2 Who is in Amelia's favorite picture?
3 What is on the shelves across from Amelia's bed?
4 Where are Liam's clothes?
5 Where are Liam's comics?
6 What is Liam's favorite thing in his room?

Culture focus

A typical home in the U.S. has two or more bedrooms, is on two floors, and covers 167 square meters. Around 16 percent of American houses have a swimming pool.

Writing

Step 1

3 Read Owen's answers to the questionnaire and then complete the description of his bedroom on the *Welcome to my bedroom* website.

Welcome to my bedroom

My bedroom is big, bright, and neat. There are two [1] ______________ in the room, and the walls are green and [2] __________. They are my favorite colors. In my bedroom, there's a bed, a wardrobe, a small table with a lamp on it, and there are some shelves, too. My bed is [3] ________ the door. The wardrobe is next to a [4] ______________. There are some [5] ______________ on the wall behind my bed. There's a [6] ______________ on the wall near the window. My favorite thing in my bedroom is [7] ______________!

1 Is your bedroom ...?
big ✓ small ☐ bright ✓
colorful ☐ neat ✓

2 How many windows are there in your bedroom?
- two

3 What furniture is there in your room?
- a bed near door
- a wardrobe
- a small table and a lamp,
- some shelves

4 Draw the furniture in your room.

5 What color are the walls?
- green and yellow

6 What's on the walls?
- clock near window
- poster of favorite bands behind bed

7 What's your favorite thing in your room?
- My bed!

Step 2

4 Answer the questions in the questionnaire in exercise 3 with information about your bedroom or your ideal bedroom.

Writing strategy

Planning your writing

Before you write, it is a good idea to make notes and plan. Make a list of things you want to include, and how you want to describe them. For example:

Bedroom: small but cool
Bed: big and comfortable
Desk: in front of window
Wardrobe: too small because my brother's things are in it!

Step 3

5 Write a description of your own bedroom or your ideal bedroom for the *Welcome to my bedroom* website. Use Owen's description in exercise 3 to help you.

My bedroom / ideal bedroom is ...

Challenge

Imagine the bedroom (or another room in the house) of a famous person. What's in the room? Write a paragraph using *there is / isn't / are / aren't* and *some / any*.

Culture p.108

4 Do you have my sunglasses?

In this unit we will ...

- talk about possessions
- talk about prices
- ask and answer questions about family, pets, and possessions
- write about our interests and possessions

1 048 **Read and listen** **Who does Mason ask about his sunglasses?** ____________

Rubi and Jacob are at homework club when Mason comes in ...

Jacob Look! I have Simon Jackson's new video on my phone.
Rubi Not now, Jacob! We have homework.
Jacob I don't have my planner. What homework do we have for tomorrow?
Rubi I have my planner here. We have French and Math.
Jacob I'm really bad at French.
Rubi OK, Math first.
Jacob Oh, I don't have a calculator.
Rubi Well, Lola's calculator is on the desk over there.
Jacob Do you have a pen?
Rubi No, I don't. Jacob, why do you never have a pen?

Mason enters.

Rubi Hi, Mason. What's up?
Mason Jacob, where are my sunglasses?
Jacob Don't ask me! I don't have your stupid sunglasses.
Mason Liar! Yes, you do!
Rubi Mason, he doesn't have your sunglasses! What's your problem?
Mason I don't have a problem!
Jacob Yes, you do, Mason. You're jealous! I'm in the finals and you aren't. Deal with it!

2 **Comprehension** **Match the people with their possessions.**

1 Jacob — c	a a planner
2 Lola	b a calculator
3 Mason	c a cell phone
4 Rubi	d sunglasses

Link to life **People sometimes argue with other people in their family. Is there a good way to stop this?**

Check it out!

Find these phrases and check their meaning.

Not now	Don't ask me!
I'm really bad at	Liar!
What's up?	Deal with it!

Step 1

3 **Find and underline the phrases in the dialogue in exercise 1.**

> **I have** Simon Jackson's new video on my phone. **I don't have** a calculator.
> **We have** homework. **he doesn't have** your sunglasses! **Do you have** a pen?
> Lola's calculator is on the desk **No, I don't.**

4 049 **Find and underline the incorrect parts of the dialogues. Then correct the mistakes. Listen and check.**

1

Rubi Not now, Jacob! We have homework.

Jacob I don't have my backpack. What homework do we have for tomorrow?

Rubi I have my planner here. We have French and History.

I don't have my planner.

1 ______________________________

2

Jacob Oh, I don't have a ruler.

Rubi Well, Lola's calculator is on the desk over there.

Jacob Do you have a pencil?

Rubi No, I don't. Jacob, why do you never have a pen?

2 ______________________________

3 ______________________________

3

Rubi Mason, he doesn't have your calculator! What's your problem?

Mason I don't have a problem!

Jacob Yes, you do, Mason. You're jealous!

4 ______________________________

049 **Now listen again and repeat.**

5 **Use the instructions to write your own dialogue.**

A Say you have homework.

____

B Ask what homework you have for tomorrow.

____

A Say what homework you have (say two subjects).

____

B Say which subject you want to do first.

____

6 **Pairwork** **Practice your dialogues in exercise 5.**

Workbook p.W22

My things

1 050 **Look at the pictures of Carter's favorite things. Match the words with the numbers in the pictures. Then listen and check.**

skateboard	1	camera	____
planner	____	game console	____
sunglasses	____	bike	____
soccer ball	____	guitar	____
phone	____		
tablet	____		

Vocabulary strategy

Vocabulary games

When you learn new vocabulary, it is good to play games with the new words. Work in pairs. Write the words without vowels, then swap for your partner to complete the missing vowels.

2 051 **Listen to three teenagers talking about their favorite things. Complete the lists.**

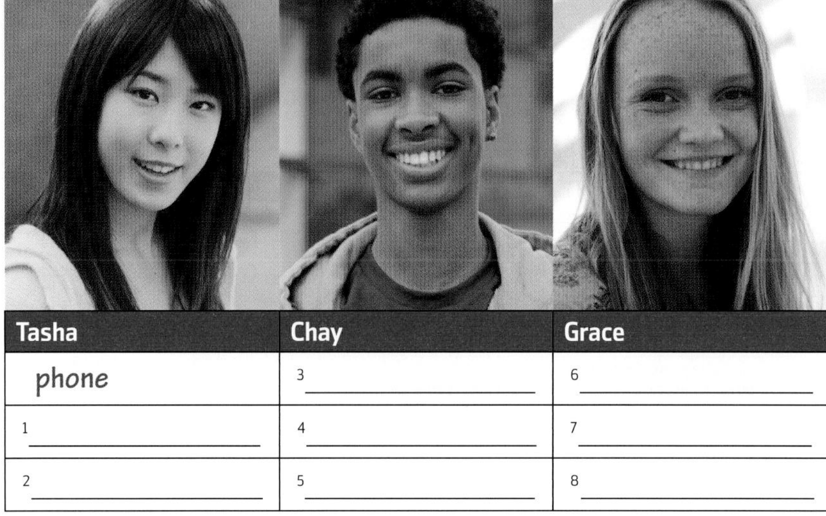

Tasha	Chay	Grace
phone	3 ____	6 ____
1 ____	4 ____	7 ____
2 ____	5 ____	8 ____

3 **Pairwork** **Choose your three favorite things from the objects in exercise 1. Compare your favorite things.**

What's your favorite thing?

My favorite thing is my phone.

What's your second- / third-favorite thing?

It's my …

Workbook p.W22

have: Simple present

Affirmative

I **have** my planner here.
Lola **has** a calculator.

have
I **have**
you **have**
she / he / it **has**
we **have**
you **have**
they **have**

Think!

Choose the correct alternatives.

With third person singular pronouns (*he*, *she*, *it*), we use [1]**have / has**.

With all other subject pronouns, we use [2]**have / has**.

Rules p.W20

1 Write sentences with the prompts and the correct form of *have*.

I / eight cousins
I have eight cousins.

1 They / an apartment in Pittsburgh
____
____

2 I / a good camera
____

3 Beatriz / green eyes
____

4 We / Math homework
____

5 Sam / three sisters
____

Look!

We use *have*:

- to talk about possession.
  *She **has** a skateboard / homework.*
- to talk about family.
  *I **have** a sister.*
- to describe physical appearance.
  *Tom **has** brown hair.*

Negative

I **don't have** a calculator.
He **doesn't have** your sunglasses!

Full form	Short form
I / you **do not have**	I / you **don't have**
he / she / it **does not have**	he / she / it **doesn't have**
we / you / they **do not have**	we / you / they **don't have**

Rules p.W20

2 Rewrite the sentences with the negative short form of *have*.

I have a game console.
I don't have a game console.

1 Cesar has a brother.
2 I have a Chilean friend.
3 Our apartment has two bathrooms.
4 They have a new Art teacher.
5 Tina has my calculator.
6 You have Music at school today.

3 Sophie has a tree house in her backyard. Look at the picture and use the prompts to write affirmative and negative sentences with *have*.

(guitar) *She doesn't have a guitar.*
1 (camera) ______________________
2 (TV) ______________________
3 (tablet) ______________________
4 (game console) ______________________
5 (soccer ball) ______________________
6 (skateboard) ______________________

Challenge

Look at exercise 3 again. Write sentences to say if you have or don't have the things.

I don't have a guitar. I have a camera.

Puzzles p.119

Prices and paying for things

1 **Match the prices in the box with the pictures. Use the *Culture focus* box to help you.**

35 cents ~~6 cents~~ $1.50 $2.30 $4.55

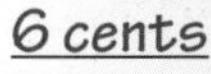
6 cents 

1 __________

2 __________

3 __________

4 __________

Culture focus

In the U.S., they have coins for:

1 cent

2 cents

5 cents

dime = 10 cents

quarter = 25 cents

50 cents

The paper money, or "dollar bills," comes in these quantities: $1, $2, $5, $10, $20, $50, and $100.

Speaking strategy

Saying prices

When we talk about money in the U.S., we say prices like this:

$5	*five dollars*
$10	*ten dollars*
$1.50	*one fifty*
$15.99	*fifteen dollars ninety-nine* OR *fifteen ninety-nine*

2 052 **Now listen and check your answers in exercise 1. Then listen again and repeat.**

3 053 **Watch, listen, or read** **Arianna and Dominic are in the shopping mall. Choose the correct prices.**

1

Arianna Excuse me. How much is this bag, please?
Assistant It's **$13.49** / **$30.49**.
Arianna It's nice. I'll take it.
Assistant OK, that's [1] **$13.49** / **$30.49**, then.
Arianna Here you are.
Assistant Thank you. Here's [2] **51 cents** / **61 cents** change, and here's your receipt.
Arianna Thank you. Goodbye.

2

Dominic Excuse me. How much is this game, please?
Assistant It's [3] **$13.99** / **$30.99**.
Dominic Oh, that's expensive! No, thank you.
Assistant No problem. Goodbye.
Dominic Goodbye!

4 054 **Real English** Listen and repeat.

How much is this bag, please?

It's $13.49.

It's nice. I'll take it.

OK, that's $13.49.

Here you are.

Thank you. Here's your change, and here's your receipt.

Thank you. Goodbye.

How much is this game, please?

It's $30.99.

That's expensive! No, thank you.

No problem. Goodbye.

5 **Pairwork** Imagine you are in a store and you want to buy the things in the pictures. Write short dialogues.

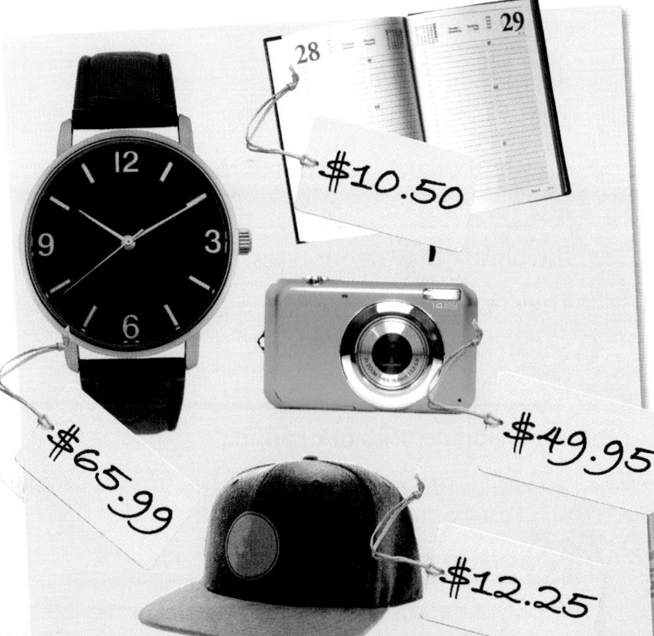

Beat the clock

With your partner, count from 1 to 100. One person counts from 1–10, then the next person from 11–20, etc. You have two minutes. How fast can you do it without making any mistakes?

6 Practice your dialogues from exercise 5. Change your roles for each dialogue.

Link it!

Think of something in a store that you really want to buy. Write a paragraph about it. Think about these things:

- What is it?
- Which store is it in?
- What color / size is it?
- How much is it?
- Is it a good price or is it expensive?

Workbook p.W24 Extra communication p.55

have: Simple present

Interrogative and short answers

Do you **have** a pen? **No**, I **don't**.
Does Lola **have** a calculator? **Yes**, she **does**.

Short answers		
Interrogative	Affirmative	Negative
Do I / you **have**?	Yes, I / you **do**.	No, I / you **don't**.
Does he / she / it **have**?	Yes, he / she / it **does**.	No, he / she / it **doesn't**.
Do we / you / they **have**?	Yes, we / you / they **do**.	No, we / you / they **don't**.

Think!

Choose the correct alternative.

To answer a question with *have*, we use ***do*** **or** ***does*** / ***have*** **or** ***has*** in the short answer.

Rules p.W21

1 Complete the questions with the correct form of *have*. Then write affirmative (✓) or negative (✗) short answers.

Does Ellen have a watch?
(✗) No, she doesn't.

1 _______ Alonso _______ this book?
(✓) _______________________
2 _______ you _______ my calculator, Alicia?
(✗) _______________________
3 _______ the children _______ a hamster?
(✓) _______________________
4 _______ I _______ your cell phone number?
(✓) _______________________
5 _______ we ___________ English today?
(✗) _______________________
6 _______ your house _______ a garage?
(✗) _______________________

Challenge

Write five questions with *have* for your partner.

Do you have a camera?
Does your brother / sister have blue eyes?

Puzzles p.119

The possessive *'s*

Lola**'s** calculator is on the desk.
Where are Mason**'s** sunglasses?

Singular + *'s*	Plural (irregular) + *'s*
Joshua**'s** tablet.	The children**'s** tablet.
Plural (regular) + *'*	**Two subjects + *'s***
The boys**'** tablet.	Caleb and Landon**'s** tablet.

Think!

Read the example and choose the correct alternative to complete the rule.

Oliver's computer is black.

The object comes **before** / **after** the name of the person who owns the object.

Rules p.W21

2 Complete the sentences with *'s* or *'* and the word in parentheses.

It's Sarah's tablet. (Sarah)

1 What is that ___________ name? (boy)
2 Mr. Klein is ___________________________ teacher. (Jack and Débora)
3 Is this ___________ planner? (Norie)
4 These are the _____________ books. (students)
5 This is the _____________ bedroom. (children)

3 Read what the people say. Rewrite the sentences using the possessive *'s*.

Karen: "He's my brother."
He's Karen's brother.

1 Ryan: "She's my mom."
She's _______________________.
2 Amy and Chloe: "It's our bedroom."
It's _______________________.
3 the boys: "They're our bikes."
They're _______________________.
4 Sofia: "It's my cell phone."
It's _______________________.
5 the children: "He's our cousin."
He's _______________________.

Challenge

Write five descriptions of possessions in the classroom.

Alfredo's backpack is gray and black.
Lina's pencil case is pink.

Puzzles p.119

Step 1

1 055 **Listen to the short conversations. Choose the correct answers.**

How many brothers and sisters does Jackson have?
a one b two (c) three

1 What's Lily's sister's name?
a Daniel b Brooklyn c Logan

2 What pets does Ryan have?
a a dog and a cat b two dogs c a dog and a hamster

3 What is Savannah's favorite type of music?
a hip-hop b pop c rap

4 What color is Julian's new bike?
a blue and black b yellow and black c blue and yellow

5 What is Zilda's favorite video game?
a *Fashion Party* b *Just Dance* c *Super Smash Bros.*

Listening strategy

Identifying speakers

Before you do a listening exercise, read the first exercise carefully. Sometimes you can see how many people are speaking, and who is speaking. Are they boys or girls?

Step 2

2 056 **Listen to Christopher answering questions about his family and things. Complete the chart with the missing information.**

Name	Christopher
Number of brothers Name(s)	One ________
Number of sisters	________
Pet(s)	dog ☐ cat ☐ fish ☐ no pets ☐
Possessions	phone ☐ guitar ☐ bike ☐ game console ☐

Step 3

3 **Pairwork** **Do you know your partner? Complete the information for him / her on your own. Then ask questions to check your answers.**

- Name
- brothers and sisters
- names of family members
- pets?
- favorite possession
- cell phone?
- game console?
- bike?
- favorite color
- favorite game
- favorite music

Do you have any brothers and sisters?

Yes, I do. I have one brother. / Yes, I do. I have a brother and a sister.

What's his name? / What are their names?

4 **Presentation** **Tell the class about your partner. Use the information from exercise 3.**

Cléber has a brother, but he doesn't have a sister. His brother's name is Evandro…

Workbook p.W24

My passions

Home | Profiles | News | Events | Contact

Personal profiles

Hi! My name's Yuki Sakamoto, and I'm 15 years old. I'm really into technology, and Computer Science is my favorite subject at school. At home, I have a computer, a laptop, and a tablet, but my favorite thing is my phone. It has hundreds of songs on it. I'm a big fan of Ariana Grande. She's an American singer. I have all her songs. My favorite song is *7 rings*. She's cool! All my friends love my music, too! We always listen to my playlists!

Hello, I'm Abi Wilson, and I'm 14. My favorite subject at school is Spanish. I have a Chilean penfriend, Marisol. My Spanish isn't very good, but Marisol's English is perfect! I'm also into sports, in particular tennis and soccer–my soccer ball is my favorite thing! I'm on a soccer team, and my uncle is our coach. He's a great soccer player and has about fifty trophies at home! He's my hero!

Hi there! My name's Manuel Torres, and I'm 13 years old. I'm really into music. I have a guitar and a piano, and I'm in a band, Just Rock. We aren't very good, but it's fun! I'm also a scout, and I'm a member of a scout troop in Michigan. We always do fun activities. I'm really into sports, and my bike is my favorite thing.

Teen life summer activities

1

International Scout Jamboree

West Virginia, U.S. July 22nd–August 2nd

A twelve-day jamboree for scouts from all over the world! Group games, sports, and outdoor activities during the day, with karaoke, dance, and rock bands in the evening!

Click here for an application form.

2

Learn to be a DJ

July 13th–17th

A five-day DJ course for teenagers in Portland, Oregon, U.S.! Bring it on!

Click here for an application form.

3

Worldteen Sports course

August 10th–23rd

Learn a sport and a language! Activity courses for teenagers in the U.S., Canada, Mexico, and Brazil.

Click here for an application form.

Reading

Check it out!

Find these words and phrases and check their meaning.

I'm really into   penfriend   fun   Bring it on!   learn

1 057 **Read and listen to the three personal profiles. Choose the correct answers.**

1 Yuki's favorite thing is her
- a computer.
- b tablet.
- c laptop.
- d phone.

2 Abi's Spanish
- a is very good.
- b is good.
- c isn't very good.
- d is perfect.

3 Manuel is
- a 12 years old.
- b 14 years old.
- c 13 years old.
- d 15 years old.

2 Read the profiles again and look at the summer activities. Match the people (Yuki, Abi, Manuel) with the activities.

International Scout Jamboree ____________

Learn to be a DJ ____________

Worldteen Sports course ____________

3 Answer the questions.

What's Yuki's favorite school subject?
It's Computer Science.

1 How many songs does Yuki have on her phone?

2 What's Yuki's favorite Ariana Grande song?

3 Where is Abi's penfriend from?

4 Who is Abi's soccer coach?

5 What does Abi's uncle have at home?

6 What musical instruments does Manuel have?

7 What's Manuel's favorite thing?

Writing

Step 1

4 Connor wants to apply to the Worldteen Sports course in Brazil. Complete his application form with information from the fact file.

Teen life summer activities

Application form

Course	Worldteen Sports course
Date	August 10th–23rd
Location	U.S. / Canada / (Brazil) / Mexico
First name	1 ___________ **Last name** 2 ___________
Email address	cwilson14@gmail.us
Mom's / Dad's cell phone number	(555) 555-7624

About you

My name is Connor Wilson, and I'm 3 _____ years old. I'm 4 ___________ and I'm from 5 ___________, in Washington in the U.S. My favorite school subjects are 6 ___________, in particular Spanish and French.

I have a sister, but I don't have a 7 ___________. My sister's name is 8 ___________. She's 9 _____ years old, and she's very different from me, but she's nice.

I'm crazy about 10 ___________. I have a 11 ___________, and I'm in a skaters' club in Seattle. It's fantastic! My skateboard is one of my favorite 12 ___________. I'm also into 13 ___________, and I have a cool 14 ___________ and a game console. I have about 30 video games! My favorite is *Fortnite*. It's awesome!

Fact File

Name	Connor Wilson
Age	12
Nationality	American
Town	Seattle, Washington, U.S.
Brothers	0
Sisters	one–Katie, 14
Interests	sports and technology
Favorite things	skateboard, cell phone, game console
Favorite school subjects	languages–Spanish and French
Course name and location	Worldteen Sports course, Brazil

Step 2

5 Imagine that you want to apply to one of the courses on page 52. Copy the fact file from exercise 4 into your notebook and complete it with information about you.

Step 3

6 Now complete the application form with information about you. Use Connor's text in exercise 4 to help you.

Challenge

Choose one of the courses on page 52 for a family member or friend and write a text about them for the *About you* section of the application form.

Application form

Course ___________

Date ___________

Location ___________

First name ___________

Last name ___________

Email address ___________

Mom's / Dad's cell phone number ___________

About you

____

____

____

____

____

____

____

____

Culture p.109

B Extra practice

Vocabulary

1 Write *R* (room), *F* (furniture) or *P* (possession).

bathroom	R	dining room	9___
bike	1___	stove	10___
bookcase	2___	game console	11___
camera	3___	guitar	12___
armchair	4___	hallway	13___
cabinet	5___	kitchen	14___
sunglasses	6___	living room	15___
desk	7___	bedroom	16___
planner	8___	wardrobe	17___

2 Choose the correct alternatives.

The couch is in the **living room** / **stairs**.

1 The keys are in the **bathroom** / **hallway**.
2 My **sunglasses** / **planner** is in my backpack.
3 The **stove** / **toilet** is in the bathroom.
4 My jeans are in my **armchair** / **wardrobe**.
5 The sink is in the **bathroom** / **living room**.
6 The **fridge** / **shower** is in the kitchen.

3 Complete the possessions with the missing letters.

Érico has a g u i t a r.

1 Julia has a p ___ o n ___.
2 I have a g ___ m ___ c ___ ___ s ___ l e.
3 You have a s k ___ ___ e ___ o a ___ d.
4 They have a ___ ___ c c e r b ___ l l.
5 We have a t ___ ___ l ___ t.

Grammar

4 Rewrite the sentences with the plural form of the words in bold. Use plural forms of the verbs *some* and *any*.

There is a **man** in the hallway.
There are some men in the hallway.
There isn't a **mouse** in the kitchen.
There aren't any mice in the kitchen.

1 There is a **fish** in the ocean.
2 There isn't a **child** in the backyard.
3 There is a **box** on the table.
4 There is a **shelf** in my bedroom.
5 There isn't a **family** in the park.
6 There isn't a **tomato** in the fridge.

5 Complete the text with the prepositions of place.

~~on~~ under next to between behind across from

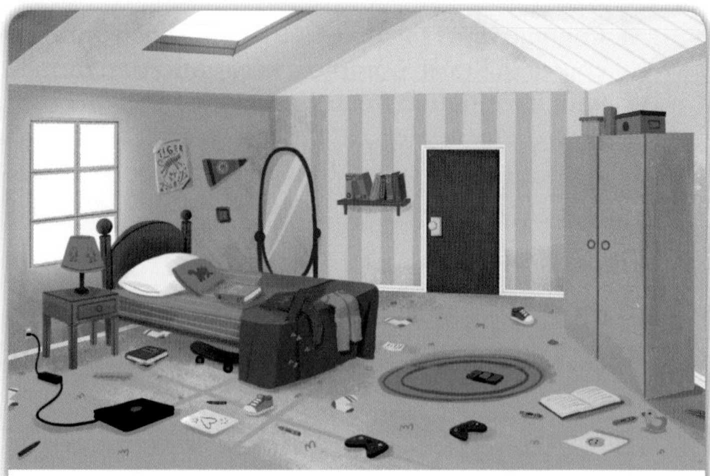

The book is on the bed. The mirror is [1]___ the bed and the door. The skateboard is [2]___ the bed. The poster is [3]___ the bed, on the wall. The table is [4]___ the bed. The bed is [5]___ the wardrobe.

6 Complete the dialogue.

Jose Are there any couches in your living room?
Ignacio Yes, [1]___. [2]___ two small couches.
Jose [3]___ a table?
Ignacio No, [4]___.
Jose [5]___ you [6]___ any armchairs?
Ignacio No, we [7]___. [8]___ any armchairs because the room is very small.
Jose [9]___ a bookcase?
Ignacio Yes, [10]___. [11]___ a shelf, too, with all my stuff on it!
Jose What [12]___ you [13]___ on the shelf?
Ignacio I [14]___ some DVDs and a camera. My brother [15]___ his game console.
Jose [16]___ he have an Xbox?
Ignacio No, he [17]___. He [18]___ a PlayStation.
Jose [19]___ a TV?
Ignacio Yes, [20]___! It's very big!

7 Underline and then correct the mistakes.

Its Sasha's planner.
It's Sasha's planner.

1 Where is there mom?
2 The childrens' teacher is in the hallway.
3 There the boys' guitars.
4 They're is a game console in my brother's bedroom.

Communication

1 058 Listen and choose the correct answers. Then listen again and check.

Érico How many students are there in your school?
Daniela There are **a** 1,200. **b** 2,000. **c** 2,200.
Érico How many floors are there in the school?
Daniela There are **a** 14. **b** 40. **c** 4.
Érico How many desks are in each classroom?
Daniela There are **a** 30. **b** 13. **c** 20.

Érico How many teachers are there at the school?
Daniela There are **a** 115. **b** 160. **c** 150.
Érico How many girls are there in your class?
Daniela There are **a** 10. **b** 12. **c** 20.
Érico How many computers are there in your class?
Daniela There are **a** 9. **b** 4. **c** 5.

2 059 Complete the dialogues with the words in the box. Then listen and check.

receipt	are	take	change	~~much~~	that's

1
Sangwoo Excuse me. How much are those sunglasses, please?
Assistant They're $39.50.
Sangwoo They're nice. I'll [1]__________ them.
Assistant OK, [2]__________ $39.50, please.
Sangwoo Here you [3]__________.
Assistant Thank you. Here's 50 cents [4]__________ and here's your [5]__________.

it's	problem	that's	this	bye

2
Jessica Excuse me. How much is [6]__________ skateboard, please?
Assistant [7]__________ $119.99.
Jessica Oh, [8]__________ expensive! No, thanks.
Assistant No [9]__________. Goodbye.
Jessica [10]__________.

Pronunciation

3 060 Read and listen to the sentences. Listen to the pronunciation of the sound /ð/. Then listen again and repeat.

Is **th**ere a bookcase in **th**eir living room?
No, **th**ere isn't.
Are **th**ere any shelves in **th**e bedroom?
Yes, **th**ere are. **Th**ey're near **th**e window.

Video link

4 061 Watch or listen
Choose the correct answers.

Ludmila's bedroom
a has two wardrobes.
(b) has a wardrobe.
c doesn't have a wardrobe.

1 Her mirror is between
a the bed and the TV.
b the TV and the window.
c the bed and the window.

2 Mario
a has a room with his brother.
b has a room with his two brothers.
c doesn't have a brother.

3 There's a big wardrobe
a between the two beds.
b for the boys' clothes.
c for his brother's clothes.

4 Clara's TV
a is across from the bed.
b is across from her desk.
c is next to her bed.

5 On her wall, there are
a lots of pictures.
b lots of posters.
c lots of shelves.

We will ...

- discuss different ideas in a group
- make a presentation confidently

Design your own youth hostel

What's up?

1 Match the words with the pictures (a–i).

1 popcorn maker ____
2 movie screen ____
3 game console ____
4 laptop a
5 pool table ____
6 skateboard ____
7 bookcase ____
8 sports equipment ____
9 beanbag ____

a

b
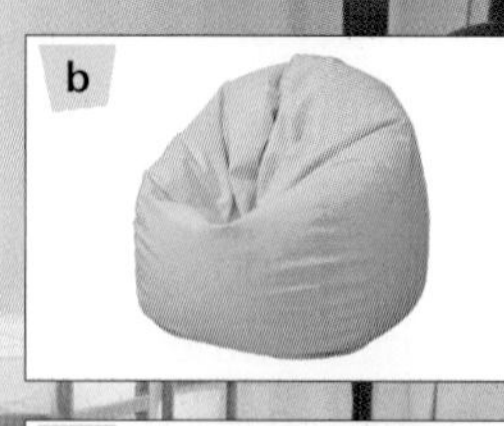

c

f

d

e

g

h

i

Get thinking

2 Read the poster. Is it about your house, or a place you can stay on vacation?

____

NEW Youth Hostel

There is a new youth hostel in your town! Imagine it is your youth hostel. You always have guests and everyone thinks it looks great! A good name is very important and we want to hear your ideas! Get involved! Send your ideas to youthtown@hostel.com

"There are colorful pictures on the walls. There are modern shower rooms, toilets, and lots of bedrooms."

"There's a kitchen with a big fridge, a stove, and lots of chairs and tables–perfect for guests to cook and have fun together."

"In the living room, there are games in the corner, musical instruments on the shelves, and sports equipment like soccer balls and skateboards."

Get involved

3 Imagine your ideal youth hostel. Make a list of five things you have in it.

The project

4 Groupwork Design your youth hostel. Make a big poster with pictures. Answer the questions.

1 How many rooms do you have in the youth hostel? What rooms are they?
2 What furniture and other things do you have in each room? Where are they?
3 What is the name of your youth hostel?

Real English

Let's have a ... in / on / next to ...
How about a ... here? That's a great idea!
I don't like that idea. I'm not sure.

5 Presentation Present your poster to the class.

Check it out!

Find these phrases and check their meaning.

youth hostel
in the corner
guests

How did you do?

Write the statements into your notebook and score yourself from 1 to 5.

I can ... talk about different things to put in a youth hostel.

1 2 3 4 5
not very well — very well

I can ... describe where things are with prepositions of place.

1 2 3 4 5
not very well — very well

Speaking competences

I can identify different rooms and furniture. (p.36)

1 Pairwork Complete the sentences with the words in the box. Then say true sentences to your partner.

~~sink~~ table and chairs wardrobe toilet couch stove

The sink is in the bathroom.

1 The ________ is in the bedroom.
2 The ________ is in the living room.
3 The ________ is in the kitchen.
4 The ________ are in the dining room.
5 The ________ is in the bathroom.

/5

I can talk about quantity. (p.38)

2 Complete the dialogue.

A How many beds are there in your bedroom?
B There [1]________ two.
A How many windows does it have?
B [2]________ has one.
A How many desks [3]________ in your room?
B There is [4]________.
A [5]________ shelves are there?
B There are four.

/5

I can talk about houses and apartments. (p.41)

3 Pairwork Choose the correct alternatives. Then read the text to your partner.

My cousin Luisa's house is big. It has five bedrooms and three **bathrooms / stairs**. In my cousin's bedroom, [1] **there are / there's** a big bed, a big wardrobe, a desk, and a laptop. In the [2] **hallway / living room**, there are two big couches, an armchair, a small table, and a big TV. My favorite room is the [3] **bedroom / kitchen**. It has a stove, a [4] **fridge / toilet**, a sink, and lots of cabinets. [5] **it / There** has a big table, with chairs, and a massive couch. I love Luisa's house!

/5

I can identify possessions. (p.46)

4 Pairwork Write the missing words in the sentences. Then, ask and answer the questions.

"Do you have a skateboard?"
1 "Is there a ________ in your bag?"
2 "Do you have your ________?"
3 "Is there a ________ under your bed?"
4 "Do you have any ________?"
5 "Is your ________ black?"

/5

I can ask about prices and pay for things. (p.48)

5 Pairwork Complete the dialogue with the words in the box. Then practice with a partner.

great here it's change take ~~that~~

Alicia Excuse me. How much is that camera?
Assistant [1]________ $80.99.
Alicia It's nice. I'll [2]________ it.
Assistant [3]________! That's $80.99, please.
Alicia [4]________ you are.
Assistant Thank you. Here's one cent [5]________ and your receipt.

/5

I can talk about family and possessions. (p.51)

6 Look at the chart and write five more sentences.

About my friend, his family, and possessions	
Name	Jaime
Family	one brother–Pedro two sisters–Camila and Lucila
Favorite thing	bike
Dogs	one dog–Fido
Cats	no cats

My friend's name is Jaime.

/5

Listening, reading, and writing competences

	Yes	I'm not sure	No
I can understand someone talking about where they live. (p.41)	○	○	○
I can read and answer questions about rooms and furniture. (p.42)	○	○	○
I can write a description of my bedroom. (p.43)	○	○	○
I can understand someone talking about their family and possessions. (p.51)	○	○	○
I can read and answer questions about different summer courses. (p.52)	○	○	○
I can complete an application form for a summer course. (p.53)	○	○	○

5 I get up at six o'clock

In this unit we will …
- talk about daily routines
- ask for and make suggestions
- write about a typical school day

1 062 **Read and listen** **Where does Jacob go after school?** ______

The girls are in the park with Jacob. He is worried …

Lola Where are the boys?
Rubi Jacob is always at dance practice– he practices every day … and Mason is probably in his bedroom.
Lola Oh, poor Mason.
Rubi I think you like Mason!
Lola Oh, stop it, Rubi!
Rubi Well, he is cute …
Lola Yeah, he is …

Jacob arrives.

Rubi Hi, Jacob! What a surprise! We never see you now.
Jacob I know. I'm sorry, but I'm very busy … I practice all the time.
Rubi Really? All the time?
Jacob Yes, in the morning, I get up at six o'clock, I have breakfast, and then I sometimes practice some dance moves at home before I go to school.
Rubi What?! You're crazy!
Jacob Yes, I know! Then, when I finish school, I always go to the dance studio. I have a personal dance teacher now. She comes to the studio on Tuesdays and Thursdays.
Lola Wow! That's exciting!
Jacob Yes, it is. It's awesome. But …
Rubi But what?
Jacob … but I feel bad for Mason.

2 **Comprehension** **Put the sentences about Jacob's daily routine in the correct order.**

I go to the dance studio. ___
I finish school. ___
I have breakfast. ___
I get up. 1
I go to school. ___

Check it out!

Find these words and phrases and check their meaning.

cute	Really?
What a surprise!	You're crazy!
I'm very busy.	I feel bad

Step 1

3 **Find and underline the phrases in the dialogue in exercise 1.**

She **comes** to the studio **on** Tuesdays and Thursdays. he **practices** every day
I **practice** all the time. I **get up at** six o'clock We **never see** you now.
Then, when I **finish** school, I **always go** to the dance studio.

Step 2

4 063 **Read the dialogues and choose the correct alternatives. Then listen and check.**

1

Rubi Jacob is always at **soccer** / **dance** practice– he practices every day … and Mason is probably [1] **in his bedroom** / **at school**.

2

Jacob Yes, in the morning, I get up at [2]**six** / **seven** o'clock, I have breakfast, and then I sometimes practice some dance moves at home before I go to [3]**school** / **the dance studio**.

Rubi What?! You're [4]**a star** / **crazy**!

3

Jacob I have a [5] **personal dance teacher** / **new partner** now. She comes to the studio on [6] **Tuesdays and Thursdays** / **Tuesdays and Fridays**.

Lola Wow! That's [7]**expensive** / **exciting**!

063 **Now listen again and repeat.**

Step 3

5 **Complete the sentences with information about your daily routine.**

I get up at ______________________________.

I have breakfast at ______________________________.

I go to school at ______________________________.

I finish school at ______________________________.

6 **Pairwork** **Use the sentences from exercise 5 to tell your partner about your daily routine.**

I get up at 7:00. And you?

I get up at 6:20, and I have breakfast at 7:00.

Workbook p.W28

Vocabulary

Daily routines

1 064 **Look at the pictures of Sofia's daily routine. Match the sentences (a–l) with the pictures 1–12. Then listen and check.**

a I have lunch at twelve thirty.
b I do my homework at four fifteen.
c I go to bed at nine thirty.
d I get home at three fifteen.
~~e I get up at six twenty.~~
f I watch TV at seven thirty.
g I take a shower at six thirty.
h I start school at eight o'clock.
i I have breakfast at seven o'clock.
j I finish school at two forty-five.
k I get dressed at six forty-five.
l I have dinner at six o'clock.

e

____

____

____

____

____

____

____

____

____

____

____

2 **Pairwork** **Talk about your daily routines during the week. Is it different on weekends? Compare with your partner.**

During the week, I get up at six thirty, but on weekends I get up at ten o'clock. And you?

Vocabulary strategy

Categorizing vocabulary

Writing new vocabulary in different colors can help you visualize the new words and remember them more easily. Try using a different color for each topic.

Workbook p.W28

Simple present

Affirmative

She **comes** to the studio.
He **practices** every day.

I	**live**
you	**live**
he / she / it	**lives**
we	**live**
you	**live**
they	**live**

Think!

Complete the rule.
In the third person singular (*he, she, it*),
we add _____ to the base form of the verb.

Rules p.W26

1 Read the sentences and add -*s* to the verbs where necessary.

He play*s* tennis.
1 We live_____ in Rome.
2 He speak_____ English.
3 I visit_____ my grandparents on Sundays.
4 It start_____ at 6 p.m.
5 You listen_____ to music in your bedroom.
6 She get_____ up at 7 a.m.
7 They practice_____ every day.
8 He play_____ soccer on Saturdays.

2 Complete the sentences. Use the correct form of the verbs in the box.

~~get~~ read play listen get start live

My dad *gets* up at 10:00 on Saturdays.
1 Oliver ________ video games in his bedroom.
2 My mom ________ to classical music.
3 My parents ________ home at 6:00.
4 Kerry's grandparents ________ in Ohio.
5 Before I go to bed, I ________ a book.
6 Class ________ at nine o'clock.

Spelling variations

do	do**es**	kiss	kiss**es**
go	go**es**	study	stud**ies**
watch	watch**es**	have	ha**s**
finish	finish**es**		

Rules p.W26

3 Rewrite the sentences with the subject pronouns in parentheses.

I do my homework in the afternoon. (He)
He does his homework in the afternoon.
1 They study Spanish. (She)
2 We finish school at 3:30 p.m. (He)
3 She has breakfast in the backyard. (They)
4 Mom watches TV after dinner. (Mom and I)
5 Jenny and I go to school. (My sister)

4 Look at the picture of Jamie's bedroom. Write sentences about what he does in his free time.

~~go to~~ play read eat study

He goes to the gym.

5 065 **Pronunciation Listen to the verbs and check (✓) the correct column. Then listen again and repeat.**

	/s/	/z/	/ɪz/
works			
teaches			
has			
reads			
likes			

Challenge

Look at the illustrations on page 60.
Write sentences about Sofia's routine.
She gets up at 6:20 a.m.

Puzzles p.120

Asking for and making suggestions

1 066 **Watch, listen, or read** **Match the pictures with the conversations.**

a

____

b

____

c

____

2 066 **Listen again and complete the dialogues with the expressions in the box.**

~~play *Super Mario*~~ go to the movies watch TV have a snack do our homework

1

Arianna I'm bored. What do you want to do?
Dominic Let's play *Super Mario*.
Arianna OK, great. I love that game.

2

Arianna What do you want to do?
Dominic Let's [1]__________________.
Arianna Oh ... OK, but do you want to [2]__________________ first?
Dominic OK, that's a good idea. I'm hungry!

3

Arianna I'm bored. What do you want to do?
Dominic Let's [3]__________________.
Arianna There aren't any good shows on TV. Let's [4]__________________ instead.
Dominic Cool. I want to see the new Star Wars movie.

Speaking strategy

Saying *no* politely

It's important to say *no* to a suggestion or idea politely. First, say why you don't want to do something, and then suggest an alternative plan.

Let's go to the park.

Hmm ... it's very cold today. Let's play video games instead.

3 067 **Real English** **Listen and repeat.**

What do you want to do?

Let's play *Super Mario*.

Do you want to have a snack first?

OK, cool! / OK, great!

OK, that's a good idea!

No, let's go to the movies instead.

No, I'm sorry, but I'm busy.

Sorry, I'm tired / I have homework.

4 068 **Listen and complete the sentences with the phrases in the box. Then listen again–do the people say *yes* or *no* to the idea? Choose the correct answers.**

have some ice cream	clean up	~~do some homework~~	meet up

It's Monday tomorrow. Do you want to *do some homework*? **yes / (no)**

1 I'm hungry. Let's ______________________. **yes / no**

2 It's a mess in here. Do you want to help me ______________________? **yes / no**

3 I'm bored. Do you want to ______________? **yes / no**

Beat the clock

In two minutes, think of ideas of things to do. Use the verbs in the word map to help you.

go watch play listen

5 Pairwork **Look at the *Real English* phrases in exercise 3 and your answers from *Beat the clock*. Write two dialogues similar to exercise 2.**

6 **Practice your dialogues from exercise 5 with your partner.**

Link it!

Pairwork **One person is Student A. One person is Student B.**

Student A: Say you're bored. Say what you want to do.

Student B: You aren't happy with the idea. Say no, and say why.

Student A: Say OK and give another idea.

Student B: You aren't happy with this idea. Say no, and say why.

Repeat. How long can you continue the conversation?

Link to life **Sometimes people make suggestions that you don't like. When is it better to be honest and suggest something different? When is it better to agree to do what the other person wants?**

Workbook p.W30 Extra communication p.79

Grammar

Prepositions of time: *at, in, on*

In the morning, I usually get up **at** six o'clock.
She comes to the studio **on** Tuesdays and Thursdays.

at	**at** six thirty / eight o'clock
	at night
in	**in** the morning / afternoon / evening
	in December / March / July
	in the summer / fall / spring
	in 2030
on	**on** Saturday(s) / Tuesday(s)
	on the weekend / **on** weekends
	on July 17th / September 24th
	on Christmas Day / Valentine's Day

Think!

Complete the rule with *at* and *in*.

In English, we say [1]___ *the morning,* [2]___ *the afternoon,* [3]___ *the evening,* but [4]___ *night.*

Rules p.W27

1 **Complete the expressions with the correct preposition of time. Which one is different?**

in the summer   in 2020   (at) 6 p.m.

1 ____ 5:20   ____ the winter   ____ night
2 ____ Sundays   ____ Christmas Day   ____ April
3 ____ Tuesday   ____ September   ____ the spring
4 ____ 2 p.m.   ____ the evening   ____ the fall
5 ____ August 18th   ____ August   ____ my birthday

2 **Complete the sentences with information that is true for you. Use the words in parentheses to help you. Use the correct preposition of time.**

I get up *at seven o'clock*. (time)

1 My school day starts ________________. (time)
2 My birthday is ________________. (date)
3 I do my homework ________________. (afternoon / evening)
4 My school year starts ________________. (month)
5 I go to bed ________________. (time)
6 My 18th birthday is ________________. (year)

Adverbs of frequency

Jacob is **always** at dance practice.
We **never** see you now.

0%					100%
never	rarely	sometimes	usually	often	always

Think!

Look at the sentences. Then complete the rule with *before* and *after*.

I'm rarely late for school.
I always do my homework before dinner.

Adverbs of frequency go [1]__________ the verb *be* and [2]__________ all other verbs.

Rules p.W27

3 **Rewrite the sentences with the adverbs of frequency.**

I study with my friends. (often)
I often study with my friends.

1 We go to the movies on the weekend. (usually)
2 Marcelo listens to the radio. (sometimes)
3 Aubrey is happy. (never)
4 I go to bed before 10 p.m. (rarely)
5 Grandpa is in the backyard. (always)

4 **Read Riley's answers to the questionnaire. Write sentences about her daily routine.**

What's your daily routine?

Name Riley Morgan

1 I get up before 7 a.m.
a never   b sometimes   (c) usually
2 I take the school bus to school.
a never   (b) always   c sometimes
3 I'm late for school.
a sometimes   b rarely   (c) never
4 I do my homework in the afternoon.
a always   b usually   (c) often
5 I play video games in the evening.
(a) rarely   b never   c often

Riley usually gets up before 7 a.m.

Challenge

Do the questionnaire in exercise 4. Then write your own answers.

I never get up before 7 a.m..

Puzzles p.120

Listening and speaking

Step 1

1 069 **Listen to people talking about after-school activities. Match the names in the box with the after-school clubs a–e.**

Ichiro Liliana James ~~Ryan~~ Olivia

a volleyball club ________
b book club ________
c dance club *Ryan*
d computer club ________
e photography club ________

2 069 **Listen again and complete the sentences.**

1 Ryan finishes school at ________________.
2 He goes to an after-school club on ________________.
3 Liliana usually goes home on the ________________.
4 She always gets home ________ on Fridays.
5 Ichiro always goes to practice on ________________ and Wednesdays.
6 The two teams sometimes have ________ together after their game on Saturday.
7 James is at a new ________.
8 James goes to a club and they sometimes ________________.
9 Before she does her homework, Olivia usually ________________.
10 Olivia learns to make ________________ at her after-school club.

Step 2

3 070 **Listen and complete the chart about Logan's routine with the correct form of the phrases in the box.**

watch a movie go to drama club finish his homework ~~have a snack~~ listen to music play video games start his homework go to basketball practice watch TV have dinner

At his grandma's house	At his house	Wednesdays	Fridays
He *has a snack*. He [1] ________. He [2] ________. He [3] ________ ________.	He [4] ________. He [5] ________ ________. He [6] ________. He [7] ________.	He [8] ________ ________ ________.	He [9] ________ ________.

Step 3

4 Pairwork **Tell your partner about what you do after school. Use the activities in the box to help you. Take notes about your partner.**

go home watch TV use the computer play sports chat online watch movies listen to music meet friends do homework send text messages have a snack

I get home at 2 p.m. I usually …

5 Presentation **Tell the class about your partner's afternoon.**

After Vitória gets home at 2 p.m., she usually …

Culture focus

In the U.S., many students go to after-school clubs. They are activities that the school organizes, but they aren't in normal school hours. Drama, music, sports, and arts and crafts are popular after-school clubs.

Workbook p.W30

Addison's blog

My family | My friends | **My school** | My pets

1 I go to Lincoln Junior High School. It's a big school with 1,500 students and we wear our own clothes. We go to school five days a week, from Monday through Friday, but our school day is long! School starts at eight forty in the morning, and it finishes at four o'clock in the afternoon.

2 When I get to school, I go to homeroom. This is a period every morning when Mrs. Weston, our homeroom teacher, calls out the students' names in the class roster. After that, the classes start. The classes are 45 minutes long. On Thursdays, some of our classes are 30 minutes, and we finish school at three o'clock.

3 I'm in 7th grade, and I study twelve subjects. My favorite subjects are Computer Science and English. We have a different teacher for every subject, and we move around the school for different classes. My favorite teacher is Mrs. Hamilton. She teaches the Computer Science class. Her classes are always interesting. We sometimes make video games in her class, and then we play them! It's so much fun!

4 There's a big cafeteria in our school. It opens at seven o'clock because some students have breakfast there before school starts. The food in the cafeteria isn't bad. On Wednesdays, we have pizza! Some students prefer to bring their lunch from home. It's usually a sandwich and a drink. We have one hour for lunch. I have my lunch, and then I usually go outside with my friends.

Check it out!

Find these words and phrases and check their meaning.

homeroom   call out   move around
period   class roster   cafeteria

Reading strategy

Understanding numbers in a text

Numbers in a text are often important. If you are trying to understand a text with lots of numbers in it, underline or circle the numbers, and then find what they refer to in the text. This can help you to understand the text quickly, too.

Reading

1 071 **Read and listen** to Addison's blog post about her school. Match the topics with the paragraphs.

school day / week   paragraph 1
lunch at school   paragraph ____
school subjects   paragraph ____
homeroom / classes   paragraph ____

Culture focus

Children in the U.S. go to school for a minimum of thirteen years.

Normally, you start elementary school when you are 5 years old, and you finish in 8th grade, when you are 14.

You start high school in 9th or 10th grade, and you finish high school in 12th grade. High school students are 14–18 years old.

It is sometimes different in different parts of the country. Some states also have junior high school or middle school. These schools are for grades 5–9.

2 **Are the sentences true (T) or false (F)? Correct the false sentences.**

Addison goes to Lincoln Junior High School. T
It's a small school. F   *It's a big school.*

1 Addison goes to school Monday through Saturday. ____
2 On Thursdays, she starts school at 8:40 a.m. and she finishes at 4 p.m. ____
3 Mrs. Weston is her homeroom teacher. ____
4 The classes are 50 minutes. ____
5 She studies twelve subjects. ____
6 The school cafeteria isn't open at 7 a.m. ____
7 She likes the food in the cafeteria. ____

Writing

Step 1

3 Complete the text about Morgan's school day with the information in the questionnaire.

Name: Morgan
School: Jefferson Middle School
Number of students: 500
School day:
Get up: 7:30 a.m.
Leave home: 8:10 a.m.
Start school: 8:40 a.m.
Daily schedule:
Morning: four classes
Lunch: 12:00–12:30 p.m. (lunch from home)
Afternoon: four classes
Favorite school day: Wednesday
Favorite classes: Spanish and History
After-school clubs: On Mondays, I go to the after-school Movie and Creative Writing Club. We watch movies and write stories.

Hi, I'm Morgan. I'm a student at Jefferson Middle School. It's a small school with 500 students. On school days, I [1]__________ __________ at 7:30 a.m., and then I take a shower before breakfast. I [2]__________ __________ at 8:10 a.m. and I [3]__________ __________ at 8:40 a.m. First, I go to homeroom, and after that, I go to my classes. I have [4]__________ __________ before we have lunch. Lunch is at [5]__________ o'clock. The food in the cafeteria isn't very good. I usually bring my [6]__________ from home. My favorite school day is [7]__________ because we have [8]__________ and [9]__________. They are my favorite classes of the week. I hate Tuesdays–we have Math, Science, and finally a long period of Geography. On Mondays, I go to the after-school [10]__________ and [11]__________ __________ Club. We watch movies and [12]__________ __________. It's fun!

4 Find and underline the sequencing words in Morgan's text in exercise 3.

Step 2

5 Complete the questionnaire with information about your school and your school day.

Writing strategy

Sequencing events

When we want to talk about the order of events, we can use words like: *first, before, after, then, after that,* and *finally.*

***First**, I get up, **then** I take a shower. **After that**, I get dressed, and **finally**, I leave the house at eight thirty.*

*I take a shower **before** breakfast. **After** breakfast, I get dressed.*

Name: ______________________________
School: ______________________________
Number of students: ______________________________
School day:
Get up: ______________________________
Leave home: ______________________________
Start school: ______________________________
Daily schedule:
Morning: ______________________________
Lunch: ______________________________
Afternoon: ______________________________
Favorite school day: ______________________________
Favorite classes: ______________________________
After-school clubs: ______________________________

Step 3

6 Use the information in the questionnaire to write a blog post about your school and your school day. Use sequencing words.

Hi, I'm … I'm a student at …

Challenge

Imagine you are at elementary school again. Write a paragraph to describe your typical day. Think about these things:

- What time does school start and finish?
- What classes do you have?
- Do you have lunch at school or at home?
- What do you usually do after school?

Culture p.110

6 You don't know him

In this unit we will ...
- talk about your typical daily meals
- talk about likes and dislikes
- ask about habits
- write about a popular food in your country

1 072 **Read and listen** Who are Sam and Brody talking about? ___________

Mason hears something in the school cafeteria that makes him angry ...

Lola What's on the menu today?
Mason It's Friday, so it's nachos with cheese today.
Lola Nachos with cheese? My favorite!
Mason I love them, too!
Lola Hey, listen to this. What do you call cheese that isn't your cheese?
Mason I don't know. What do you call cheese that isn't your cheese?
Lola Nacho cheese! Not ... your ... cheese!
Mason Oh, Lola ... that's awful!
Cook Do you want any salad? Corn, carrots, tomatoes?
Mason No, I don't, thanks.
Lola Yes, please–carrots and corn for me. I love them.

Later ...

Lola Oh, there's Jacob.
Mason So what? I hope he doesn't sit here.
Sam I can't stand him.
Brody Who? Jacob?
Sam Yes, he's a real show-off.
Brody Yeah, he thinks he's great, but he's very annoying.
Mason What?! Shut up, you two! You don't know him.
Sam Who are you?
Mason I'm his brother. And he isn't a show-off. He's a great guy!
Lola You're right, Mason. Jacob is great. Tell him!

2 **Comprehension** Complete the sentences.

Lola and Mason love nachos.
1 ___________ wants nachos but not vegetables.
2 ___________ wants carrots and corn with the nachos.
3 ___________ is angry with two boys.
4 ___________ defends Jacob.

Link to life Sometimes people you don't know seem annoying. Is it bad to judge people on first impressions?

Check it out!
Find these words and phrases and check their meaning.

awful	he's a real show-off
So what?	annoying
I can't stand him.	Shut up

Step 1

3 **Find and underline the phrases in the dialogue in exercise 1.**

What do you call cheese ...? **Do you want** any salad? **You don't know** him. **I don't know. No, I don't**

Step 2

4  **Put the words in order to make sentences or questions. Then listen and check.**

1

Lola do / cheese / call / you / What / that isn't your cheese?
What do you call cheese that isn't your cheese?

Mason know. / I / don't
1 ____________
What do you call cheese that isn't your cheese?

Lola Nacho cheese!

2

Cook any / you / Do / salad? / want
2 ____________

Mason thanks. / don't, / No, / I
3 ____________

Lola Yes, please–carrots and corn for me. them. / I / love
4 ____________

3

Mason Shut up, you two! him. / You / know / don't
5 ____________

Sam Who are you?

Mason I'm his brother. And he isn't a show-off. He's a great guy!

073 **Now listen again and repeat.**

Step 3

5 **Pairwork** **Ask and answer questions about food. Write a dialogue. Use the words in the box to help you.**

tuna cheese chicken peas carrots corn

Do you want any tuna?

Yes, please.

Do you want any cheese?

No, I don't, thanks.

6 **Pairwork** **Practice your dialogues from exercise 5.**

Workbook p.W34

Vocabulary

Food and drink

1 074 **Look at the school lunches and match the food words in the box with the pictures 1–24. Then listen and check.**

peach pear apple bread carrots cheese chicken fries eggs grapes ham ice cream ~~milk~~ orange juice peas potato chips potatoes salad salmon soda corn tomatoes tuna water

1 milk
2 ______
3 ______
4 ______
5 ______
6 ______
7 ______
8 ______
9 ______
10 ______
11 ______
12 ______
13 ______
14 ______
15 ______
16 ______
17 ______
18 ______
19 ______
20 ______
21 ______
22 ______
23 ______
24 ______

Vocabulary strategy

Matching images with new words

Matching images with new words is a great way to remember new vocabulary. Draw small pictures of the different food items in your vocabulary notebook and write the English words next to them.

Lunch A

Lunch B

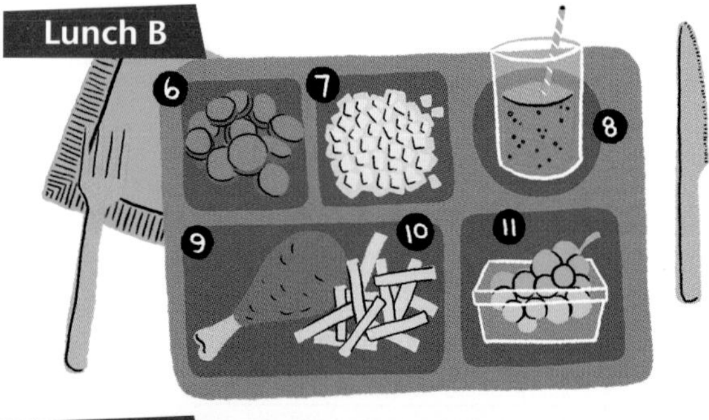

Lunch C

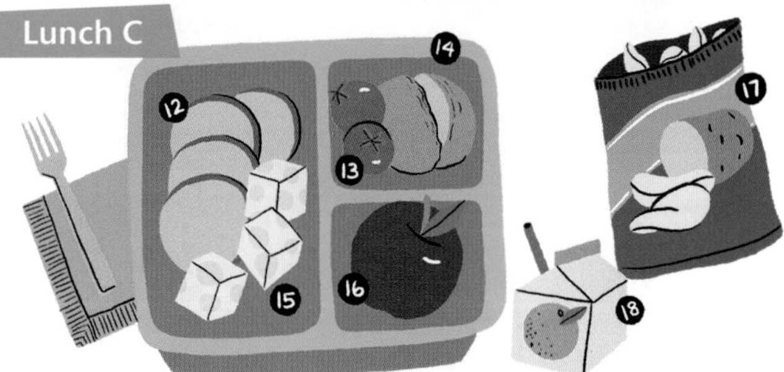

Lunch D

2 Copy the word map and complete it with the food in exercise 1.

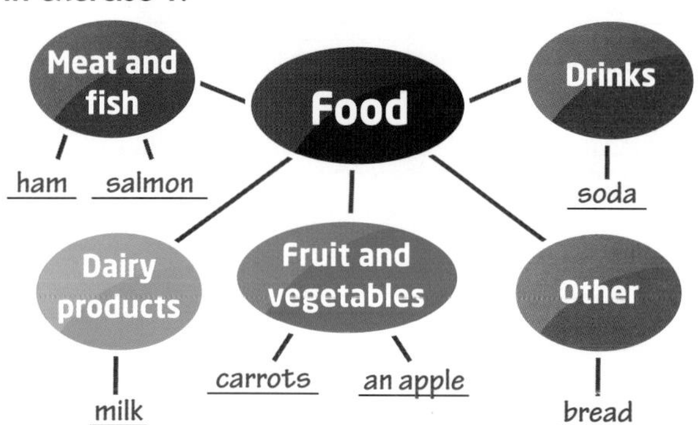

Look!

Some nouns have singular and plural forms, but we can only talk about some nouns in the singular form.

Singular	Plural	Singular only
an apple	apples	milk
a carrot	carrots	bread

3 Pairwork **Look at the lunches A–D in exercise 1. Put the lunches in order from 1 (your favorite) to 4 (your least favorite). Compare with your partner.**

What's your favorite lunch?

It's lunch A. It has salmon, potatoes, peas …

My favorite lunch is A, too. / My favorite lunch is lunch C. It has …

What's your second-favorite lunch?

It's …

Culture focus

In the U.S., children stay at school for lunch. Most of them have hot school lunches, but some bring their lunch from home.

Workbook p.W34

Simple present

Negative

You **don't** know him.
Mason **doesn't** want any vegetables.

Full form	Short form
I **do not** swim	I **don't** swim
you **do not** swim	you **don't** swim
he **does not** swim	he **doesn't** swim
she **does not** swim	she **doesn't** swim
it **does not** swim	it **doesn't** swim
we **do not** swim	we **don't** swim
you **do not** swim	you **don't** swim
they **do not** swim	they **don't** swim

Think!

Complete the sentences with *don't* or *doesn't*.

I / You / We / They [1] __________ play.

He / She / It [2] __________ play.

Rules p.W32

1 Choose the correct alternatives.

My cousin **don't** / **(doesn't)** speak English.

1 I **don't** / **doesn't** study Spanish at school.
2 We're vegetarians. We **don't** / **doesn't** eat meat.
3 Dad **don't** / **doesn't** work in the evenings.
4 My best friend **don't** / **doesn't** go to my school.
5 The children **don't** / **doesn't** like carrots.
6 The movie **don't** / **doesn't** start at 8 p.m.

2 Write the sentences in the negative form. Use *don't* and *doesn't*.

I live in London.
I don't live in London.

1 Katie goes to bed at 10 p.m.
2 We visit our uncle on Sundays.
3 My dog likes fish.
4 My mom cleans my bedroom.
5 The boys play basketball on Fridays.
6 I get home at 4 p.m.
7 Matteo has lunch at school.
8 Holly eats salad.

Interrogative and short answers

Do you **want** any salad? No, I **don't**.
Does Lola **want** any carrots? Yes, she **does**.

Interrogative	Short answers	
	Affirmative	Negative
Do I swim?	Yes, you **do**.	No, you **don't**.
Do you swim?	Yes, I **do**.	No, I **don't**.
Does he swim?	Yes, he **does**.	No, he **doesn't**.
Does she swim?	Yes, she **does**.	No, she **doesn't**.
Does it swim?	Yes, it **does**.	No, it **doesn't**.
Do we swim?	Yes, you **do**.	No, you **don't**.
Do you swim?	Yes, we **do**.	No, we **don't**.
Do they swim?	Yes, they **do**.	No, they **don't**.

Think!

Choose the correct alternatives.

- In simple present questions, *do* and *does* go [1] **before** / **after** the subject.
- In third person singular questions, we [2]**add** / **don't add** an *-s* to the main verb.

Rules p.W32

3 Complete the questions and short answers with *do, does, don't,* or *doesn't*.

Do you like tuna? Yes, I *do*.

1 ________ Mr. Black teach Art? No, he ________.
2 ________ the girls start school at 9 a.m.? Yes, they ________.
3 ________ Oscar like ice cream? Yes, he ________.
4 ________ you and your family speak German? No, we ________.
5 ________ you get up at 7:30? No, I ________.
6 ________ Lily play sports after school? Yes, she ________.
7 ________ you and Dani want pasta for lunch? Yes, we ________.
8 ________ they live in an apartment? No, they ________.

Challenge

Write five questions for the students in your class. Use the verbs.

like play start finish have

Do you like tomatoes?

Puzzles p.120

Likes and dislikes

1 075 **Watch, listen, or read** **Complete the dialogues with the words in the box. Then listen again and check.**

Katy	carrots	don't like	chicken
Bieber	~~menu~~	potatoes	love

1

Arianna What's on the menu today?
Dominic It's chicken with [1]__________ and carrots. Do you like [2]__________?
Arianna Yes, I do. I love it. What about you?
Dominic I like it a lot, but I can't stand [3]__________!
Arianna Oh, I really like them!

2

Arianna Do you like [4]__________ Perry?
Dominic No, I don't like her very much. What about you?
Arianna I really like her! Her new album's great!
Dominic What do you think about Justin [5]__________?
Arianna He's fantastic! I [6]__________ him!
Dominic Really? I [7]__________ him at all!

Speaking strategy

Using a variety of expressions

When you speak, it is nice to use different adjectives and expressions to say you like / don't like something.

I really like watching soccer. I think it's great / fantastic / awesome.

I can't stand Math class! It's very boring / difficult. / It isn't interesting.

The phrases in exercise 2 will help you.

Look!

To ask someone their opinion on the same question, you can say *And you?* or *What about you?*

2 076 **Real English** **Listen and repeat.**

Do you like chicken?
Yes, I do. / No, I don't.
What do you think about Justin Bieber?
☺ I like him.
☺☺ I like him a lot / very much.
☺☺☺ I really like him.
☺☺☺☺ I love him.
☹ I don't like him very much.
☹☹ I don't like him at all.
☹☹☹ I can't stand him.

3 077 **Match the questions and answers. Then listen and check.**

1 Do you like apples? _c_
2 What do you think about Bruno Mars? ____
3 Do you like Math? ____
4 Do you like me? ____
5 What do you think about Emma Watson? ____

a Yes, I do. I love it!
b I like her a lot.
~~c No, I don't like them very much.~~
d I really like him!
e Yes, I do! I think you're great!

Beat the clock

You have two minutes to write down all the food words you can think of. Put them in the correct circle. Compare with your partner. Do you have any of the same things?

Love   Like   Hate

4 **Pairwork** **Ask your partner about what he / she likes. Use the ideas in the box and your own ideas.**

Marta da Silva grapes Science basketball eggs Art Shawn Mendes tennis ham Ariana Grande

Do you like grapes?

Yes, I do. I like them a lot. What about you?

I love them! What do you think about Marta da Silva?

Link it!

Pairwork **Write a dialogue about food and drinks you like and don't like. Use your ideas from *Beat the clock*.**

Workbook p.W36 Extra communication p.79

Question words + simple present

What do you call cheese that isn't your cheese?

What	do	they	study?
Where	does	she	live?
When	does	he	have lunch?
What time	do	we	start school?
How	do	you	make pasta?

Rules p.W32

1 Complete the questions with the correct question word in the box and *do* or *does*.

~~how~~ what when what time where

How do you spell your last name?
T-O-R-R-E-S.

1 ________ Savannah go to school?
She goes to school in Washington, D.C.

2 ________ Bruna have gym class?
She usually has gym class on Tuesdays.

3 ________ you have for dinner?
We usually have fish or chicken.

4 ________ you get home?
I usually get home at 4 p.m.

How often ...?

How often do you eat nachos? **Once a week.**
How often does Jacob practice? **Every day.**

Question word	Expressions of frequency	
How often ...?	every	morning / day / week
	once / twice	a day / week / month / year
	three / four times	

Rules p.W33

2 Write questions and answers about Cole and Amy's diet and lifestyle. Use the information in parentheses.

Amy / eat fish? (2x a week)
How often does Amy eat fish?
She eats fish twice a week.

1 Cole / eat fish? (every week)
2 Cole and Amy / drink cola? (1x a week)
3 Cole / eat fruit and vegetables? (2x a day)
4 Amy / eat fruit and vegetables? (5x a day)
5 Cole and Amy / buy potato chips? (3x a week)
6 Cole and Amy / play sports? (2x a week)

Object pronouns

Do **you** want any carrots or corn?
Yes, please. **I** love **them**.

Subject pronouns	Object pronouns
I	**me**
you	**you**
he	**him**
she	**her**
it	**it**
we	**us**
you	**you**
they	**them**

Think!

Read the examples, then complete the rules with *after* and *before*.

We *study Math with Mr. Collins.*
Mr. Collins teaches ***us*** *Math.*

- Subject pronouns go [1] ________ the verb.
- Object pronouns go [2] ________ the verb.

Rules p.W33

3 Choose the correct alternatives.

Mom meets **we** / **(us)** after school.

1 **He** / **Him** cooks lunch on the weekend.
2 Freya is nice. I like **she** / **her**.
3 **I** / **Me** don't want ice cream, thanks.
4 I see **they** / **them** every day.
5 Miss Lopez teaches **we** / **us** History.

4 Complete the sentences with the correct object pronoun.

"Where's my tablet?" "Jessie has *it*."

1 "Do you want my peas? I don't like ________."
2 "Do you know Bella?" "No, I don't know ________."
3 "There's Jorge. Ask ________ about the party."
4 "We always help Natália and Marc, but they never help ________."
5 "Is that you, Chloe?" "Yes, it's ________."

Challenge

Write questions with *How often ...?* and words from the box. Then write answers.

drink water eat salad make cakes play sports
cook for your mom sleep eight hours or more

How often do you drink water?
I drink it three times a day.

Puzzles p.120

Step 1

1 078 **Listen to four students talking about what they have for breakfast. Match the pictures (1–4) with the names.**

Luis 1 Mercedes ____ Sophie ____ Daniel ____

Listening strategy

Using pictures

When a listening activity has pictures, look at them carefully before you listen. It can help you think about the vocabulary that you will hear.

1

2

3

4

Look!

In English, we usually use the verb *have* (not *eat*) when we talk about meals.

*What do you **have** for breakfast?*

*I **have** some cereal and some orange juice.*

Step 2

2 079 **Listen to Stella and Kyle talking about what they have for lunch and dinner. Choose the correct answers.**

1 What time does Stella have lunch on school days?
 a at 12:30 **b** at 1:00

2 Where does she have lunch?
 a at home **b** at school

3 Who does she have lunch with?
 a her family **b** her friends

4 What does she usually have for lunch?
 a meat and vegetables **b** sandwiches and fruit

5 What time does Kyle usually have dinner?
 a at 6:00 **b** at 7:00

6 Where does he have dinner?
 a at home **b** in a restaurant

7 Who does he have dinner with?
 a his mom, dad, and sister **b** his mom and sister

8 What does he often have for dinner?
 a pasta and vegetables **b** chicken and fries

Step 3

3 Pairwork **Ask your partner questions about his / her meals. Use the prompts to ask questions about breakfast, lunch, and dinner.**

- What time?
- Where?
- Who with?
- What?

What time do you have dinner?

I usually have dinner at 7:30.

Where do you ...?

4 Presentation **Tell the class about your partner's meals.**

Workbook p.W36

This week: Strange food from the U.S.!

What do American people eat? We eat food from all over the world. We love Italian, Chinese, and Japanese food. Mexican food is very popular, too. But there are some things that you usually only find in the U.S., and they're quite unusual.

- Let's start with the country's favorite sandwich: the **peanut butter sandwich**! The popular peanut butter recipe that we all love is about 100 years old. For lunch, American children sometimes have a peanut butter and jelly sandwich, but some people prefer a peanut butter and banana sandwich! Why do we like it? It's that special sweet and salty combination that makes it popular.
- The next food looks quite strange, but it's surprisingly delicious! This food is **jerky**. No one knows where jerky comes from–it's a mystery. Some people think it's a native American food. It's dried, salted meat–usually beef–but you don't eat it in the normal way. You keep it in your mouth for a long time, like salty chewing gum!
- **Grits** are another very popular meal in the U.S., and I love them! Grits are corn that you cook in milk or water. Sometimes they are sweet, and sometimes they are salty. Americans like to eat grits with shrimp. It is also common to eat grits with cheese, ham, eggs, or meat. Some people eat them with sugar, too. It's strange, but it tastes delicious!
- Finally, **s'mores**. These delicious snacks are typical when you go camping. You make them with two graham crackers and then put chocolate and a marshmallow in the center. You cook the marshmallow on a fire first, and then you put it between the crackers. They taste great! Where do they come from? S'mores (meaning *some more*) are an invention of some American Girl Scouts in 1927. They're very popular in the U.S., and there's even a National S'mores Day–on August 10th!

Check it out!

Find these words and check their meaning.

peanut butter   jelly   sweet   salty   beef   graham cracker   marshmallow

Reading

1 080 **Read and listen** **Answer the questions.**

Which food … sometimes contains fruit?
peanut butter sandwiches

1 is made of meat? ___________
2 isn't always salty? ___________
3 has its own special day? ___________

Reading strategy

Looking for key words

When you first read a text, look for the key words: nouns and adjectives. Key words are important words and they are often repeated in the text. This means they are important to the text and they give you a good idea of what the text is about.

2 Read the article again. Choose the correct answers.

What is the flavor of peanut butter and jelly sandwiches?
a sweet   (b) sweet and salty   c salty   d special

1 What is the flavor of jerky?
a sweet   b horrible   c salty   d It's a mystery.

2 How do you cook grits?
a in milk or water   c in milk and water
b only in milk   d with shrimp

3 When do Americans typically eat s'mores?
a 1927   c when camping
b at Scouts   d every day in August

3 Answer the questions.

What food from other countries is popular in the U.S.?
Italian, Chinese, Japanese, and Mexican food is popular.

1 How old is the recipe for peanut butter and jelly sandwiches?
2 What meat is typical in jerky?
3 What examples of food can you eat with grits?
4 What do you put between two graham crackers in a s'more?

Writing

Step 1

4 Complete the text with the words in the box.

different comes from countries ~~empanadas~~ ham it make delicious fillings

Culture focus

In the U.S., empanadas are very popular as a form of street food. A lot of food trucks in New York City sell them. They are also popular in large cities like San Antonio in Texas, and Los Angeles in California.

THE EMPANADA!

I quite like the food in my country, but my favorite dish is the empanada. Empanadas are a popular food in many countries in Latin America. People say that it 1 ______________ Spain and Portugal, but now, in some Latin American 2 ______________, it's the national dish!

You 3 ______________ empanadas with pastry, and you put lots of 4 ______________ things inside of 5 ______________. Some people like vegetables with cheese, and others like 6 ______________ like meat, for example chicken or 7 ______________.

There is a small store near my house. They have empanadas and I like to have them for lunch. It's difficult to go a whole week without an empanada. They're 8 ______________ and I love them! What's your favorite filling?

Step 2

5 Answer the questions with information that is true for you.

1 What is a popular food in your country that you enjoy?

____

2 How often do you eat it?

____

3 When and where do you usually eat it?

____

4 What ingredients does it have?

____

5 What do you think about food in your country in general?

____

Writing strategy

Using commas

We use commas to show natural pauses in sentences and to separate items in a list.

We put a comma before *too* at the end of a sentence.

We put a comma before *but*.

We don't put a comma before *because*.

Step 3

6 Write an article about a popular food in your country for a food guide. Use your answers from exercise 5.

Challenge

Write a paragraph about some unusual food that is popular in your country.

- Say when people eat it.
- Say what it tastes like.
- List the ingredients.

Culture p.111

C Extra practice

Vocabulary

1 Choose the correct alternatives.

I (get) / go up every morning at 6:30. I take a [1] **dressed / shower**, get [2] **dressed / TV,** and have an egg, some fruit, and a glass of [3] **orange juice / pear** for breakfast. I [4] **start / take** school at 8:00. I [5] **get up / have** lunch at 11:30. I usually have salad with [6] **ice cream / tuna**, tomatoes, and corn. I drink a glass of [7] **carrots / water**. School [8] **finishes / gets** at 2:45. I [9] **get / have** home at 3:30 in the afternoon, do my homework, and have [10] **bed / dinner** at 6:00.

Grammar

2 Complete the sentences with the affirmative (✓) or negative (✗) form of the verbs in the simple present.

She *doesn't have* lunch at 12:00. (have ✗)

1 We ____________ up at 7:30. (get ✗)
2 You ____________ school at 8:15. (start ✓)
3 They ____________ to school. (walk ✗)
4 He ____________ ham. (like ✓)
5 I ____________ a lot of salmon. (eat ✗)
6 The school ____________ a big cafeteria. (have ✓)

3 Write the verbs in the correct column in the third person singular form.

do carry finish ~~get~~ go play hurry like study want watch

+ s	+ es	y + ies
gets	______	______
______	______	______
______	______	______
______	______	

4 Use the prompts to write questions. Then match the questions with the answers.

1 you / go / Jefferson High? *e*
Do you go to Jefferson High?
2 how often / she / play sports? ____
3 what / they / have for lunch? ____
4 he / like / salmon? ____
5 what time / your school / start? ____
6 how / you / go to school? ____

a Tuna pasta.
b Twice a week.
c Yes, he does.
d I walk.
e ~~No, I don't.~~
f 8:45.

5 Complete the adverbs of frequency with the missing letters. Then write the words in the correct order.

u *s* u *a* l *l* y

1 n ____ v ____ ____
2 s ____ ____ e t ____ ____ e s
3 o ____ ____ e n
4 ____ a r ____ l y
5 a ____ w ____ y s

✓✓✓✓✓	______
✓✓✓✓	*usually*
✓✓✓	______
✓✓	______
✓	______
–	______

6 Look at the information in the chart and write sentences. Use the chart in exercise 5 to help you.

	How often?	Activity	When
	✓✓✓✓✓	play tennis	the summer
1	–	have drama club	the weekend
2	✓✓✓	watch TV	the evening
3	✓	have dinner	seven o'clock
4	✓✓✓✓	eat chocolate	her birthday
5	✓✓	have some orange juice	the afternoon
6	✓✓✓✓✓	do his homework	Sunday

Carla *always plays tennis in the summer*.

1 I ____________.
2 You ____________.
3 They ____________.
4 She ____________.
5 We ____________
____________.
6 He ____________.

7 Rewrite the sentences with object pronouns.

She has the book.
She has it.

1 You like Joe.
____
2 I can see the boys.
____
3 I always sit with you and Ellie.
____
4 I don't know Mrs. Brown.
____
5 You're in front of Sam and me.
____

Communication

1 081 **Choose the correct alternatives. Then listen and check.**

1

Katy I / (I'm) bored. What do you want to do?
Dave [1]**Do** / **Let's** go to the movies.
Katy Mmm ... there aren't any good movies in the movie theater right now. [2]**Let's** / **Do you want** to go shopping instead?
Dave [3]**Cool** / **No**. That's a [4]**great** / **terrible** idea. I want to buy some new sunglasses.

2

Sento Do you like Shawn Mendes?
Laia No, I can't [5]**like** / **stand** him! What [6]**about** / **do** you?
Sento I [7]**really** / **much** like him. His music is great!
Laia What [8]**does** / **do** you think about Bruno Mars?
Sento I don't like him at [9]**not** / **all**.
Laia Really? I like him [10]**very much** / **very**–I think he's fantastic!

Pronunciation

2 082 **Listen to the pronunciation of *Do you ...?* Then listen again and repeat.**

1 Do you like Shawn Mendes?
2 What do you think about Bruno Mars?
3 Do you like pasta?

3 Now practice asking the questions.

1 Do you like tuna?
2 How often do you eat fruit?
3 Where do you go to school?
4 Who do you sit next to in class?

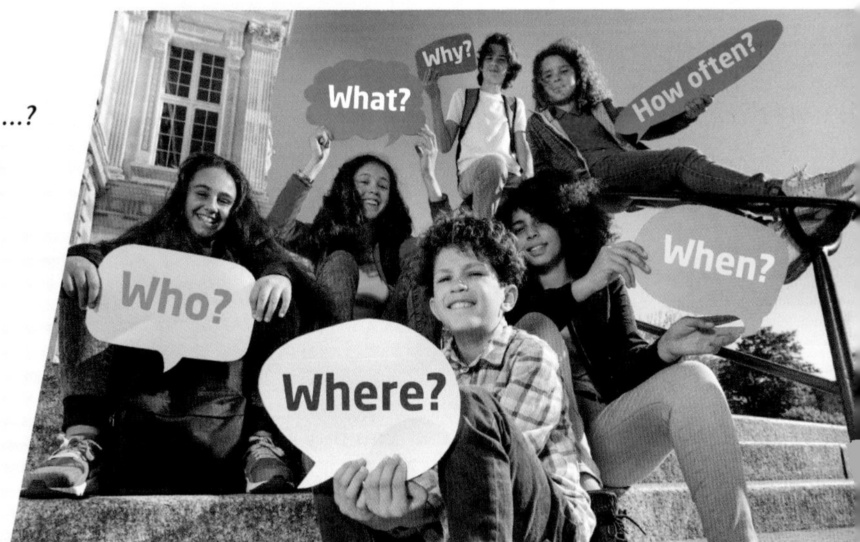

Video link

4 083 **Watch or listen Choose the correct answers.**

Mario gets up at
a 7:30 a.m.
b 6:45 a.m.
(c) 7:15 a.m.

1 Mario has ... for breakfast.
a fruit and a glass of milk
b bread and milk
c eggs and a glass of water

2 After school, Mario
a doesn't play sports.
b sometimes sees friends.
c goes to Art Club.

3 Clara doesn't
a have breakfast at home.
b have breakfast.
c have breakfast at school.

4 Clara usually has
a bread.
b fruit.
c eggs.

5 After school, Clara
a rarely goes to an after-school club.
b usually goes to an after-school club.
c doesn't go to any after-school clubs.

We will …

- be innovative when creating a new product
- give helpful feedback on options and ideas

Invent a new ice cream flavor!

What's up?

1 Match the pictures 1–9 with the food words.

vanilla 1
orange ____
lemon ____
chocolate ____
mint ____
chicken ____
ham ____
tuna ____
peach ____

1

2

3

4

5

6

7

8

9

Get thinking

2 Read the poster. Where can you buy vegetable-flavor ice cream?

____

Ice cream all over the world

The first record of ice cream in the U.S. is in a letter from 1744.

Today, ice cream is one of the country's favorite desserts. Popular flavors include vanilla, chocolate, and strawberry, but every year new flavors appear in stores and supermarkets. In Japan, you can find ice cream with meat, vegetable, and fish flavors.

Check it out!

Find these words and check their meaning.

record	flavors
dessert	appear

Get involved

3 Groupwork Write ideas for five different flavors for a new ice cream in your notebook.

Real English

Let's try mint ice cream …
What about chocolate ice cream?
I think our ice cream is great / awesome / fantastic / terrible because …
That sounds amazing / disgusting!
I'm not sure about that.

The project

4 Groupwork Choose one of your new ice cream flavors from exercise 3. Make a big poster about your ice cream. Use the questions to help you.

1 What are the ingredients?
2 Do you like your ice cream? Why?
3 What color is your ice cream?
4 What is the name of your ice cream?

5 Presentation Present your new ice cream to the class!

How did you do?

Write the statements into your notebook and score yourself from 1 to 5.

I can … talk about different flavors for a new ice cream.

1 2 3 4 5
not very well — very well

I can … explain the reasons for our choice.

1 2 3 4 5
not very well — very well

Speaking competences

I can talk about daily routines. (p.60)

1 **Complete the sentences with the words in the box.**

finish do take start ~~get~~ get

I *get* up at 7:00.

1 I ________ a shower at 7:10.
2 I ________ dressed before breakfast.
3 I ________ school at 8:50.
4 I ________ school at 2:30.
5 I ________ my homework after dinner. /5

I can ask for and make suggestions. (p.62)

2 **Pairwork** **Reorder the words in bold to complete the dialogue.**

Elisa I'm bored. **want to / Do / play / you / a / game?**
I'm bored. *Do you want to play a game?*
Javier No, [1]**instead. / a movie / watch / let's**
No, ________________
Elisa OK, [2]**a / idea. / that's / great**
OK, ________________
Javier [3]**do / you / watch? / want / to / Which movie**
____
Elisa [4]**watch / *Rogue One*? / Do / want / you / to**
____
Javier Again? No, let's [5]**instead. / *Deadpool* / watch**
Again? No, let's ________________
/5

I can talk about after-school activities. (p.65)

3 **Look at the chart and write five more sentences.**

go to play listen to do ~~watch~~ have

Person	Activity
I	TV
[1] you	video games
[2] he	basketball practice
[3] she	music
[4] we	homework
[5] they	snack

I watch TV. /5

I can identify food and drink. (p.70)

4 **Complete each group with the words.**

chicken a peach cheese ~~orange juice~~ bread carrots

Drinks	soda, water, milk, *orange juice*
Fruit	a pear, an apple, grapes, [1] ________
Vegetables	corn, peas, potatoes, [2] ________
Meat, fish	salmon, tuna, ham, [3] ________
Dairy	milk, [4] ________, ice cream
Other	[5] ________

/5

I can talk about likes and dislikes. (p.72)

5 **Pairwork** **Complete the dialogue with the words in the box. Then practice with a partner.**

~~what's~~ don't like do stand about

Isabel *What's* playing at the movie theater?
Alicia There's an Emma Stone movie. [1]________ you like her? Ryan Gosling is in it, too.
Isabel Yes, I like him, but I [2]________ like Emma Stone at all! What [3]________ you?
Alicia I [4]________ her a lot, but I can't [5]________ him!
/5

I can talk about meals. (p.75)

6 **Choose the correct alternatives.**

I usually **go** / **(have)** lunch at 12:30. I eat in the school [1]**cafeteria / classroom** with my friends, Martha and Joe. Martha always brings her [2]**breakfast / lunch** from home because she doesn't like the food in the cafeteria. She usually has a sandwich, [3]**always / but** sometimes she brings a salad. I love the school food! On Fridays, it's nachos–they're my [4]**favorite / lunch**! I [5]**eat / go** them with cheese, tomatoes, and chicken.
/5

Listening, reading, and writing competences

	Yes	I'm not sure	No
I can understand someone talking about their after-school activities. (p.65)	○	○	○
I can read and answer questions about a school in the U.S. (p.66)	○	○	○
I can write about my school. (p.67)	○	○	○
I can understand someone talking about meals. (p.75)	○	○	○
I can read and answer questions about food from the U.S. (p.76)	○	○	○
I can write a paragraph about a popular food in my country. (p.77)	○	○	○

7
You can talk to girls!
In this unit we will ...
talk about sports
talk about ability
talk about sports our partner can play
write about our abilities

1 084 **Read and listen** **Who is good at sports: Mason or Jacob?** ___________

Mason and Jacob finally talk again ...

Jacob What do you want? Are you here to make fun of me?
Mason No, I'm not. Come on, let's stop this.
Jacob But you hate me.
Mason Don't be stupid. I don't hate you. You're my brother.
Jacob Then why are you angry?
Mason Because you can dance really well, and I can't.
Jacob But, Mason, you can do lots of things really well and I can't do them at all!
Mason Like what?
Jacob Can I do karate?
Mason No, you can't.
Jacob Can I play soccer?
Mason No, you can't.
Jacob You're great at sports, Mason! You can do karate and you can play soccer really well!
Mason I guess ...
Jacob And you can talk to girls.
Mason So, is your dance routine ready?
Jacob No, it isn't. I can't do this move.
Mason OK, then. Show me! Do it slowly.

2 **Comprehension** **Check (✓) the things the boys can do and put an ✗ next to the things they can't.**

	talk to girls	dance	play soccer	do karate
Jacob	✗			
Mason	✓			

Check it out!

Find these phrases and check their meaning.

make fun of
Like what?
Don't be stupid.
I guess

Link to life **Sometimes a friend or family member feels bad about themselves because they think they can't do things well. How do you help them to feel better?**

Step 1

3 Find and underline the phrases in the dialogue in exercise 1.

Because **you can dance really well**, and **I can't**.
you can do lots of things **really well** **I can't do** them **at all**!
You can do karate and **you can play** soccer really well! **Can I do** karate? **No, you can't.**

Step 2

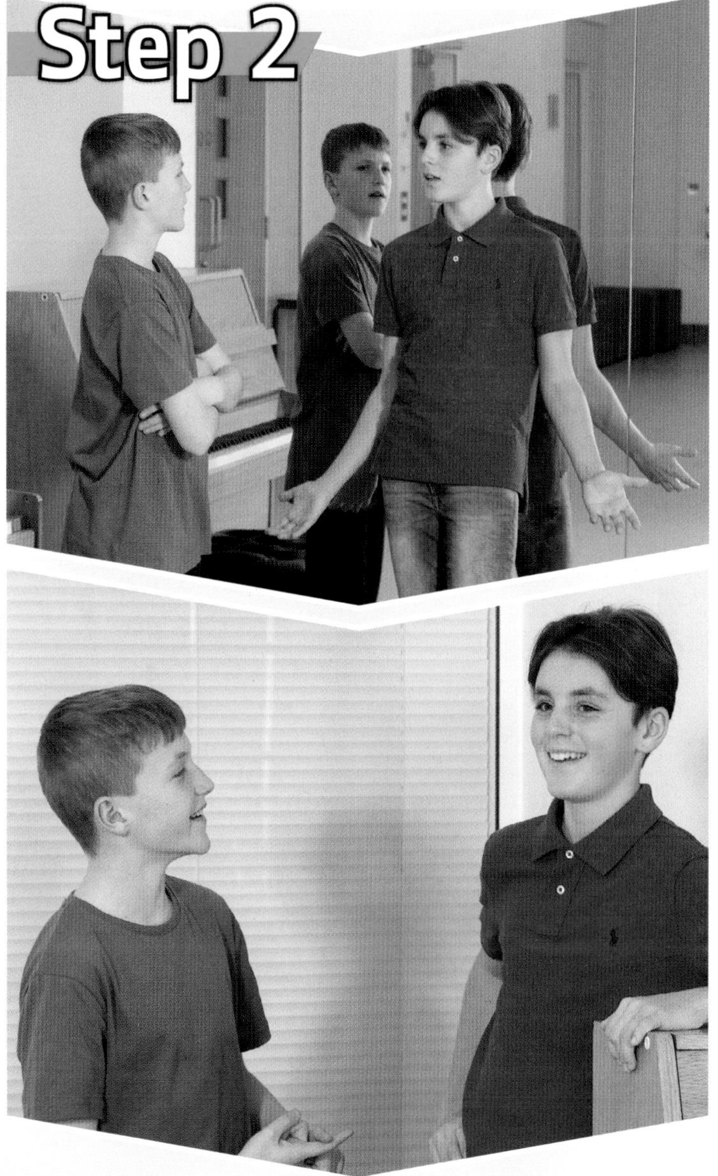

4 085 **Find and underline the incorrect parts of the dialogues. Then correct the mistakes. Listen and check.**

1

Mason Don't say that. I don't hate you. You're my friend.

Jacob Then why are you happy?

Mason Because you can play the guitar really well, and I can't.

Don't be stupid. I don't hate you. You're my brother.

1 ______________________________

2 ______________________________

____

2

Jacob Can I play tennis?

Mason No, you can't.

Jacob You're great at music, Mason! You can sing and you can play the piano really well!

3 ______________________________

4 ______________________________

5 ______________________________

____

085 **Now listen again and repeat.**

Step 3

5 **Complete the sentences with information about you. Use the phrases in the box to help you.**

play soccer speak English use a computer ride a bike sing dance

I can play soccer and I can ride a bike.

I can dance, but I can't sing.

I can ______________________________

______________________________.

I can't ______________________________

______________________________.

6 **Pairwork** **Look at your sentences from exercise 5. Tell your partner what you can and can't do.**

Workbook p.W40

Sports

1 086 **Look at the pictures. Complete the phrases with the sports in the box. Then listen and check.**

tennis basketball skiing biking track and field gymnastics volleyball karate ~~soccer~~ baseball swimming field hockey

Sports are good for you!

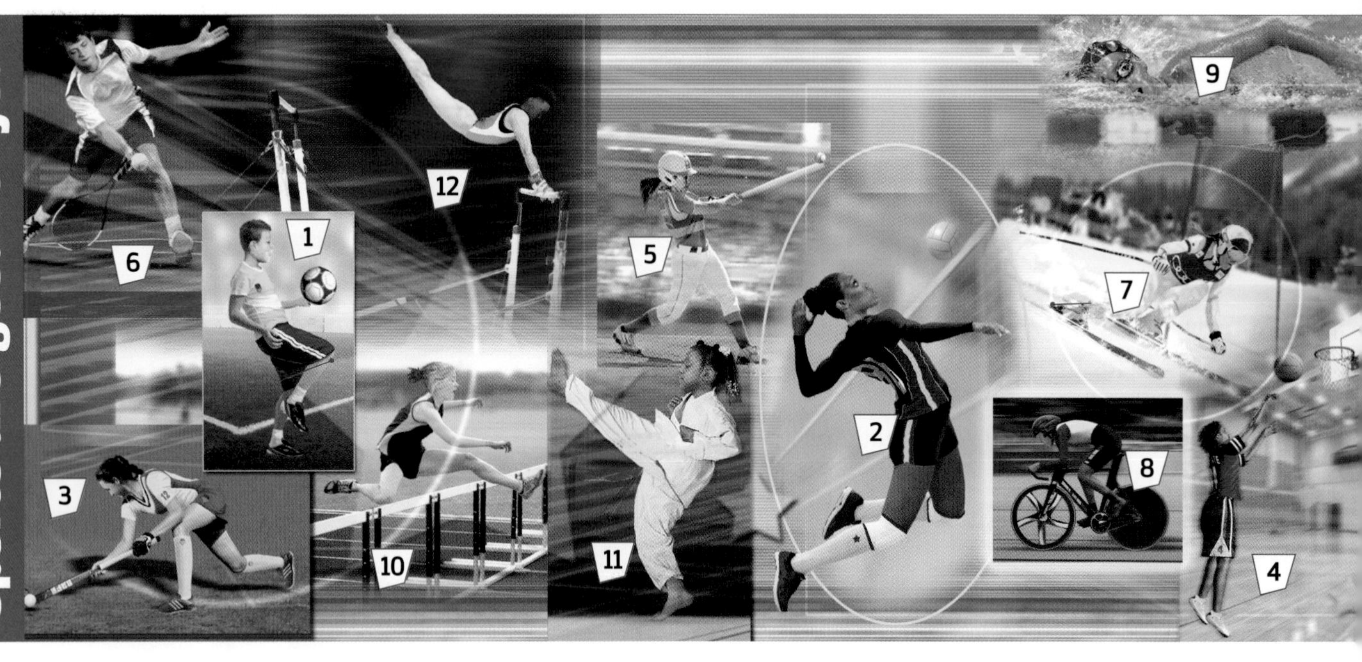
1
2
3
4
5
6
7
8
9
10
11
12

1 play *soccer*
2 play ________
3 play ________
4 play ________
5 play ________
6 play ________
7 go ________
8 go ________
9 go ________
10 do ________
11 do ________
12 do ________

2 Complete the mind map with the sports in the box.

karate gymnastics ~~tennis~~ skiing volleyball biking

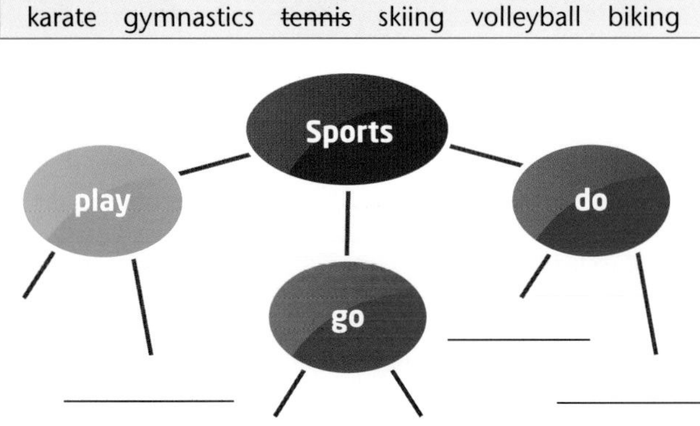
Sports
play
do
go

Look!

We normally use **play** with team sports or sports you play with a ball.

***play** soccer* ***play** volleyball*

We use **go** + ***-ing*** form, or **do**, to talk about other activities.

***go** skiing* ***do** track and field*

3 **Pairwork** **Ask your partner if he / she does the sports in exercise 1. If the answer is *yes*, ask how often he / she does it.**

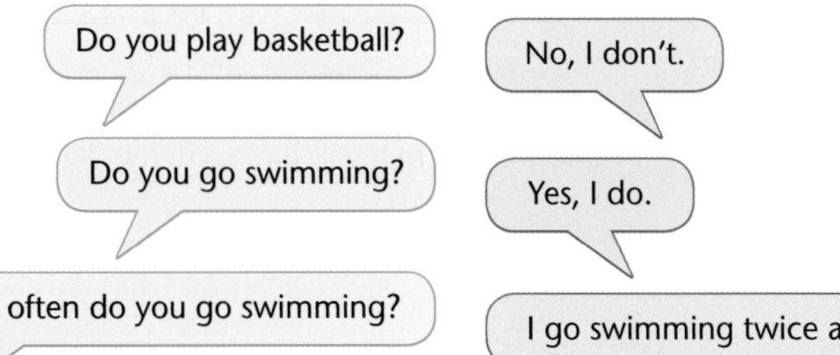
Do you play basketball?
No, I don't.
Do you go swimming?
Yes, I do.
How often do you go swimming?
I go swimming twice a week.

Vocabulary strategy

Collocations

In English, there are some fixed phrases. For example:
do karate NOT ~~*play karate*~~
go biking NOT ~~*do biking*~~

When you write phrases like these in your vocabulary book, always write the whole phrase, not just the key word. This will help you to remember which words to use together.

 Workbook p.W40

can (ability)

Affirmative and negative

You **can** dance really well.
I **can't** do them at all.

Affirmative	Negative
I **can** dance.	I **can't** dance.
You **can** dance.	You **can't** dance.
He **can** dance.	He **can't** dance.
She **can** dance.	She **can't** dance.
It **can** dance.	It **can't** dance.
We **can** dance.	We **can't** dance.
You **can** dance.	You **can't** dance.
They **can** dance.	They **can't** dance.

Look!

Short form	**Full form**
can't	**cannot**

We usually use **cannot** in formal contexts.

We normally use the short form (**can't**) in conversation.

Think!

Choose the correct alternatives.

- The form of *can* is the [1]**same** / **different** for all subjects.
- After *can*, we always use the infinitive verb [2]**with** / **without** *to*.

Rules p.W38

1 Use the prompts to write sentences with *can* ☺ and *can't* ☹.

ride a horse ☹ ride a bike ☺

Leon *can't ride a horse, but he can ride a bike*.

1 speak Portuguese ☺ speak Spanish ☹
Maria ______________________________
______________________________.

2 play soccer ☺ play baseball ☹
You ______________________________
______________________________.

3 sing ☺ dance ☹
I ______________________________.

4 do karate ☺ do gymnastics ☹
They ______________________________
______________________________.

5 swim ☹ ski ☺
We ______________________________.

Interrogative and short answers

Can I do karate? No, **you can't**.
Can Mason play soccer? Yes, **he can**.

Interrogative	Short answers	
	Affirmative	Negative
Can I sing?	Yes, you **can**.	No, you **can't**.
Can you sing?	Yes, I **can**.	No, I **can't**.
Can he sing?	Yes, he **can**.	No, he **can't**.
Can she sing?	Yes, she **can**.	No, she **can't**.
Can it sing?	Yes, it **can**.	No, it **can't**.
Can we sing?	Yes, you **can**.	No, you **can't**.
Can you sing?	Yes, we **can**.	No, we **can't**.
Can they sing?	Yes, they **can**.	No, they **can't**.

Rules p.W38

2 Use the prompts to write questions and affirmative (✓) or negative (✗) short answers with *can* and *can't*.

Luis / cook
Can Luis cook?
(✓) *Yes, he can*.

1 you and your friends / play baseball
______________________________?
(✗) ______________.

2 Cauê and Flora / dance
______________________________?
(✓) ______________.

3 your grandparents / speak English
______________________________?
(✗) ______________.

4 Brittany / speak Spanish
______________________________?
(✗) ______________.

5 Ana / do this exercise
______________________________?
(✓) ______________.

Challenge

Use the ideas in the box to write questions with *can*. Then give personal answers.

you / sing a song in English? your mom / swim?
your dad / speak Spanish?
you / say "hello" in Portuguese?
your best friend / play a musical instrument?
you / count to ten in three different languages?

Can you sing a song in English?
Yes, I can. / No, I can't.

Puzzles p.121

Grammar link

Workbook p.W40

Ability

1 087 **Watch, listen, or read** **Complete the dialogues with the missing questions. Then listen and check.**

1

~~How well can you swim~~	What about soccer
Can you play well	What other sports can you play

Arianna How well can you swim, Dominic?
Dominic I can swim quite well.
Arianna [1] ______?
Dominic I can play basketball, and tennis, too. I'm not very good at it, but I love it.
Arianna [2] ______?
Dominic I can't play soccer at all. I'm awful at it! Can you?
Arianna Yes, I can.
Dominic [3] ______?
Arianna Yes, I can. I'm on the school team.

Look!

We can use adverbs with *can* to talk about ability and how good we are at something.

really / very well
pretty / quite well
well
not very well
not at all

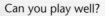

2

How well can you play the piano	~~Can you sing~~
Can you play a musical instrument	Can you read music

Dominic [4] Can you sing?
Arianna Yes, I can. I can sing really well. I'm in a band.
Dominic Oh, really?
[5] ______?
Arianna Yes, I can play the piano.
Dominic [6] ______?
Arianna I'm pretty good at it.
Dominic [7] ______?
Arianna Yes, I can, but not very well. It's really difficult!

2 088 **Real English** **Listen and repeat.**

Can you play well?
Yes, I can. / No, I can't.
How well can you swim?
I can swim very well / really well / well / pretty well.
I can't swim very well / at all.
I'm great / good at soccer.
I'm not very good at soccer / I'm awful at soccer.

3 089 Listen to three conversations. Complete the chart with the activity and then choose the correct alternatives.

Matteo	play volleyball	[1] really well / pretty well
Benjamin	[2] ______	[3] not very well / not at all
Valentina	[4] ______	[5] well / pretty well

Speaking strategy

Using emphasis in questions

When we ask a question, we normally put emphasis on the most important words in the question.
Can *you play* ***tennis well****?*
How well *do you play* ***tennis****?*

4 Pairwork Take turns to ask and answer questions with *can* or *can't*. Say how well you can do the activity.

play field hockey draw sing dance cook ski swim speak English

How well can you play field hockey?

I can play field hockey (very well). And you?

I can't play field hockey (at all).

Beat the clock

Look at the pictures. In two minutes, write the sports that you play with a ball and any sports that don't use a ball. Then compare your answers with your partner. How many are the same?

Link it!

Pairwork Write a dialogue about sports and abilities. Use your ideas from *Beat the clock* in your dialogue. Try to include one of the phrases from the box below.

very well really well great at pretty well well
good at not very well not good at not at all awful at

Workbook p.W42 Extra communication p.103

Grammar

Imperatives

Show me! **Don't be** stupid.

Affirmative	Negative
Stop!	Don't stop!

Think!

Complete the rule.

To form the negative imperative, we put ________ before the base form of the verb.

Rules p.W39

1 Complete the sentences with the affirmative or negative form of the imperative.

~~swim~~ touch run wear bring play

Don't swim here! The water isn't safe.

1 ____________ the correct clothes to karate.

2 ____________ to the end of the track.

3 ____________ ball games here!

4 ____________ the ball with your hand!

5 ____________ sunglasses when you go skiing.

Adverbs of manner

Regular adverbs

Do it **slowly**!

Think!

Complete the rules.

- To form most adverbs, we add [1]____ to the adjective.

slow – slowly *bad – badly*

- For adjectives ending in *-y*, we change the *-y* to [2]____ and then add *-ly*.

happy – happily *lucky – luckily*

Rules p.W39

Why? / Because ...

Why are you so angry?
Because you can dance and sing really well.

2 Complete the mini-dialogues with the questions and answers in the box.

~~Because it's funny.~~ Why do you like Tuesdays?
Why is Lea the captain of the soccer team?
Because the classes are interesting.
Because his favorite sport is skiing.
Because she goes to bed late.

Why is *Futurama* your favorite TV show?
Because it's funny.

1 Why is Hannah always tired in the mornings?
____

2 ____________________
Because she's an amazing player.

3 Why does Tyler prefer winter to summer?
____

4 ____________________
Because I go to Drama Club after school.

5 Why do you like History?
____

Irregular adverbs

Adjective	Adverb
good	well
early	early
late	late
fast	fast
hard	hard

3 Use the adjectives in the box to make adverbs. Complete the sentences.

easy ~~beautiful~~ hard fast early slow

She plays the piano beautifully.

1 She gets up ________ every morning–at 5:00!

2 My horse is amazing. It can run ________.

3 Joshua is a good student. He studies ________ for his tests.

4 Grandpa is a careful driver. He drives ________.

5 I love reading! In one weekend, I can ________ read two books.

Challenge

Write true sentences about you or your family using the adverbs in the box.

slowly badly well hard early late

Puzzles p.121

Listening and speaking

Step 1

1 090 **Listen to Paige and Bryson answering questions about sports. Choose the correct alternatives.**

> **Listening strategy**
>
> **Listening for key information**
>
> When a listening exercise contains answer options, read them before you do the exercise, and think about how they sound. This will help you listen for the correct information.

Paige

She can play volleyball **very well** / **well**.

1 She can play basketball **really well** / **pretty well** .
2 She's on the school **volleyball** / **basketball** team.
3 She plays volleyball **twice** / **three times** a week.
4 She plays volleyball on **Thursdays** / **Wednesdays** after school.
5 She **doesn't watch** / **watches** sports on TV.

Bryson

1 Bryson **is** / **isn't** very good at sports.
2 He **can** / **can't** play soccer very well.
3 He **sometimes** / **never** plays soccer with his friends.
4 He watches **basketball** / **track and field** on TV.
5 He **is** / **isn't** very interested in sports.
6 He plays the **guitar** / **piano**.

Step 2

2 091 **Listen again and complete the questions the interviewer asks Paige.**

What sports can you play, Paige?

1 ______________ can you play them?
2 Are you on ______________, or do you play with ______________?
3 ______________ do you play?
4 Do you watch sports ______________?
5 ______________ a favorite sports star?

Step 3

3 **Pairwork** **Take turns to ask and answer the questions in exercise 2. Make notes about your partner's answers.**

What sports can you play?

I can …

How well can you play them?

4 **Presentation** **Use your notes from exercise 3 and prepare a short presentation. Then tell the class about your partner.**

Workbook p.W42

Trending topics Reading and writing competences

Welcome to our street fair!

The first Saturday in August is a very special day in the town of Greenvale! It's the day of our street fair. The street fair is a big party with music, sports, arts and crafts, and lots of delicious food. It starts at one o'clock in the afternoon and finishes at six o'clock. Come and have fun with us!

AUG Mark your calendar for the first Saturday in August! Don't miss a great day! For more information, contact greenvalecommittee@post.us

Music and performance

You can sing in your bedroom or in the shower, but can you sing in front of 100 people and three judges? Don't be shy! Come and take part in our Star Song Karaoke Contest.

Do you have a special talent? Can you sing, dance, or write poems? Then take part in Greenvale's *Stars of the Future!* Share your special talent with the world.

Arts and crafts

Are you artistic? Can you paint or draw really well? Share your paintings and pictures with us in our Art exhibition, *Show and Share.*

Are you into fashion? Show the town your talent! Join the Fashionista Workshop and design a T-shirt for charity. Then we sell them at the fair. Don't forget–the money goes to local charities.

Sports

Can you run fast? Enter our 5-kilometer Superhero Fun Run. Start training, and remember your costume! Be your favorite superhero and take part in our run.

Can your dad play baseball? Can your mom ride a bike? Can your grandma run 100 meters? Take part in our Family Olympic Games! Be the town champions!

Food and cooking

How well can you cook? Are you great at making cakes or cookies? Take part in our Greenvale Bake-Off and bake a delicious cake for our judges. Every year, at the end of the competition, we sell the cakes for charity.

Check it out!

Find these words and phrases and check their meaning.

town	champions	design
take part	arts and crafts	bake a cake
training	exhibition	miss

Culture focus

A street fair is a public event where people can play games, take part in small contests, and buy food and drink. The money from the fair normally goes to local charities or is used to help the local community.

Reading

1 092 **Read and listen** **Find one event for each category.**

Music and performance Star Song Karaoke Contest / Greenvale's Stars of the Future

Sports ______________________

Arts and crafts ______________________

Food and cooking ______________________

2 Answer the questions.

Which month is the street fair? The street fair is in August.

1 What time does the street fair start and finish?

2 How many judges are there at the Star Song Karaoke Contest?

3 What is the theme of the Fun Run?

4 Where can you show your paintings?

5 What do they do with the cakes after the final of the Greenvale Bake-Off?

Writing

Step 1

3 Read the fact file. It has true information about Ivan. Then read the text. Find and underline the mistakes. Rewrite the text with the correct information.

Ivan can cook very well. He knows over 50 recipes ...

Fact File

Name: Ivan	**Specialty:** chocolate cake
Cook: very well	**Dad:** chef in a hotel
Recipes: over 50	**Event:** Greenvale Bake-Off

Ivan can cook very well. He knows over ten recipes, and his specialty is curry! His dad is a teacher in a school near the town. Ivan wants to take part in the Fun Run.

Step 2

4 Read the sentences and connect them using *and* or *but*.

My family likes watching cooking shows on TV. We always learn lots of new recipes.
My family likes watching cooking shows on TV, and we always learn lots of new recipes.

1 I love baking. My favorite thing to make is cookies.
2 I want to go to the karaoke contest. I'm awful at singing.
3 I'm very good at basketball. I'm not on the school team.
4 My sister wants to do the five kilometer run. She can run very fast.
5 My friends and I are into music. We can't play any musical instruments.

Writing strategy

Using connecting words

When you use notes or answers to questions as a guide for a writing exercise, remember to use words like *and* or *but* to connect your ideas.

I'm musical. I can't sing. =
I'm musical, but I can't sing.

I can cook. I prepare a lot of meals. =
I can cook, and I prepare a lot of meals.

Step 3

5 Answer the questions with information about you. Use your answers to write a text about your abilities in music, art, sports, and cooking.

Music
- Can you sing, dance, or play an instrument?
- Who's your favorite music star?
- How many songs are there on your cell phone?

Art
- Are you creative?
- Can you paint and draw well?

Sports
- How many sports can you play? What are they?
- How often do you play sports?
- Do you play with your friends, or are you on a team?

Food
- How well can you cook?
- How often do you help prepare meals at home?
- How many recipes do you know?

I'm musical. I can sing very well, and I can dance ...

Challenge

Imagine that you are super talented. Write a paragraph about yourself and the amazing things you can do. Use the ideas in the box to help you.

speak 20 languages
play fifteen musical instruments
run 100 meters in ten seconds
swim across the Atlantic Ocean
speak to animals

I'm super talented! I can speak 20 languages. I can speak Chinese very well and Arabic well ...

Culture p.112

8 The music's starting!

In this unit we will ...
- talk about clothes
- go shopping for clothes
- talk about what people are wearing
- write about school uniforms

1 093 **Read and listen** **What is special about Jacob's T-shirt?**

____

It's time for Jacob's performance at the *Dance for the U.S.* finals ...

Rubi It's Jacob's turn–I'm very excited!
Lola Me too! Oh, look! There's Jacob!
Rubi Wow, he looks great! Cool pants, new sneakers ...
Lola Hey–is he wearing your T-shirt, Mason? I love it!
Mason Yes, he is. It's my favorite T-shirt. It's for good luck.
Lola Aww, Mason! That's so cute!
Rubi Shh! The judges are talking to him.
Lola What's Jacob saying?
Rubi I don't know. He isn't talking very loudly.
Mason Oh no, he's nervous ... Come on, Jacob!
Lola The music's starting!
Mason He's dancing very well! You can do it, Jacob!

Later ...

Judge And the winner is ... Jacob Spencer from New York City!
Lola Way to go, Jacob!
Jacob I can't believe it! Thanks for coming!
Rubi I'm so happy for you!
Mason Well, I'm not!
Lola What? Mason! Are you kidding?
Mason Of course I'm kidding! My brother is the American dance champion!
Jacob Yes!

2 **Comprehension** **Answer the questions.**

Where are Rubi, Lola, and Mason?
They're at the Dance for the U.S. finals.

1 Who has new sneakers?
2 Why does Jacob have Mason's favorite T-shirt?
3 Who is nervous?
4 Who wins the competition?

Check it out!

Find these phrases and check their meaning.

he looks great!
That's so cute!
Come on
Way to go
Are you kidding?

Link to life **Do you think clothes are important? Do you think people feel different when they wear different clothes?**

Step 1

3 **Find and underline the phrases in the dialogue in exercise 1.**

Is he wearing your T-shirt, Mason? **Yes, he is.** The judges **are talking** to him. What's Jacob **saying**? He **isn't talking** very loudly.

Step 2

4 094 **Complete the dialogues with the words in the box. Then listen and check.**

's starting ~~are talking~~ isn't talking 'm kidding 's dancing are you kidding

1

Rubi The judges *are talking* to him.
Lola What's Jacob saying?
Rubi I don't know. He [1] ________________ very loudly.

2

Mason Come on, Jacob!
Lola The music [2] ________________!
Mason He [3] ________________ very well! You can do it, Jacob!

3

Rubi I'm so happy for you!
Mason Well, I'm not!
Lola What? Mason! [4] ________________?
Mason Of course I [5] ________________! My brother is the American dance champion!

094 **Now listen again and repeat.**

Step 3

5 **Pairwork** **Role-play one of the activities in the box. Can your partner guess the activity?**

dancing skiing swimming drawing painting singing cooking studying riding a bike playing baseball

You're skiing!

Yes, that's right. / No, I'm playing baseball.

Workbook p.W46

Fashion

fall / winter

spring / summer

What's cool this year?

Clothes

1 095 **Match the clothes (1–18) in the picture with the words. Then listen and repeat.**

hat 1	pants ____	boots ____
baseball hat ____	T-shirt ____	leggings ____
top ____	hoodie ____	shirt ____
dress ____	coat ____	shoes ____
scarf ____	sneakers ____	sweater ____
shorts ____	skirt ____	jacket ____

We use the simple present (**wear** / **wears**) to talk about clothes that a person usually has on.

*I always **wear** jeans to school. I **wear** skirts on the weekend.*

We use the present progressive (**I'm wearing**) to talk about clothes we have on at that moment.

*Today, **I'm wearing** pants and a top.*

2 096 **Listen to Ellie and Oscar talk about what they wear in their favorite season. Complete the fact files with the missing items of clothing.**

Ellie
I love winter!
My clothes: jeans
1
2
3
4
5
6
Oscar
Summer rules!
My clothes:
7
8
9
10
11

3 Pairwork **Tell your partner what you are wearing today.**

I'm wearing jeans, sneakers, …

Workbook p.W46

Present progressive

Affirmative

The music**'s** start**ing**.
The judges **are** talk**ing** to him.

Full form			Short form	
I	**am**	reading	I**'m**	read**ing**
you	**are**		you**'re**	
he / she / it	**is**		he**'s** / she**'s** / it**'s**	
we / you / they	**are**		we**'re** / you**'re** / they**'re**	

Think!

Complete the rule.

We use the present progressive to talk about actions that are happening now.

We form the present progressive with the present tense of the verb [1]______ and the base form of the verb [2]________.

Rules p.W44

Spelling variations

Base form	*-ing* form
walk	walking
write	writing
run	running
study	studying

Rules p.W44

Look!

We can add the short form of ***is*** (*'s*) after nouns and question words.

*The music'**s** starting.*

*What'**s** Kenji doing?*

We sometimes use the short form of ***is*** after names, but only in informal conversation.

1 Complete the sentences with the present progressive form of the verbs in the box.

study play use get up write have ~~make~~

Sophie *is making* a cake.

1 The children ______________ breakfast.
2 Ana ______________ the guitar.
3 I ______________ a text message.
4 Kenji ______________ the computer.
5 Bruno and Oliver ______________ Geography.
6 It's 7:30 a.m. and Chloe ______________.

Negative

Jacob **isn't talking** very loudly.
You **aren't dreaming**.

Full form			Short form	
I	**am not**	**reading**	**I'm not**	**reading**
you	**are not**		you **aren't**	
he / she / it	**is not**		he / she / it **isn't**	
we / you / they	**are not**		we / you / they **aren't**	

Think!

Choose the correct alternative.

To make the negative form of the present progressive, we put *not* **before** / **after** *am*, *are*, and *is*.

Rules p.W44

2 Complete the sentences with the present progressive form of the verbs in parentheses. Use the short form.

Toby *isn't listening* to the teacher. (not / listen)

1 I ______________ my homework. (not / do)
2 We ______________ for clothes. (not / shop)
3 You ______________ your dinner. (not / eat)
4 The students ______________ Math now. (not / study)
5 Lucila ______________ an email. (not / write)

3 Correct the sentences using the information in parentheses. Write one negative (✗) sentence and then an affirmative (✓) sentence. Use the short form.

Dylan is reading. (he / use the computer)
Dylan isn't reading. He's using the computer.

1 The girls are watching a movie. (they / listen to music)
2 Henry is getting dressed. (he / take a shower)
3 You're studying. (you / play games on your cell phone)
4 Dad is working in the backyard. (he / chat to Mom)
5 We're running in the park. (we / play soccer)

Challenge

Imagine you are preparing for a party. What are your friends doing? Write affirmative and negative sentences.

We are preparing for my birthday party. I'm organizing the music. Tom is making food. Katya is …

Puzzles p.121

Shopping for clothes

1 097 **Watch, listen, or read** **Arianna and Dominic are shopping. Complete the dialogues with the words in the box.**

~~help~~ medium jeans big try thanks rooms top

1

Store clerk Can I <u>help</u> you?
Arianna No, [1]__________. I'm just looking.

Later ...

Arianna Excuse me. How much is this [2]________, please?
Store clerk It's $19.99.
Arianna Can I try it on?
Store clerk Yes, of course. What size are you?
Arianna I'm a [3]__________.
Store clerk Here you are. The fitting rooms are over there.

Later ...

Store clerk Is it OK?
Arianna Yes, it is. I'll take it.
Store clerk OK, come with me.

2

Store clerk Can I help you?
Dominic Yes, please. How much are these [4]________?
Store clerk They're $39.99.
Dominic Can I [5]________ them on?
Store clerk Yes, of course.
Dominic Where are the fitting [6]________?
Store clerk They're over there.
Dominic Thank you.

Later ...

Store clerk Are they OK?
Dominic No, they aren't. They're too [7]________. Thanks anyway.

Look!

There are two ways to say prices. For example, you can say *$5.99* as **five ninety-nine**. This is the most common way to say it.

You can say **five dollars and ninety-nine cents**, but it is less common.

To say *$0.25*, you would say **twenty-five cents**.

2 098 **Real English** **Listen and repeat.**

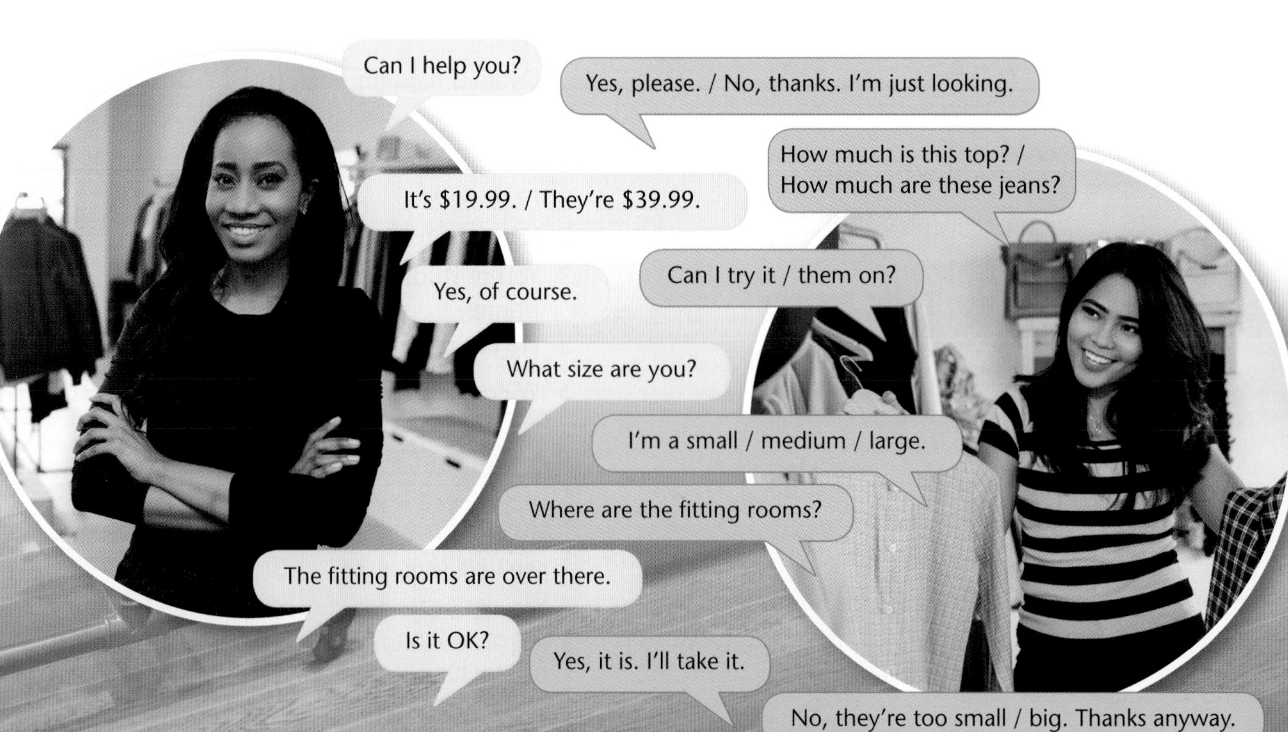

Can I help you?
Yes, please. / No, thanks. I'm just looking.
How much is this top? / How much are these jeans?
It's $19.99. / They're $39.99.
Can I try it / them on?
Yes, of course.
What size are you?
I'm a small / medium / large.
Where are the fitting rooms?
The fitting rooms are over there.
Is it OK?
Yes, it is. I'll take it.
No, they're too small / big. Thanks anyway.

3 **Pairwork** Imagine you are shopping and you want to try on some clothes. Write two dialogues between you and the store clerk. Use the information in the chart.

Clothing item	Price	Size / fit
a sweater	$34.99	small / too small
some jeans	$47.99	medium / OK
a T-shirt	$14.49	large / too big
some pants	$32.50	small / OK

Can I help you?

Yes, please. How much is this sweater?

It's $34.99.

Speaking strategy

Using polite language

When you are speaking to a store clerk, it is important to use phrases that sound polite.

Can I try it on, please? NOT ~~*I want to try it on.*~~
Thanks anyway. NOT ~~*I don't want it.*~~

If you are answering the question *Is it OK?*, say:
Yes, it is. I'll take it. NOT ~~*Yes.*~~

4 Practice your dialogues from exercise 3. Take turns being the store clerk.

Beat the clock

In two minutes, complete the word map for clothes you wear in summer, clothes you wear in winter, and clothes you wear to parties. Then compare with a partner.

Winter — scarf

Summer

Parties

Link it!

Imagine you are going to a formal party. Write a dialogue about the clothes you want to wear to the party.

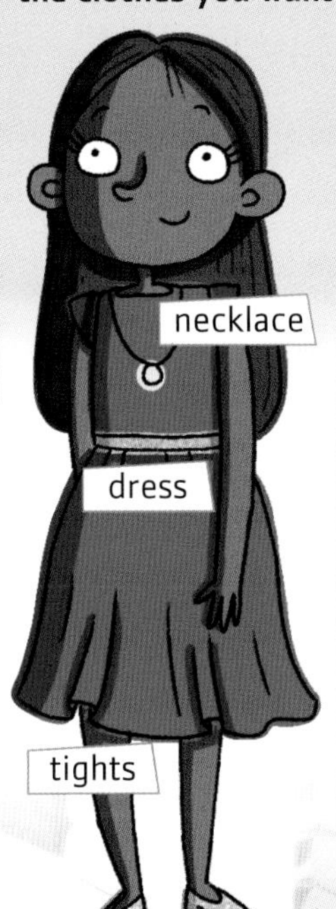

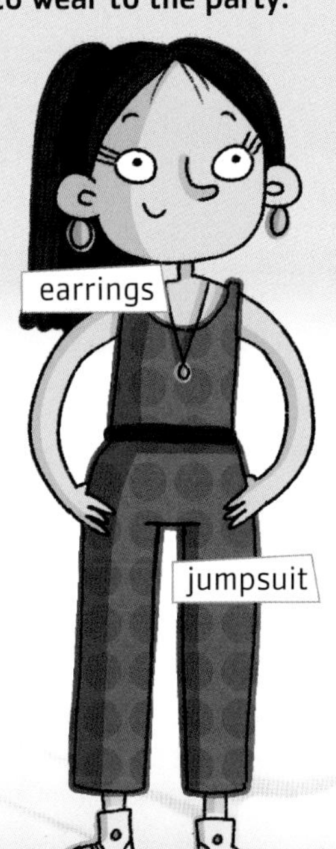

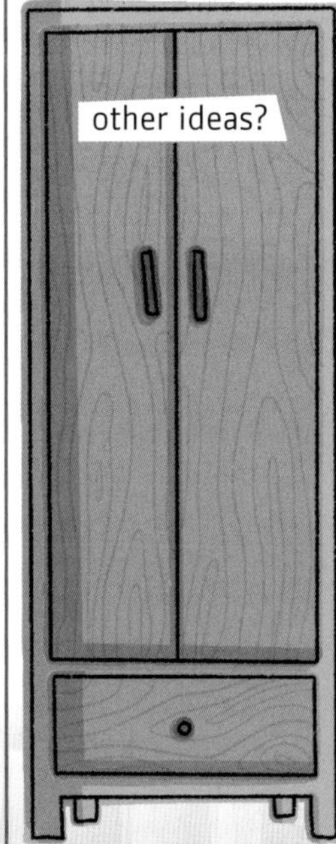

Workbook p.W48 Extra communication p.103

Present progressive

Interrogative and short answers

Is he **wearing** your T-shirt? Yes, he **is**.

Interrogative	Short answers	
	Affirmative	Negative
Am I **going**?	Yes, you **are**.	No, you **aren't**.
Are you **going**?	Yes, I **am**.	No, I**'m not**.
Is he **going**?	Yes, he **is**.	No, he **isn't**.
Is she **going**?	Yes, she **is**.	No, she **isn't**.
Is it **going**?	Yes, it **is**.	No, it **isn't**.
Are we **going**?	Yes, you **are**.	No, you **aren't**.
Are you **going**?	Yes, we **are**.	No, we **aren't**.
Are they **going**?	Yes, they **are**.	No, they **aren't**.

Rules p.W45

1 **Put the words in order to make questions. Then write short affirmative (✓) or negative (✗) answers.**

tablet? / Is / her / using / Amy (✓)

Is Amy using her tablet? Yes, she is.

1 lunch? / having / you / Are (✓)
2 George / jeans? / wearing / Is (✗)
3 you / this book? / reading / Are (✗)
4 Is / starting? / the / class (✓)
5 the / students / Are / a test? / taking (✓)
6 a shower? / taking / Megan / Is (✗)

2 **Complete the mini-dialogues with the present progressive form of the verbs in the box.**

~~play~~ watch make clean talk do

A Is Ricky playing basketball?
B Yes, he is. He always plays basketball on Fridays.

1 A _______ you ___________ this movie?
B Yes, ________________. It's very good.

2 A _______ the boys ___________ their room?
B No, ________________. They're in the backyard.

3 A _______ Mercedes ___________ dinner?
B No, ________________. She can't cook!

4 A _______ you ___________ your homework?
B Yes, ________________. I have French for tomorrow.

5 A _______ Jordan ___________ to Grandma?
B No, ________________. He's talking to a friend.

Question words + present progressive

What's Jacob saying?
Who's he talking to?

Question words	Present progressive
What	are you doing?
Where	is he going?
Who	is she talking to?
Why	are you leaving?

Rules p.W45

3 **Use the prompts to write questions. Then use the words in parentheses to write answers.**

What / they watch? (Avengers movie)

What are they watching?

They're watching an Avengers movie.

1 Where / you go? (movie theater)

____

____

2 What / he eat? (tuna salad)

____

____

3 What / she sing? (a Dua Lipa song)

____

____

4 Who / you call? (Aunt Alison)

____

____

5 Why / you / run (because / bus / come)

____

____

4 **Write true answers to the questions.**

1 What are you wearing?
2 Where are you sitting?
3 Who are you sitting next to?
4 Why are you holding a pen or pencil?

Challenge

Use the questions in exercise 4 to write questions about another student in your class. Then write answers to the questions.

What is Cesar wearing?

He's wearing jeans, a shirt, and a sweater.

Puzzles p.121

Listening and speaking

Step 1

1 099 **Look at the picture and listen to six people talking about what they are doing. Then choose the name of the person who is speaking.**

1 Joe / Mario
2 Mary-Kate / Ellen
3 Joe / Zac
4 Amber / Jessica
5 Connor / Tony
6 Ellen / Abigail

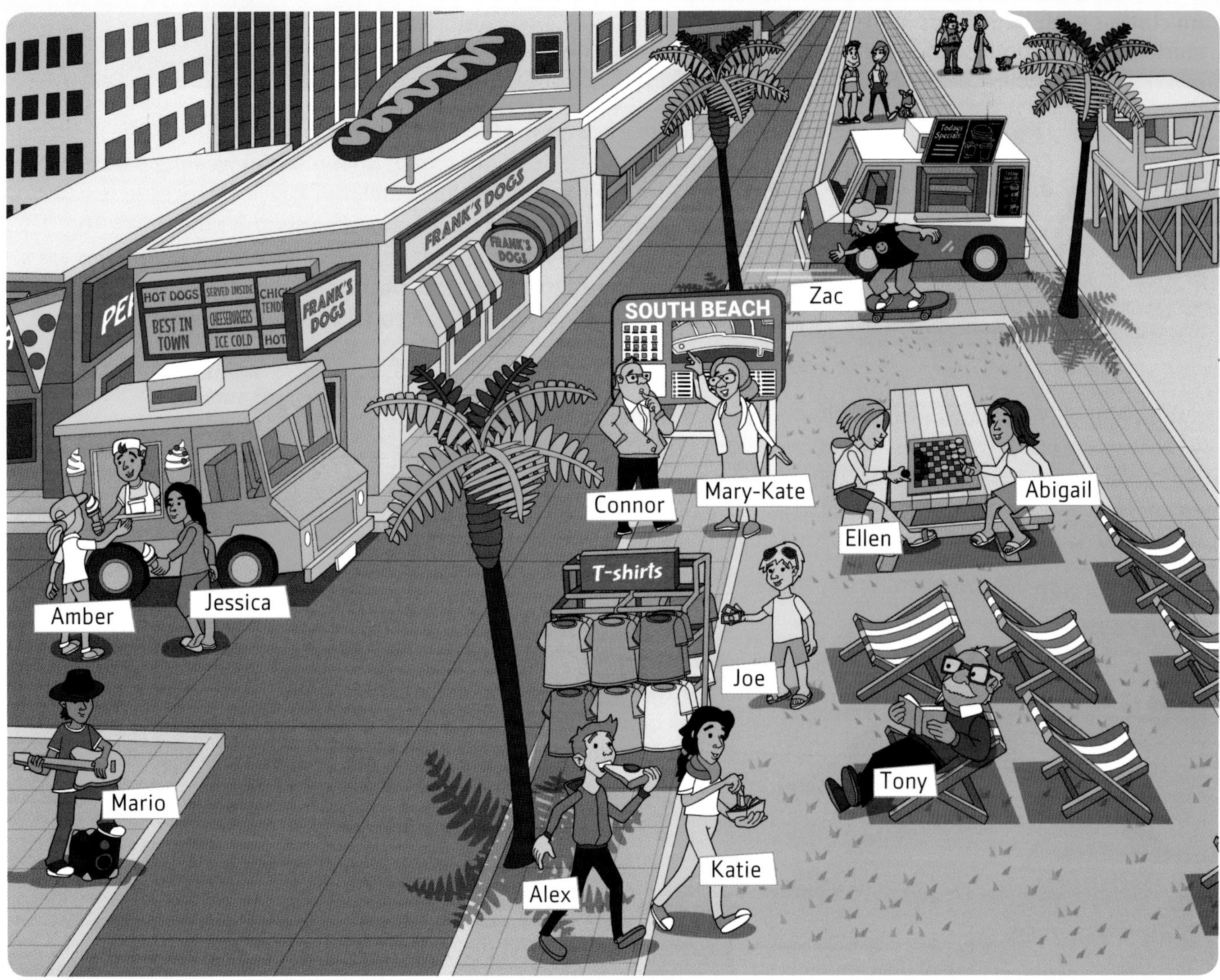

Step 2

2 100 **Listen to two people playing the "Guess who?" game. For each conversation, write the name of the person they are talking about.**

Joe 1 ________ 2 ________ 3 ________ 4 ________

Step 3

3 Pairwork **Play the "Guess who?" game. Choose a person from the picture in exercise 1. Your partner can only ask five questions. Can they guess the correct person?**

Guess who I am!

Are you buying an ice cream?

No, I'm not.

Are you ...?

Workbook p.W48

School uniforms: what's your opinion?

Are you at school today? Are you wearing a school uniform? In the U.S., about 20 percent of students wear school uniforms. In other schools, students wear their own clothes, but there are often rules, for example, no short skirts, and no clothes with bad words on them. It's interesting to know what American students think about school uniforms. Here are some of their opinions!

This is a picture of me with my friends Steffan, Chris, and Mauro. We're sitting in the schoolyard, and we're in our school uniforms! I'm wearing pants and a white polo shirt. I'm not wearing a sweater, but I have a dark blue sweater, too. We can choose between different-colored pants and polo shirts. The girls can choose different-colored pants or skirts. I think school uniforms are a good idea. In my school, there are students from rich and poor families, but we all wear the same uniform. We're all equal at school. *Samuel (13)*

In this picture, I'm having lunch at school with my friends, Peyton and Jennifer. We're wearing our own clothes–I'm wearing jeans and a yellow sweater. I think that uniforms are a bad idea. Your clothes tell people about you and your personality, and a uniform can't do that! At my school, you can wear what you want every day. There are some rules, but that's OK by me! *Lyla (12)*

Our school has a very strict uniform, but I like it! In this picture, I'm with my science partner in class. We're doing a test, and we're wearing the uniform: a dark blue jacket, a white shirt, and a dark-blue-and-light blue tie. I think uniforms are a good idea. When I'm wearing my uniform, I concentrate on what I'm doing and not on what I'm wearing, and I think I get better grades because of this. *Jay (14)*

Check it out!

Find these words and check their meaning.

schoolyard equal tie
polo shirt strict concentrate

Culture focus

Some people think school uniforms are good because they have positive effects on students' behaviour.

In 1994, the district of Long Beach, California, asked all students at elementary and middle schools to wear uniforms. After this, there was less crime in schools.

Reading

1 101 **Read and listen** **Choose the correct answers.**

1 What percentage of American students wear a school uniform?
 a 30 percent
 b 20 percent
 c 100 percent

2 Who has a sweater but isn't wearing it?
 a Jay b Samuel c Lyla

3 Who's wearing a strict school uniform?
 a Samuel b Lyla c Jay

2 Answer the questions.

Where are Samuel and his friends sitting?
<u>They're sitting in the schoolyard.</u>

1 Can Samuel and his friends wear different-colored pants and polo shirts?
2 In Samuel's opinion, how does a school uniform help students?
3 What are Lyla and her friends doing in the picture?
4 Why doesn't Lyla like school uniforms?
5 What is Jay wearing in the picture?
6 Why does he like wearing a uniform?

Writing

Step 1

3 Look at the picture of Tilly with her friends at school. Complete what Tilly says with the words in the box.

~~friends~~ wearing top jeans shirt standing jacket black pants

This is a picture of me and my friends at school. We're [1]__________ outside one of our classrooms, and we're [2]__________ the clothes that we often wear to school. I'm wearing a white-and-purple skirt, [3]__________ boots, and a gray [4]__________. My best friend, Grace, looks very cool. She's wearing a red [5]__________, a black top, and blue [6]__________. Her friend, Max, is wearing black [7]__________, a jacket, and a [8]__________.

Step 2

4 Look at the picture and answer the questions.

1 Where are the students?
2 What are the girls wearing?
3 What are they doing?
4 What is the boy wearing?
5 What is he doing?
6 Do you like their uniforms?

Writing strategy

Using adjectives

We use adjectives to describe people, things, and places. Adjectives go after the verb *be* or before a noun.
*My uniform is **old-fashioned**.*
*I love **fashionable** clothes.*
Adjectives make your writing interesting to read. Try to use a variety of adjectives in your writing. Don't always repeat the same ones.

Step 3

5 Find or think about a picture of you and your friends. Write a description. Include the answers to these questions:

- Who is in the picture?
- Where are you?
- What are you doing?
- What are you wearing?
- Are school uniforms a good or bad idea? Why?

Challenge

Imagine that you can choose your ideal school uniform. Write a description of it.

My ideal school uniform is …

Culture p.113

Vocabulary

1 Write *play*, *go*, or *do*.

go skiing
1 ________ karate
2 ________ swimming
3 ________ baseball
4 ________ track and field
5 ________ tennis
6 ________ volleyball
7 ________ biking
8 ________ gymnastics

2 Complete the sports and clothing items with the missing letters.

When I play t e n n i s, I wear white [1]s ___ o ___ t s, a white [2]t ___ p, and [3]s ___ e a ___ ___ r s. I can run fast and hit the ball very hard!

When I go [4]s ___ i ___ n g, I always wear a [5]j ___ c ___ e t, [6]p ___ n ___ s, a [7]h ___ ___, and ski [8]b ___ ___ t s. I ski very fast, but I get very cold!

When I go [9]b ___ k ___ ___ g, I wear [10]l ___ ___ g ___ n g ___ and a [11]T - s ___ ___ r t. With these clothes, I can ride my bike easily.

When I do [12]t r ___ ___ k a ___ ___ f ___ e ___ d, I always wear a [13]h ___ o ___ ___ e at the beginning of practice. It keeps me nice and warm!

Grammar

3 Look at the information in the chart. Write questions and short answers.

	Dance	Ski	Swim	Sing
I	✓			✗
[1]you		✗	✗	
[2]he		✓		✗
[3]she	✗		✓	
[4]we	✓			✓
[5]they		✗	✓	

Can I sing? No, you can't.

4 Look at the emojis and write the imperatives.

to the . Walk to the beach.

1 your  . ____________

2 in class. ____________

3 the  ! ____________

4 at the  ! ____________

5 Write the imperatives from exercise 4 in the negative form.

Don't walk to the beach.

6 Complete the mini-dialogues with the words.

uniform cold soccer sport ~~wear~~ people

A Why do you wear a jacket in winter?
B Because it gets [1]__________.

A Why do [2]__________ wear white clothes for karate?
B Because it's their [3]__________.

A Why does Dad play [4]__________ every weekend?
B Because it's his favorite [5]__________.

7 Complete the sentences with the adverb form of the adjectives in the box.

good fast easy ~~late~~ quiet happy

I never arrive late for school!
1 I can't sing very __________.
2 Talk to your partner, but please speak __________.
3 The children are smiling and laughing. They are playing __________.
4 My sister always wins races because she can run very __________.
5 This exercise isn't difficult and we can do it __________.

8 Choose the correct alternatives.

I **'m not** / **don't** doing karate.
1 **Are** / **Do** you listening to music?
2 **Where** / **What** are you going?
3 He **are** / **'s** playing field hockey.
4 We **aren't** / **doesn't** watching the volleyball game.
5 What are they **talk** / **talking** about?
6 You **'re** / **'s** doing gymnastics.
7 She **doesn't** / **isn't** riding her bike.
8 It's **start** / **starting** now.

Communication

1 102 **Complete the dialogue with the words in the box. Then listen and check.**

do ~~you~~ awful soccer good play can

William Can *you* swim fast?
Amara Yes, I [1]________. I'm on the school team.
William Really? Can you [2]________ other sports well, too?
Amara Yes, I can. I can [3]________ track and field.
William Are you [4]________ at it?
Amara Yes, I am.
William Can you play [5]________?
Amara No, I'm [6]________ at soccer!

2 103 **Complete the dialogue. Then listen and check.**

~~help~~ thanks much too try fitting over course is

Assistant Can I *help* you?
Amara Yes, please. How [1]________ is this dress?
Assistant It's $47.99.
Amara Can I [2]________ it on, please?
Assistant Yes, of [3]________.
Amara Where are the [4]________ rooms?
Assistant They're [5]________ there.
Amara Thank you.

Later ...

Assistant [6]________ it OK?
Amara No, it isn't. It's [7]________ small.
[8]________ anyway.

Pronunciation: *can* and *can't*

3 104 **Listen to the pronunciation of *can* and *can't*. Then listen again and repeat.**

/ə/	/æ/
I **can** play tennis	I **can't** play soccer.

4 105 **Listen and choose the correct alternatives.**

They **can** / **can't** ski. (circled: can't)

1 We **can** / **can't** do gymnastics.
2 Kate **can** / **can't** dance.
3 He **can** / **can't** do karate.
4 You **can** / **can't** swim.
5 I **can** / **can't** speak French.
6 Roy **can** / **can't** do track and field.

Video link

5 106 **Watch or listen** **Choose the correct answers.**

Clara is wearing
a a skirt, a T-shirt, and black shoes.
(b) a skirt, a shirt, and black shoes.
c a shirt, pants, and black shoes.

1 Clara is wearing these clothes because
a she doesn't have any other clean clothes.
b they're her school uniform.
c they're her favorite clothes.

2 Mario is wearing these clothes because
a he goes biking on Wednesdays.
b he plays soccer on Wednesdays.
c he doesn't have school today.

3 Ludmila is wearing
a jeans and a top.
b a dress and a cardigan.
c leggings and a top.

4 Ludmila
a always wears them to school.
b only wears them on weekends.
c can't wear them to school.

D Global skills

We will ...
- think about people's needs
- make suggestions clearly
- work collaboratively

Design an Olympic uniform

What's up?

1 Match the pictures 1–9 with the clothes words.

__1__ tracksuit
____ scarf
____ hoodie
____ T-shirt
____ baseball hat
____ sneakers
____ jacket
____ shorts
____ boots

1 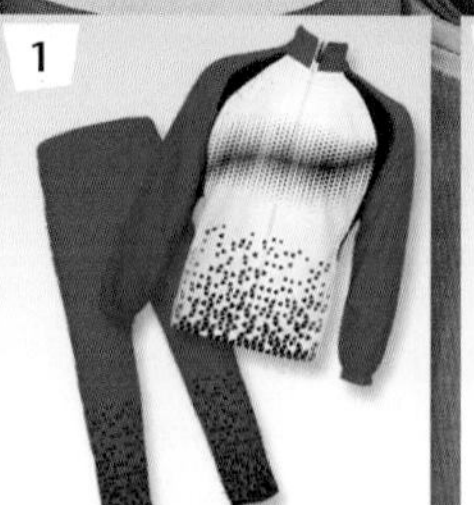
2 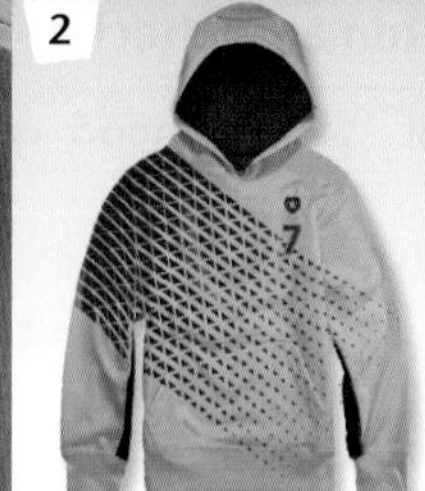
3 
4 
5 
6 
7 
8 
9 

Get thinking

2 Read the text. Why are uniforms for the Olympic Games important?

Every two years, the Olympics or the Winter Olympics happen. These events are very important. The athletes represent their country, and millions of people are watching them, so it's very important that the athletes look great!

Olympic sports stars need clothes for competitions, training, and warm-ups, and, of course, the very special opening and closing ceremonies. For this reason, fashion designers spend a lot of time designing clothes that are perfect for the event. They usually cost a lot of money, too!

Now it's your turn! Who is your favorite sports star? Imagine he or she is going to the Olympic Games. What is his or her sport? What clothes does he or she need? Think carefully–it's possibly the uniform of a future Olympic champion!

Real English

I think he / she needs ...
... are perfect for warming up / training.
In a ..., he / she can run / swim / ski easily.
They can / can't wear ... for a sports event.
The national colors are ...
I think a ... and ... looks nice / awful.
Sorry, I don't agree!

Get involved

3 Groupwork In groups, think about different athletes and their sports. Write notes about each person. Discuss what clothes they need.

- Formal uniform for ceremonies
- Clothes for training and warming up
- Clothes for sporting events

The project

4 Groupwork In groups, choose one athlete and design his or her Olympic uniform.

1 What clothes are part of his or her uniform?
2 What are the colors?
3 Are the clothes for training or competitions?
4 Why are they perfect for their different uses?

5 Presentation Make a poster of your designs. Present your Olympic uniform to the class.

How did you do?

Write the statements into your notebook and score yourself from 1 to 5.

I can ... work in a group to design a new Olympic uniform for my favorite sports star.

1 2 3 4 5
not very well — very well

I can ... present my designs to the class.

1 2 3 4 5
not very well — very well

Speaking competences

I can talk about different sports. (p.84)

1 Pairwork Complete the sports words. Then say true sentences to your partner.

I often play b a s e b a l l.

1 I can do k ___ r ___ t ___ very well.
2 I can play v ___ l ___ e ___ b ___ l l.
3 I often do g y ___ n a ___ t ___ c s.
4 I can s ___ ___ very fast.
5 I'm good at t ___ a c ___ ___ n ___ f i ___ ___ d.

/5

I can talk about ability. (p.86)

2 Pairwork Complete the dialogue with the phrases in the box. Then practice with your partner.

at | can you play | ~~how well~~ | I can play | I can't | I can

Amara: How well can you play tennis?
William: [1] ___ it very well.
Amara: What other sports [2] ___?
William: I often go skiing, but [3] ___ ski very well.
Amara: What about soccer?
William: I'm awful [4] ___ soccer. Can you play it?
Amara: Yes, [5] ___. I'm on the school team.

/5

I can talk about sports my partner can do. (p.89)

3 Pairwork Look at the chart and the code. Write five sentences. Then write similar clues for different activities and ask your partner to say the sentences.

👎 = not at all 👎👍 = not very well
👍 = pretty well 👍👍 = very well

Name	Sport	How well?
Levi	tennis	👎
Maria	ride a bike	👍👎
Juan	swim	👍
Yuki	play basketball	👍👍
Ben	do gymnastics	👍👎
Silvia	ski	👎

Levi can't play tennis at all.

/5

I can identify clothes. (p.94)

4 Complete the diagram with the words.

pants | jacket | sneakers | ~~hat~~ | skirt | sweater

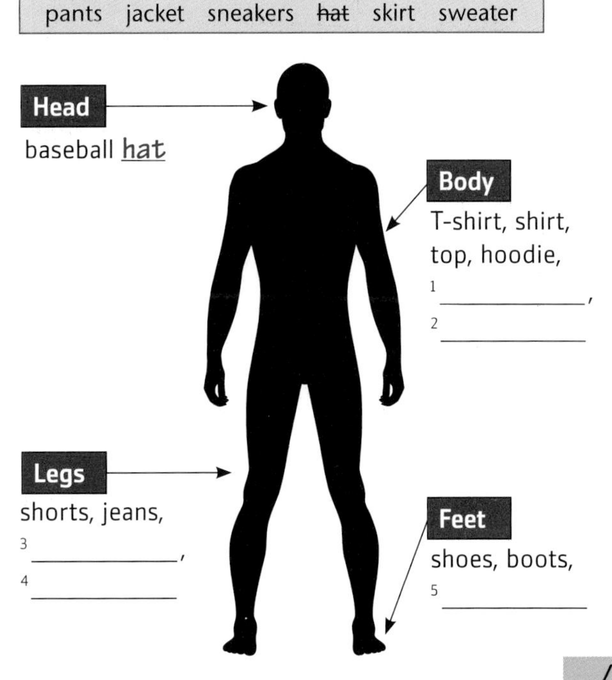

/5

I can talk about shopping for clothes. (p.96)

5 Pairwork Choose the correct alternatives. Then practice with a partner.

William: How **many** / **much** is this sweater?
Assistant: It's $29.99.
William: Can I try it [1] **on** / **up**, please?
Assistant: Yes, [2] **for** / **of** course. What [3] **big** / **size** are you?
William: I'm a small.
Assistant: Here you [4] **are** / **have**. The fitting rooms are [5] **over** / **under** there.

/5

I can talk about activities and what people are wearing. (p.99)

6 Pairwork Write five sentences in your notebook about what your classmates are wearing. /5

Listening, reading, and writing competences

	Yes	I'm not sure	No
I can understand someone talking about sports and abilities. (p.89)	○	○	○
I can read and answer questions about a street fair. (p.90)	○	○	○
I can write about my abilities. (p.91)	○	○	○
I can understand two people talking about what people are wearing. (p.99)	○	○	○
I can read and answer questions about school uniforms in the U.S. (p.100)	○	○	○
I can write about what my friends are wearing in a picture. (p.101)	○	○	○

Famous people from around the world

ZAYN MALIK is from the U.K., and his family home is in the city of Bradford, in the north of England. His father's family is from Pakistan, and his mother is part British and part Irish. Now Zayn's homes are in the U.S.–in Los Angeles, Pennsylvania, and New York City.

MEGHAN MARKLE is a member of the British Royal Family. Her home is Kensington Palace, in London, and she's in British newspapers nearly every day. She is American, and her childhood home is in Los Angeles, California. Meghan's mom is African-American, and her dad's family is from Ireland and the Netherlands.

KEANU REEVES's family is very interesting. He is Canadian, but his mom is British, and his dad has family from China and Hawaii. The influence of Portuguese, British, Irish, and American cultures is important to Keanu, for example Chinese art and British TV shows!

ALICIA VIKANDER is the star of many English-speaking movies, and her British English accent is perfect! But she isn't from the U.K. In fact, she's from Sweden, and her home is in Portugal!

SEAN PAUL is a singer. He is from Jamaica, and his father is part Portuguese, part Afro-Caribbean. His mother is part British, Chinese, and Jamaican.

Check it out!

Find these words and phrases and check their meaning.

part newspaper star in fact
member childhood accent

1 107 **Read and listen** **Match the sentence halves.**

1 Zayn Malik is d
2 Meghan Markle is ____
3 Alicia Vikander is ____
4 Sean Paul is ____
5 Keanu Reeves is ____

a Swedish.
b from Canada.
c from the U.S.
d ~~British.~~
e from Jamaica.

2 Complete the sentences with the words in the box.

Hawaii	~~Ireland~~	the U.K.	Chinese	Irish

Zayn Malik's mom is from the U.K. and Ireland.
1 Megan Markle's home is now in ____________
2 Megan Markle's dad is part ____________.
3 Sean Paul is part ____________.
4 Keanu Reeves's dad is from ____________.

3 Answer the questions.

Where are Zayn Malik's homes?
They are in the U.S.
1 Where is Megan Markle's childhood home?
2 Where is Alicia Vikander's home?
3 Is Sean Paul's family from the same country?
4 What part of Chinese culture is important to Keanu Reeves?

4 **Presentation** **Prepare a presentation about your family or the family of another celebrity. Use the questions to help you. Give your presentation to the class.**

- Who is the celebrity or person?
- Where is he / she from?
- Where are his / her homes?

The U.K.'s biggest family

What is the average number of children in a family in your country? In the U.S., it's 2.4 children, and in the U.K., it's 1.9 children. Of course, some families are very small, and some are very big. But one British family is really big, with a mom, a dad, and 20 children!

Sue and Noel Radford love children. They are mom and dad to eleven boys and nine girls. Nineteen of these children are uncles and aunts because their eldest sister, Sophie, is mom to three children: Daisy, 5, Ayprill, 3, and Leo, 2. Families are sometimes complicated–for example, Archie is Sophie's little brother. He is only nine months old, but he is uncle to Daisy, Ayprill, and Leo.

The Radfords' home is a big house in Lancashire, England. At home, the children are always with their brothers and sisters, so life is never boring.

Perhaps for some people, the Radfords' lifestyle is too busy and noisy, but it is very interesting to the British public! They are often on TV, and their videos on YouTube are very popular. On Instagram, the mom, Sue, has 60,000 followers.

With every new baby, Sue says that this one is the last. But is this true? Wait and see!

Check it out!

Find these words and phrases and check their meaning.

average	busy	the last
eldest	noisy	Wait and see!

The Radford family in numbers

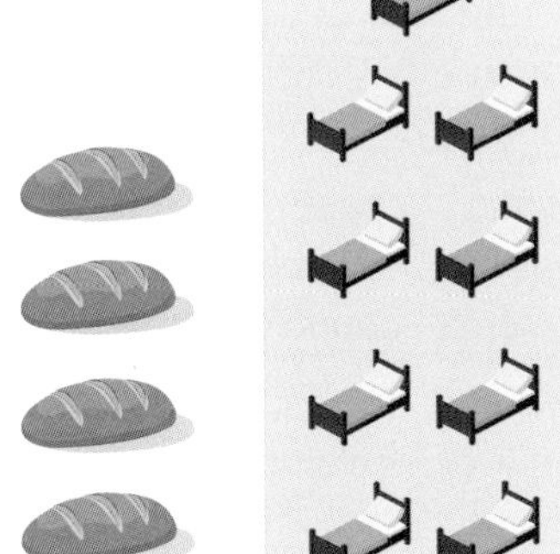

4 loaves of bread a day

9 bedrooms

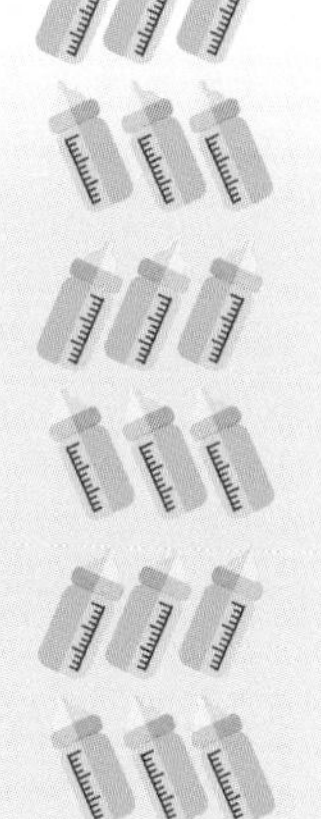

15 seats in the car

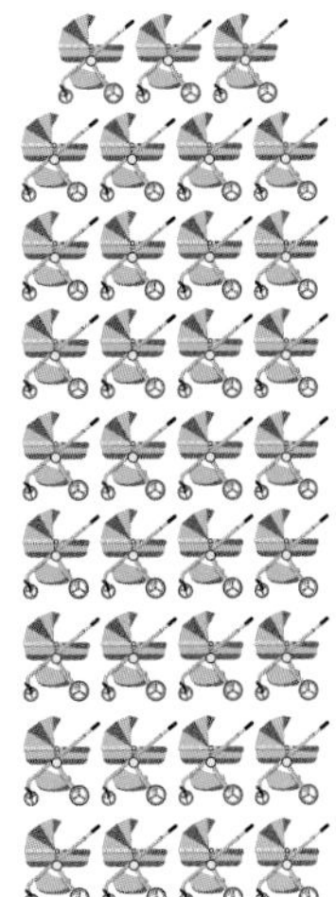

18 bottles of milk a day

35 strollers

62 pairs of shoes

1.5 kg of pasta per meal

1 108 **Read and listen** **Complete the sentence.**

Leo has __________ aunts and __________ uncles.

2 Choose the correct alternatives.

In the **U.K.** / (**U.S.**), there are 2.4 children in a typical family.

1. Noel and Sue Radford are **a mom and dad** / **brother and sister**.
2. Sophie is mum to **nineteen** / **three** children.
3. Daisy, Ayprill, and Leo have eleven **brothers** / **uncles.**
4. British people **are** / **aren't** interested in the Radfords.
5. The Radford family **is** / **isn't** popular on Instagram.

3 Answer the questions with short answers.

Are there twenty children in the Radford family?
Yes, there are.

1. Is the Radford family big?
2. Are Sue and Noel grandparents, too?
3. Is Leo Archie's uncle?
4. Is the Radfords' house small?

4 **Presentation** **Research a famous family from your country. Prepare a presentation about them. Use the questions to help you. Present the family to the class.**

- What is the family's name?
- Where are they from?
- How many children are there?
- Are there grandparents, aunts, uncles, and cousins?
- Are they popular on TV / YouTube / Instagram?

Watch the culture video

1 🔊 109 **Read and listen** **What are *fusuma* and where are they from?**

____

____

2 **Are the sentences true (T) or false (F)?**

American homes are normally big. T

1 The population of Japan is big. ____
2 An open-plan space doesn't have a dining area. ____
3 A Japanese room is always one type of room. ____
4 Sinks aren't normally in Japanese bathrooms. ____

3 **Complete the sentences with the correct words.**

Homes in the U.S. are normally bigger than homes in Japan.

1 For a Japanese person, a __________ home is normal.
2 The uses of __________ in the U.S. and Japan are very different.
3 In a Japanese bathroom, there is only one piece of furniture: the __________!
4 In a Japanese home, there __________ any toilets in bathrooms.

4 **Presentation** **Research a typical home in another country. Prepare a presentation about it. Use the questions to help you. Present the home to the class.**

- Where is the home?
- Is it big or small?
- How many rooms are there?
- What furniture is in each room?

Around the world, homes come in different shapes and sizes. In some countries, like the U.S., typical homes are big–and getting bigger. The American home is now 56 percent bigger than the typical American home from 1973. Normally, Japanese homes are small: half the size of an American home. Why is there such a big difference in homes between the two countries?

One of the main reasons is space. There is lots of space in the U.S., so it isn't a problem to build a big house. Japan is a small country with a lot of people, so small homes are necessary!

One of the big differences between Japanese and American homes is the use of each room. In an American home, one room is the bathroom. Another room is the living room. Another room is the dining room, and so on. Lots of houses are now "open-plan," so the kitchen, dining room, and sometimes the living room is one big room.

In a Japanese home, things are different! It is possible for one room to be lots of different things, for example, a living room by day and a bedroom by night. With furniture in different places and sliding doors called *fusuma*, living areas can be different in an instant. A typical Japanese bathroom is also different from an American one. Only the bathtub is in the bathroom! The sink is normally in another room, and the toilet is always in a separate room.

Which do you like? The question is simple: is a big house really better, or is a small home beautiful?

Find these words and check their meaning.

shapes	half	space
sizes	reasons	sliding

Toys from the past...

Imagine a time before phones or iPods. Imagine a living room or bedroom without a TV or laptop. This is life for teenagers of the past. Instead of playing with a game console, teenagers played with games and toys. Inside the Museum of Childhood in London, there is everything you need to know about old toys and games. It is free to go into the museum and you can learn a lot about the history of games here!

One of the oldest games in the museum collection is marbles. This game is from ancient Egypt and Rome. The idea is to hit the other person's marbles or to shoot them into a goal.

A magic lantern is a gadget that projects pictures onto a wall. The first ones are from the 17th century. They are for stories or for education. The images don't move, but in the past, magic lanterns were very popular.

The Slinky is from the U.S. It is a spring that can make a walking movement. It's still fascinating to watch a Slinky "walk" down the stairs!

Many people have the game of chess, but do you know where it comes from? It's actually from 7th-century India! Today, the typical board is black and white, but the traditional boards are red and white. Although we usually think that chess has one set of rules, there are in fact a lot of different ways of playing it.

Now imagine that you are in the past and you only have these games. Choose one of them. Which one is your favorite?

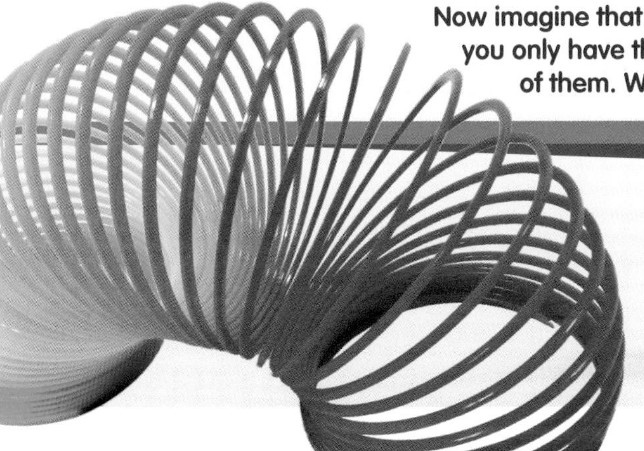

Check it out!

Find these words and check their meaning.

marbles	goal	projects
shoot	lantern	chess

1 110 **Read and listen** **How many toys from the past does the text mention?**

____

2 Choose the correct answers.

In _____, there are more games and activities.
(a) the 21st century b the past c museums

1 The Museum of Childhood in London is _____.
a free b expensive c cheap

2 Marbles is a _____ game.
a very old b new c modern

3 A magic lantern is for _____.
a movies b pictures c books

4 The perfect place for a Slinky is _____.
a a museum b the stairs c the floor

5 There _____ rules for the game of chess.
a is only one set of b aren't any c are lots of

3 Answer the questions.

Where is the Museum of Childhood?
It's in London.

1 Where is the game of marbles from?
2 Which century are the first magic lanterns from?
3 What are magic lanterns for?
4 Which country is the Slinky from?
5 What are the more traditional colors of a chess board?

4 **Presentation** **Think of a traditional game that you enjoy playing. Prepare a presentation about it. Use the questions to help you. Present your game to the class.**

- What is it called?
- Where is it from?
- How old is it?
- How do you play it?
- Why do you like it?

School days around the world are very different. So let's compare the school days of two students in two countries: the U.S. and China.

Cameron is at a middle school in the U.S., with students aged 13 to 16. Yu Yan is at a high school in China, for students from age 12 to 18.

Cameron lives at home with her parents. She gets up at about 7:00 a.m., takes a shower, and has breakfast. Students at Cameron's school start classes at about 8:00 a.m. They have four classes before lunch, and each class is 50 minutes long. Lunch is at 11:30a.m., for half an hour, and then students have four more classes. School finishes at about 3:30 p.m. Students then go home on the school bus, or do different activities, for example, sports or music. They do about an hour of homework, and then they relax: they watch TV, play video games, and have dinner.

Now let's look at Yu Yan's typical school day.

In China, a lot of people live in rural areas, so sometimes there isn't a school close to their house. For this reason, a lot of students go to boarding schools. This means they live and go to school in the same place. Yu Yan goes to boarding school. Here they get up and have breakfast at about 6:00 a.m., because their classes start at 7:00 a.m.

After five classes, students stop for a long break at about 12:00 p.m.–they have lunch, and they sleep, too. In the afternoon, students have four more classes, and they have a break at about 5:45 p.m. Then they have dinner and study time. This is when they do their homework. On some days, high school students finish school at 11:00 p.m.

These are two examples of a typical school day around the world. What is your school day like?

Check it out!

Find these words and phrases and check their meaning.

let's compare   rural
relax   boarding school

1 111 **Read and listen** **How many classes does Yu Yan have in one day?**

____

2 Choose the correct alternatives.

Cameron's middle school is for students aged **(13–16)** / **12–18**.

1 In Cameron's middle school, there are **six** / **eight** classes in a day.
2 The American students **don't have any** / **have** free time in the evenings.
3 Many Chinese students live in boarding schools **far** / **near** from their homes.
4 In Yu Yan's school, students sometimes **get up** / **start** school at 7:00 a.m.
5 Students at Yu Yan's school **don't finish** / **finish** studying at 5:45 p.m.

3 Answer the questions.

How old are the students in Yu Yan's school?
They are 12–18 years old.

1 How long are the classes in Cameron's school?
2 What time do the American students finish school?
3 How much homework do the American students do?
4 How many classes do the Chinese students have before lunch?
5 What do the Chinese students do during their break in the middle of the day?
6 What time do they sometimes finish school?

4 **Presentation** **Research a typical school day in another country. Prepare a presentation about it. Use the questions to help you. Present the school day to the class.**

- Which country is it in?
- What time does school start and finish?
- How many classes are there in one day?
- Do the students have lunch at school?

The world's youngest restaurant critic

In the world of restaurants, everybody knows Andrew Knowlton. He is an editor for the famous food magazine *Bon Appétit*. He visits restaurants to try their food. When Andrew Knowlton walks into a restaurant, chefs get nervous. What does he think of their pasta? What is his opinion of their salmon or chicken? The answer is often in his next article for *Bon Appétit.*

But now, there's another restaurant critic next to Knowlton, and she's very scary, too. Say hello to Julep Knowlton, Andrew Knowlton's daughter. When she tries food in a restaurant, chefs know they need to do their best!

Julep is only 10 years old, but she knows exactly what she likes. She loves trying food in restaurants with her dad, and she isn't worried about giving chefs her opinion. Normally a 10-year-old says their favorite food is burgers and fries, but Julep is not a typical 10-year-old. Julep eats everything, and her dad says it is because she always eats the same things as her parents.

So why does Andrew Knowlton take Julep with him to restaurants? The answer is simple–Andrew thinks it is important to try different food. He wants Julep to enjoy eating food because people who enjoy different types of food are happy people!

Find these words and check their meaning.

editor critic everything
chefs scary

1 112 **Read and listen** **Who takes Julep Knowlton to restaurants?** ______

2 Match the sentence halves.

1 Andrew Knowlton *b*
2 Julep Knowlton ____
3 Chefs get nervous when ____
4 Julep eats ____
5 Julep knows ____
6 Andrew Knowlton believes that ____

a food makes you happy.
b ~~writes about food.~~
c what she likes to eat.
d the same food as her parents.
e is a very young food critic.
f the Knowltons visit their restaurants.

3 Answer the questions.

What is Andrew Knowlton's magazine called?
It's called Bon Appétit.

1 Where do chefs find Andrew Knowlton's opinion of their food?
2 How old is Julep Knowlton?
3 Does she like giving chefs her opinions?
4 What do most 10-year-olds like?

4 Presentation Imagine you are going to a restaurant for dinner. Prepare a presentation about your ideal meal, with a first, second, and third course. Use the questions to help you. Present your meal to the class.

- What kind of restaurant is it?
- What food is in each course?
- What adjectives can you use to describe the food?

Petrúcio Ferreira

With only one arm, life can sometimes be difficult for Petrúcio Ferreira, but he can run very fast and he is a member of Brazil's Paralympic track and field team.

Petrúcio has this disability because of an accident at the age of two. But it doesn't stop him from doing what he wants. He is the winner of the 100-meter sprint at the 2016 Paralympic Games in Rio de Janeiro, and is the fastest Paralympic runner in the world! He has a world record to show it.

Petrúcio is from a family that doesn't have a lot of money, but he has people around him who help him a lot. With their help, he has a nice home, and he can train and take part in races. Training isn't easy for him–sometimes he is very tired, so he can't even take a shower! But every time he wins a race, he knows that it is worth the effort.

In the future, Petrúcio doesn't want to stop playing sports. He knows that he can help people, too, and wants to become a coach. Hopefully, in the future, he can train Paralympic athletes, and help to make future champions.

Petrúcio is one example of people with disabilities who are top athletes. Thanks to organizations like the Paralympic committee, people with disabilities have more opportunities than in the past.

Check it out!

Find these words and phrases and check their meaning.

disability	it is worth the effort
world record	coach
to train	athlete
race	

1 113 **Read and listen** **Which organization helps athletes like Petrúcio Ferreira?**

____

2 Are the sentences true (T) or false (F)?

Petrúcio can run very fast. T

1 He can't run in the Paralympics. ____

2 He has a world record. ____

3 Petrúcio's family can't give him lots of money. ____

4 Petrúcio is usually very tired, so he can't train. ____

5 He wants to continue with sports in the future. ____

3 Answer the questions.

What is Petrúcio's disability? He only has one arm.

1 Which country does he run for?

2 What type of race does he run?

3 How does he find training?

4 What job does he want to do in the future?

4 **Presentation** **Research another Paralympic athlete and prepare a presentation about him / her. Use the questions to help you. Present the athlete to the class.**

- What is his / her name?
- Where is he / she from?
- What is his / her disability?
- What is his / her sport?
- What does he / she hope to do in the future?

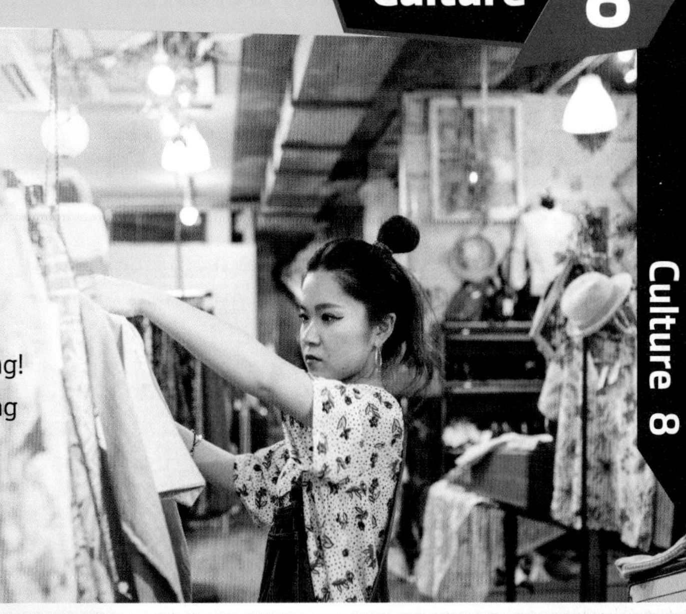

It's a sunny Saturday morning in New York City and Annabel and her best friend, Gemma, are shopping for clothes. They aren't visiting the popular stores on the main street or in malls. Instead, they're doing something quite different: they're thrifting!

Thrifting means shopping in thrift shops. In thrift shops, nothing is new–it's all second-hand. This means that everything is cheaper, some items are old, and the pants, skirts, shirts, and dresses aren't always the latest fashion. Why are the girls doing this?

The first reason is that Annabel and Gemma are teenagers, so they don't have a lot of money. Second, they don't want to look the same as everyone else. But the third reason is maybe the most important: they know about the effects of clothing companies on the environment.

Every year, globally, we buy 80 billion items of clothing. But we often buy things we don't want, or cheap clothes that don't last very long. This is bad for the environment.

Thrifting is one way to help the environment, and in the U.S. it's very popular. Companies like Goodwill and the Salvation Army have thrift shops all over the U.S., and money from the shops goes to charities. Right now, Annabel is holding a beautiful red jacket, and Gemma is trying on a pair of black pants. The girls are helping the planet–and they're looking good!

Check it out!

Find these words and phrases and check their meaning.

second-hand	environment
latest	globally
companies	to last

1 114 **Read and listen** **What is *thrifting*?**

____

2 Choose the correct answers.

Annabel and Gemma are shopping for _____ clothes.
a new
(b) second-hand
c expensive

1 Annabel and Gemma _____.
a don't want to buy clothes
b only want cheap clothes that don't last long
c know that people buy a lot of clothes

2 In the U.S., thrifting is _____.
a only for teenagers
b popular
c unpopular

3 In the U.S., there _____ thrift shops.
a are lots of Goodwill and Salvation Army
b are only Goodwill and Salvation Army
c aren't many

4 The thrift shops give the money from sales to _____.
a teenagers
b clothing companies
c charities

3 Answer the questions.

What kind of shop are Annabel and Gemma shopping in?
They're shopping in a thrift shop.

1 How are the clothes different from those in main street stores?
2 Why don't Annabel and Gemma have much money?
3 How many items of clothing do people buy each year?
4 What is one good thing about shopping in a thrift shop?

4 **Presentation** **Imagine you are running a new thrift shop in your town. Prepare a presentation about it. Use the questions to help you. Present your new thrift shop to the class.**

- Why is a thrift shop a good idea in your town?
- What is the name of your thrift shop?
- What are you selling in there? (It doesn't have to be only clothes!)
- Who can shop in your thrift shop?

A very *special* care home

In London, there's a care home called Nightingale House. It is a home to very old men and women–a lot of them are about 90 years old, or maybe older!

But there's something very special about this care home. It is the first care home in the U.K. to have a nursery for young children. Here, everybody–young and older people–comes together for different activities.

Every day, the children arrive at 7:30 a.m. and do painting, drawing, cooking, music, and other activities with the residents. They all eat together and listen to stories together. Finally, at 6:30 p.m., the children go home.

But why does this care home have a nursery? The answer is that spending time with young children helps older people, and it is a very positive experience for them. Some residents don't have grandchildren, so they love the visits from the small children. Old age is often difficult, but time with young children makes older people happier–they forget their problems, they eat more food, and their health improves! It is also a great experience for the children. Some children don't have grandparents, so at Nightingale House, they can spend time with older people and learn from them, too.

The idea isn't new. There are care homes like Nightingale House in Japan, Australia, the U.S., and across Europe. Now it is a very popular idea in the U.K., and more care homes with nurseries are opening. It helps many people, and everybody is happy!

Check it out!

Find these words and check their meaning.

care home, old, nursery, young, resident, health, improves

1 115 **Read and listen** **What is different about this care home?**

____

2 Complete the sentences with the words in the box.

idea ~~residents~~ children nursery lunch good

The *residents* are very old.

1 The __________ opens at 7:30 a.m.

2 There are activities for the residents and __________.

3 The children have __________ with the residents.

4 The __________ for the care home isn't new.

5 The children help the old residents to feel __________.

3 Answer the questions.

Where is Nightingale House? *It's in London.*

1 How old are most of the residents?

2 What activities do the residents do with the children?

3 What is one positive thing for the older people at Nightingale House?

4 What is one positive thing for the children at Nightingale House?

5 What other countries have homes like Nightingale House?

4 Presentation **Prepare a short presentation about an older family member or friend. Use the questions to help you. Give your presentation to the class.**

- How old is he / she?
- Where does he / she live?
- What does he / she like doing?
- What activities do you do together?
- Is he / she happy?

What are **Fuego**, **Misti** and **Cotopaxi**?

Yes, they are all volcanoes.

A volcano is a **mountain** with a **crater** at the top. Inside the mountain, there is very hot rock called **magma**. When the volcano erupts, **lava**, gas, and a cloud of black **ash** come out of the crater. Lava is the same as magma, but we call it lava when it is outside the volcano.

The Ring of Fire, Pacific Ocean

There are three types of volcano: an active volcano, a dormant volcano, and an extinct volcano. An active volcano often erupts; a dormant volcano is inactive, or sleeping; and an extinct volcano can't erupt again.

Volcanoes are dangerous, but some people live near them. Volcanoes are good for tourism. Also, many farms are near volcanoes because the ash from volcanoes is good for the soil. This makes it easy for fruit and vegetables to grow.

The most active volcanoes on Earth are in the Ring of Fire in the Pacific Ocean. Many of these volcanoes are in South and Central America: Fuego in Guatemala, Cotopaxi in Ecuador, and Misti in Peru. Some volcanoes are under the ocean, and there are also volcanoes on other planets, like Venus and Mars!

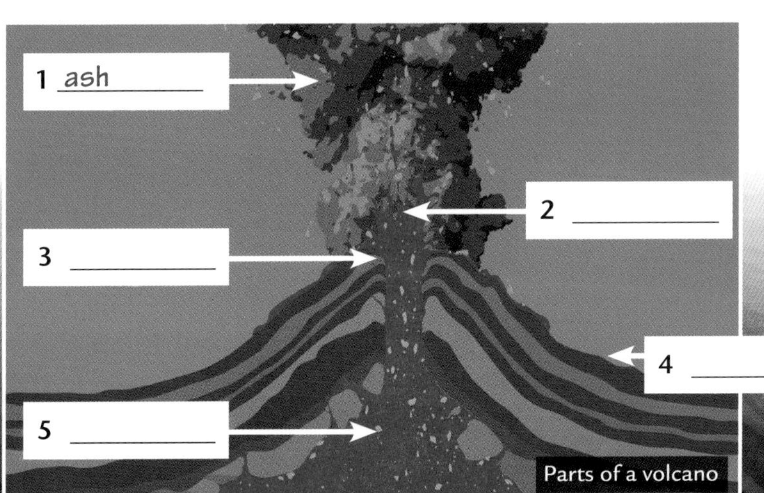

Parts of a volcano

Check it out!

Find these words and check their meaning.

erupts tourism
ash soil
farm

1 116 **Read and listen** Where is Cotopaxi?

______

2 Label the picture of the volcano with the **bold** words in the text.

3 Answer the questions.

What three things come out of the top of a volcano? *Lava, gas, and ash.*

1 What is the difference between lava and magma?
2 What do you call a "sleeping volcano"?
3 What is ash good for?
4 Where are most active volcanoes?
5 What three planets are mentioned in the text?

4 **Link it!** Research a volcano and make a fact file about it. Illustrate your fact file with pictures and use the questions to help you.

- What is your volcano's name?
- Which country is it in?
- How tall is it?
- Is it active or dormant?
- What is the date of its last eruption?
- If active, how often does it erupt?
- Do people live near the volcano? What are the names of the cities, towns, or villages?

CLIL Computer science

A helping hand

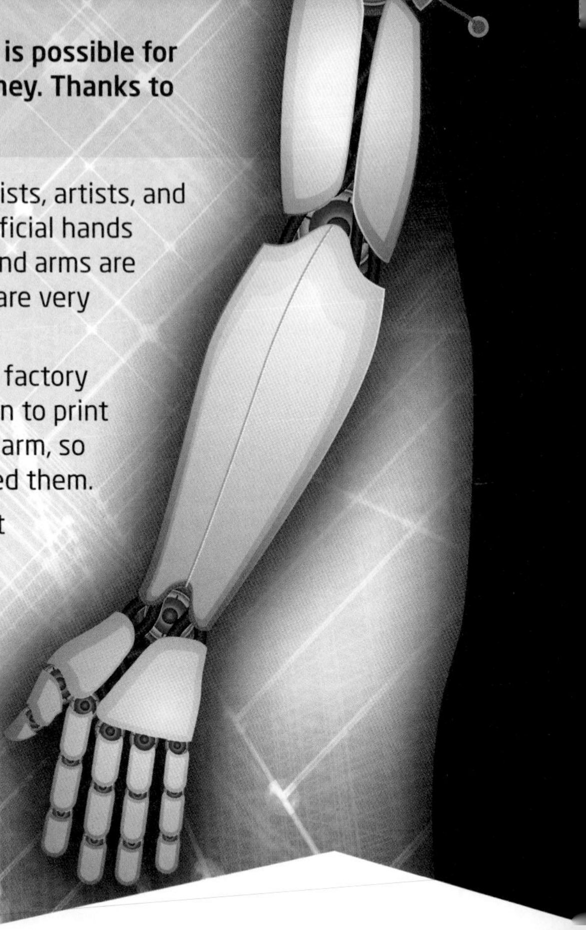

Every year, many children are born without hands or arms. It is possible for their families to buy artificial ones, but they cost a lot of money. Thanks to an organization called e-NABLE, things are changing.

e-NABLE is an international group of engineers, teachers, scientists, artists, and computer engineers. These people use computers to design artificial hands and arms for children in many countries. These artificial hands and arms are different from normal ones: they look like robot arms and some are very colorful! Children love them.

It isn't expensive to make the hands and arms. You don't need a factory with lots of equipment. All you need is a 3-D printer and a person to print it for you! e-NABLE wants everyone to be happy with their new arm, so e-NABLE doesn't sell them–they are free for the people who need them.

e-NABLE artificial hands and arms aren't perfect, and they aren't forever, but children often need new ones because they grow quickly, so e-NABLE is an ideal solution.

A lot of children without hands or arms often find that simple activities, like playing sports, are very difficult, but with the help of e-NABLE, these activities are now possible!

Check it out!

Find these words and phrases and check their meaning.

artificial	look like	equipment	print	forever
engineers	factory	3-D printer	sell	grow

1 117 **Read and listen** **Choose the correct answer.**

The article is about

a accidents with your hand or arm.

b why some children don't need new hands or arms.

c an organization that helps children without hands or arms.

2 Complete the sentences with the words in the box.

3-D printer computers ~~money~~ playing sports hands and arms expensive

Artificial hands and arms normally cost a lot of <u>money</u>.

1 e-NABLE designs the arms and hands using ________________.

2 e-NABLE's products look like the ________________ of a robot.

3 e-NABLE arms and hands aren't ________________ –they're free.

4 You need a ________________ to make a new arm.

5 Thanks to e-NABLE, things like ________________ are possible.

3 Choose the correct alternatives.

Families don't buy artificial arms or hands, because they **(are expensive)** / **don't help.**

1 e-NABLE is an organization of people from **all over the world / the U.S.**

2 e-NABLE's products **don't look / look** real.

3 The e-NABLE arms and hands **are / aren't** expensive.

4 Children need new arms and hands because they **break them / grow quickly**.

4 Link it! Find another object that it is possible for 3-D printers to make. Make a poster about the object. Write sentences and decorate the poster with pictures. Use the questions to help you.

- What's the name of the object?
- What can it do?
- Who is it for?
- Why is it useful?
- Can you buy this object in stores?

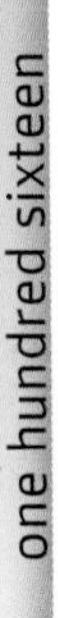

BRAZIL'S WEEK OF MODERN ART

The year is 1922. Brazil is celebrating 100 years of independence. Brazilian art still has some close links to Portugal and the rest of Europe, but Brazilian art is now creating its own unique style. Brazilian artists want to tell the world about their art, so a group of artists from São Paulo are having a week-long celebration of Brazilian art. From sculpture to poetry, from paintings to song, Brazilian artists, writers, and musicians are showing their latest work. These include painters like Di Cavalcanti and Anita Malfatti, and poet Mario de Andrade.

But there's a problem. This art is too modern for the public. People are confused, frightened, and angry about the artists' work.

Ten years later in 1932, things are changing. Generally, Brazilian people are starting to enjoy modern art. People are now talking about opening new art galleries in São Paulo and Rio de Janeiro.

The effects of the 1922 exhibition are so positive that, nearly 30 years later, Brazil is having another celebration of modern arts! The São Paulo Biennial, a large modern art exhibition, soon becomes one of the most important art exhibitions in South America. From that moment, every two years the exhibition shows art from Brazil and the rest of the world.

Today, in the 21st century, Brazil's modern art scene is still very strong and represents the different cultures in the country. It is the unique style of Brazilian art and the influence of these cultures that makes it so special.

Di Cavalcanti

Mário de Andrade

1 118 **Read and listen** **Are the effects of the week of modern art positive or negative?**

____

2 Are the sentences true (T) or false (F)?

A group of artists want to celebrate Brazil's independence. T

1 The week of modern art is only for paintings and sculpture. ___
2 At first, the public doesn't like the modern art in the celebration. ___
3 The São Paulo Biennial happens every year. ___
4 Today, Brazil has a strong modern art scene. ___

3 Answer the questions.

What is the year of Brazil's independence?
It's 1822.

1 Who is Di Cavalcanti?
2 How often is the São Paulo Biennial?
3 According to the text, why is Brazilian art special?

Check it out!

Find these words and check their meaning.

celebrating frightened strong
sculpture angry

4 **Link it!** **Find out more information online about the São Paulo Biennial. Write and record a short advert for the next São Paulo Biennial. Use the questions to help you. Share your advert with the class.**

- When is the next São Paulo Biennial?
- Which artists are in it?
- Where are the artists from?
- How much are the tickets?
- What are the opening times?
- What adjectives can you use to describe the art?
- Who is your favorite artist?

1A

Find the countries and nationalities in the wordsearch. Write them in the correct columns.

Nationality	Country
Portuguese	the ______
______	______
______	the ______
______	______
______	______
______	______
	______

S	P	A	I	N	J	M	A	F	S	C	W
A	O	A	E	R	W	A	E	W	C	H	A
S	R	U	K	F	U	B	P	R	H	I	R
W	E	S	F	M	S	F	S	A	I	L	U
E	T	T	A	H	S	A	R	S	N	E	S
F	U	R	W	E	X	E	W	M	E	W	S
B	R	A	Z	I	L	F	M	E	S	A	I
B	K	L	B	O	R	B	R	X	E	R	A
R	I	I	A	A	M	E	R	I	C	A	N
O	S	A	S	B	F	O	M	C	B	S	R
B	H	N	F	A	B	R	F	O	A	L	S
P	O	R	T	U	G	U	E	S	E	E	N

1B

Look at sentences 1–5. Use the words in the boxes to make similar sentences.

~~Japanese~~	We're	Portuguese	He's
You're	British	She's	I'm
Spanish	Chilean	~~They're~~	Chinese

Miwa and Yuki are from Japan.
They're Japanese.

1 Ana and I are from Spain.
______

2 Joe is from the U.K.
______

3 I come from Portugal.
______

4 Lucila is from Chile.
______

5 You and Chen are from China.
______

2A

Copy the letters in black to make sentences.

1 IT'MANNOTTYAGYSFTNOOBUGUCIDETLNUT.
2 HRESIJSDNN'FTPIFENHSJCKHCOQOPL.
3 WUGEFATRBEXZN'TYREPEULCSIDSILAOWN.
4 TRXHTHEUJYEFTARFDQECVNBH'TQAOSLCD.
5 YIOPUOLAFDRGEHNN'BTXLROFLGAJ.

1 ______
2 ______
3 ______
4 ______
5 ______

2B

Draw lines to make questions.

Am I	his parents?
Are they	your cousin?
1 Is she	his sister?
2 Is he	her dad?
3 Are you	frightened?
4 Is he	their aunt?
5 Are they	their grandparents?
6 Is she	your mom?
7 Is he	your uncle?
8 Is she	your grandma?
9 Are you	your cousins?
10 Are we	his brother?

3A

Look at the picture. Complete the sentences with the missing words. Find them in the wordsnake.

BEHINDAFWARDROBEGUDESKPORLAMPWENEXTTOBGACROSSFROM

The bed is next to a table.

1 The ___________ is on the table.
2 The window is ___________ the bed.
3 There's a bag under the ___________.
4 The desk is ______________ the door.
5 There's a ___________ between the door and an armchair.

3B

In the wordsearch, find the plural forms of the nouns in the box.

~~pencil case~~ person foot box mouse
woman family shelf dress child man

P	M	B	Y	A	E	W	O	B	O	D	D
A	E	M	O	P	E	O	P	L	E	R	R
D	N	N	E	R	S	M	E	M	D	E	O
E	O	D	C	E	O	E	D	A	C	S	D
O	M	A	S	I	Y	N	B	T	H	S	E
M	I	C	E	S	L	A	R	E	I	E	A
B	E	S	R	H	M	C	O	S	L	S	F
S	M	O	A	E	D	O	A	Y	D	E	E
F	A	M	I	L	I	E	S	S	R	A	E
Y	D	R	S	V	B	R	T	R	E	B	T
M	S	E	Y	E	O	E	M	O	N	S	Y
B	O	X	E	S	R	D	A	O	E	D	M

4A

Reorder the words in boxes of the same color. Write affirmative (✓) and negative (✗) sentences with *have*.

I have a phone. (✓)

1 ______________________________. (✓)
2 ______________________________. (✗)
3 ______________________________. (✓)
4 ______________________________. (✗)

he	have	you	soccer	we	~~have~~
guitar	red	have	new	~~I~~	bike
ball	~~phone~~	they	have	a	have
a	doesn't	skateboards	a	don't	a

4B

Follow the lines from the people to their possessions. Write sentences with the possessive *'s*.

It's Jack's game console.

1 It's ______________________.
2 They're ______________________.
3 It's ______________________.
4 It's ______________________.
5 They're ______________________.

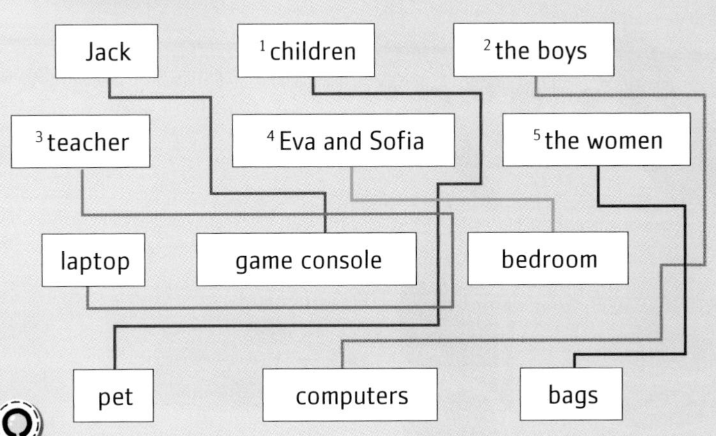

5A

Write the missing words in the crossword.

1 I finish school at 3:30.
2 I ___________ school at 8:30.
3 I ___________ TV in the evening.
4 I get ___________ at 4 p.m.
5 I take a ___________ in the morning.
6 I have ___________ at 12:00.
7 I go to ___________ at 9:30.
8 I ___________ my homework before dinner.

5B

Break the code. What time does Silvia get up in the morning?

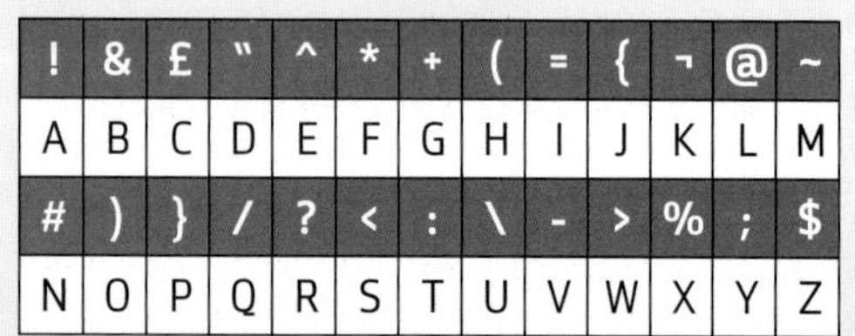

!	&	£	"	^	*	+	(	=	{	¬	@	~
A	B	C	D	E	F	G	H	I	J	K	L	M
#	)	}	/	?	<	:	\	-	>	%	;	$
N	O	P	Q	R	S	T	U	V	W	X	Y	Z

```
= \<\!@@; +^: \} !: <^-^#
:(=?:;
```

_______________________________.

Silvia gets up at ___________________.

In pairs, create two sentences using the code.

6A

**Draw lines to make sentences.
Use each box only once.**

You can go in these directions: → ← ↓ ↑

You can't go in these directions: ↗ ↙ ↘ ↖

Jack	don't	has	They	not	tuna.	You
doesn't	like	eats	don't	want	like	don't
likes	cheese.	has	wants	any	no	likes
wants	no	you	I	soda.	he	eat
eats	peas.	wants	carrots.	has	they	She
doesn't	eat	don't	want	don't	have	doesn't
Kenji	not	I	doesn't	we	any	eggs.

6B

**Look at the pictures. Write the words in the puzzle.
What is the mystery vegetable in the blue squares?**

1
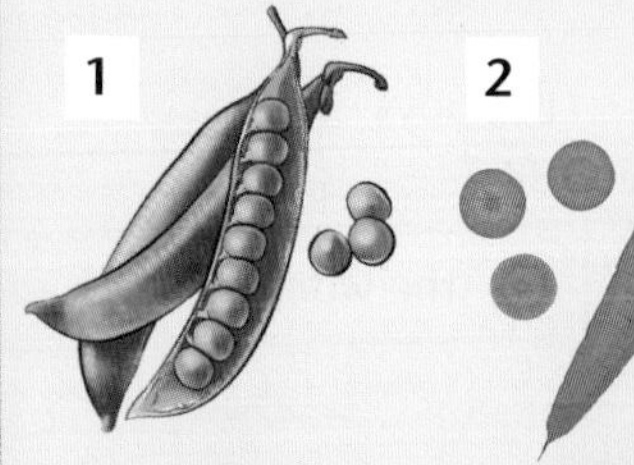
2
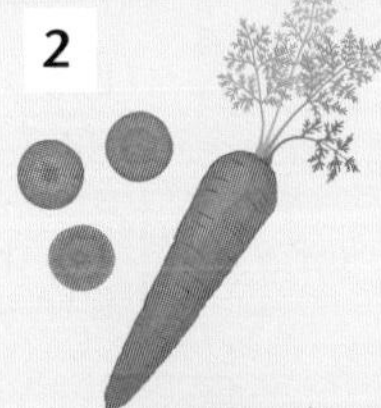
3

4

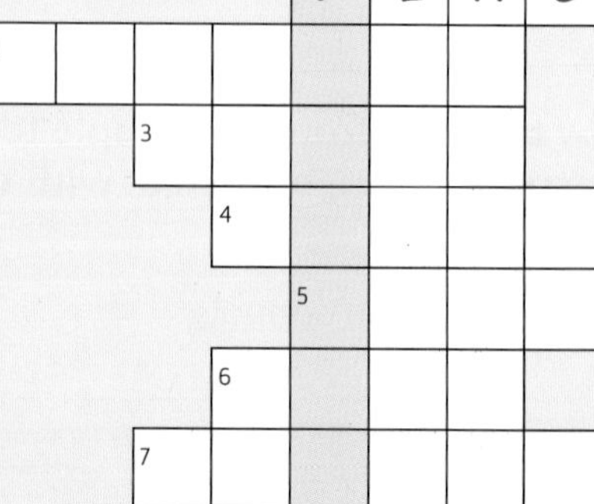

5

6
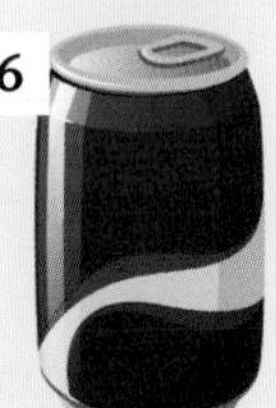
7
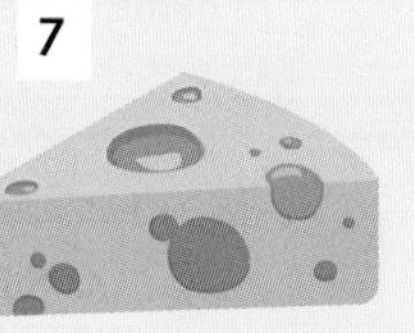
8
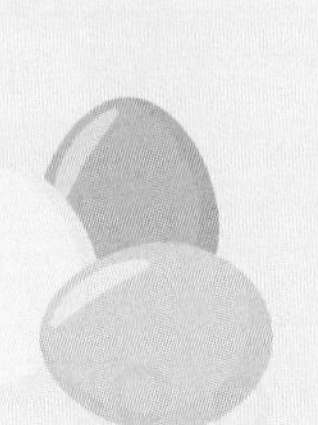

7A

Look at the pictures. Find the matching sentences in the wordsnake and write them next to the pictures.

~~ICAN'TPLAYVOLLEYBALL~~WECANDO
GYMNASTICSTHEYCANPLAYSOCCERSHECAN'TPLAYTENNIS
YOUCAN'TDOKARATEHECANPLAYFIELDHOCKEY

I can't play volleyball.

1 

______________________.

2 

______________________.

3 

______________________.

4 

______________________.

5 

______________________.

7B

Complete the sports in the crossword.

	[1] B	A	[2] S	K	E	T	[3] B	A	L	L	
											[6] S
[4] S	K		I				S				
											C
			M				B				
						[5] K		R	A	T	E
			N								
							L				

8A

What are the missing vowels? Write the complete sentences.

Sh*'s w**r*ng p*nts.

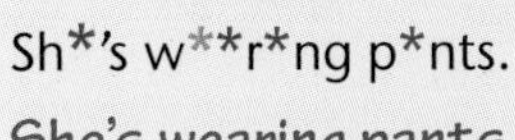

She's wearing pants.

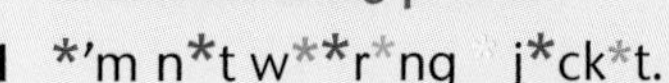

1 *'m n*t w**r*ng * j*ck*t.

____

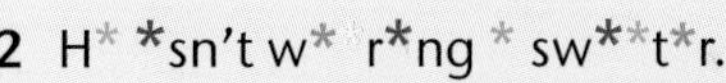

2 H* *sn't w**r*ng * sw**t*r.

____

3 Sh*'s w**r*ng * sk*rt.

____

4 Y**'r* w**r*ng n*w sn**k*rs.

____

5 Th*y *r*n't w**r*ng h**d**s.

____

8B

Match the words to make questions. Then match the questions to the answers.

What are	he wearing a scarf?	To the movies.
1 Where is	you doing?	A magazine.
2 Why is	he reading?	It's cold.
3 Who are	she going?	Their friends.
4 What is	they talking to?	Watching TV.

Word list

Welcome

Classroom language

book /bʊk/
close /kloʊz/
listen /ˈlɪsn/
look /lʊk/
open /ˈoʊpən/
read /rid/
sit down /ˌsɪt ˈdaʊn/
talk /tɔk/
write /raɪt/

Numbers

zero / oh /ˈzɪroʊ, oʊ/
one /wʌn/
two /tu/
three /θri/
four /fɔr/
five /faɪv/
six /sɪks/
seven /ˈsɛvn/
eight /eɪt/
nine /naɪn/
ten /tɛn/
eleven /ɪˈlɛvn/
twelve /twɛlv/
thirteen /ˌθərˈtin/
fourteen /ˌfɔrˈtin/
fifteen /ˌfɪfˈtin/
sixteen /ˌsɪksˈtin/
seventeen /ˌsɛvnˈtin/
eighteen /ˌeɪˈtin/
nineteen /ˌnaɪnˈtin/
twenty /ˈtwɛnti/
twenty-one /ˌtwɛnti ˈwʌn/
thirty /ˈθərt̬i/
forty /ˈfɔrt̬i/
fifty /ˈfɪfti/
sixty /ˈsɪksti/
seventy /ˈsɛvnt̬i/
eighty /ˈeɪt̬i/
ninety /ˈnaɪnt̬i/
one hundred /ˌwʌn ˈhʌndrəd/

School things

backpack /ˈbækpæk/
board /bɔrd/
calculator /ˈkælkyəˌleɪt̬ər/
chair /tʃɛr/
clock /klɑk/
colored pencils /ˌkʌlərd ˈpɛnslz/
desk /dɛsk/
door /dɔr/
eraser /ɪˈreɪsər/
laptop /ˈlæptɑp/
magic marker /ˈmædʒɪk ˌmɑrkər/
notebook /ˈnoʊtbʊk/
pen /pɛn/
pencil /ˈpɛnsl/
pencil case /ˈpɛnsl ˌkeɪs/
pencil sharpener /ˈpɛnsl ˌʃɑrpənər/
ruler /ˈrulər/
textbook /ˈtɛkstbʊk/

Days and months

Monday /ˈmʌndeɪ/
Tuesday /ˈtuzdeɪ/
Wednesday /ˈwɛnzdeɪ/
Thursday /ˈθərzdeɪ/
Friday /ˈfraɪdeɪ/
Saturday /ˈsæt̬ərˌdeɪ/
Sunday /ˈsʌndeɪ/

January /ˈdʒænyuˌɛri/
February /ˈfɛbyuˌɛri/
March /mɑrtʃ/
April /ˈeɪprəl/
May /meɪ/
June /dʒun/
July /dʒʊˈlaɪ/
August /ˈɔgʌst/
September /sɛpˈtɛmbər/
October /ɑkˈtoʊbər/
November /noʊˈvɛmbər/
December /dɪˈsɛmbər/

Pets and colors

bird /bərd/
cat /kæt/
dog /dɔg/
fish /fɪʃ/
guinea pig /ˈgɪni ˌpɪg/
hamster /ˈhæmstər/
horse /hɔrs/
mouse / mice /maʊs, maɪs/
rabbit /ˈræbət/
snake /sneɪk/

black /blæk/
blue /blu/
brown /braʊn/
gray /greɪ/
green /grin/
orange /ˈɔrɪndʒ/
pink /pɪŋk/
purple /ˈpərpl/
red /rɛd/
white /waɪt/
yellow /ˈyɛloʊ/

Parts of the body

arm /ɑrm/
ear /ɪr/
eye /aɪ/
finger /ˈfɪŋgər/
foot / feet /fʊt, fit/
hair /hɛr/
hand /hænd/
leg /lɛg/
mouth /maʊθ/
nose /noʊz/
shoulder /ˈʃoʊldər/
toe /toʊ/

Other nouns

birthday /ˈbərθdeɪ/
dictionary /ˈdɪkʃəˌnɛri/
email /ˈimeɪl/
fall /fɔl/
(last) name /(ˈlæst) ˌneɪm/
page /peɪdʒ/
partner /ˈpɑrtnər/
restroom /ˈrɛstrum/
season /ˈsizn/
song /sɔŋ/
spring /sprɪŋ/
summer /ˈsʌmər/
winter /ˈwɪntər/

Other verbs

have /hæv/
love /lʌv/
spell /spɛl/

Other adjectives

beautiful /ˈbyut̬əfl/
blond /blɑnd/
favorite /ˈfeɪvrət/

Adverbs

o'clock /əˈklɑk/
very /ˈvɛri/

Unit 1

Countries and nationalities

Australia /ɔˈstreɪlyə/
Australian /ɔˈstreɪlyən/
Brazil /brəˈzɪl/
Brazilian /brəˈzɪlyən/
Canada /ˈkænədə/
Canadian /kəˈneɪdiən/
Chile /ˈtʃɪli/
Chilean /ˈtʃɪliən/
China /ˈtʃaɪnə/
Chinese /ˌtʃaɪˈniz/
Japan /dʒəˈpæn/
Japanese /ˌdʒæpəˈniz/
Mexico /ˈmɛksɪˌkoʊ/
Mexican /ˈmɛksɪkən/
Portugal /ˈpɔrtʃəgl/
Portuguese /ˌpɔrtʃəˈgiz/
Spain /speɪn/
Spanish /ˈspænɪʃ/
the U.K. /ðə ˌyu ˈkeɪ/
British /ˈbrɪt̬ɪʃ/
the U.S. /ðə ˌyu ˈɛs/
American /əˈmɛrɪkən/
Turkey /ˈtərki/
Turkish /ˈtərkɪʃ/

Other nouns

actor /ˈæktər/
address /əˈdrɛs, ˈædrɛs/
afternoon /ˌæftərˈnun/
age /eɪdʒ/
Art /ɑrt/
audition /ɔˈdɪʃn/
ballet /bæˈleɪ/
band /bænd/
city /ˈsɪt̬i/
competition /ˌkɑmpəˈtɪʃn/
dancer /ˈdænsər/
English /ˈɪŋglɪʃ/
evening /ˈivnɪŋ/
fan /fæn/
friend /frɛnd/
grade /greɪd/
group /grup/
guy /gaɪ/
hero /ˈhɪroʊ/
hobby /ˈhɑbi/
home /hoʊm/
hometown /ˌhoʊmˈtaʊn/
judge /dʒʌdʒ/
man / men /mæn, mɛn/
Math /mæθ/
monument /ˈmɑnyəmənt/
morning /ˈmɔrnɪŋ/

Music /ˈmyuzɪk/
night /naɪt/
president /ˈprɛzədənt/
singer /ˈsɪŋər/
story /ˈstɔri/
street dance /ˈstrit ˌdæns/
student /ˈstudnt/
studio /ˈstudiˌoʊ/
style /staɪl/
subject /ˈsʌbdʒɛkt/
teacher /ˈtitʃər/
team /tim/
town /taʊn/
weekend /ˈwikɛnd/

Verbs

dance /dæns/
see /si/
watch /wɑtʃ/

Other adjectives

awesome /ˈɔsəm/
(not) bad /(ˌnɑt) ˈbæd/
big /bɪg/
contemporary /kənˈtɛmpəˌrɛri/
cool /kul/
every /ˈɛvri/
excellent /ˈɛksələnt/
famous /ˈfeɪməs/
fantastic /fænˈtæstɪk/
fine /faɪn/
good /gʊd/
great /greɪt/
intelligent /ɪnˈtɛlədʒənt/
interesting /ˈɪntrəstɪŋ/
international /ˌɪntərˈnæʃənl/
little /ˈlɪt̬l/
next /nɛkst/
nice /naɪs/
ready /ˈrɛdi/
same /seɪm/
young /yʌŋ/

Adverbs

here /hɪr/
later /ˈleɪt̬ər/
now /naʊ/
today /təˈdeɪ/
together /təˈgɛðər/
well /wɛl/

Unit 2

Family

aunt /ænt/
brother /ˈbrʌðər/
cousin /ˈkʌzn/
dad /dæd/
grandma /ˈgrænmɑ/
grandpa /ˈgrænpɑ/
grandparents /ˈgrænˌpɛrənts/
mom /mɑm/
parents /ˈpɛrənts/
sister /ˈsɪstər/
uncle /ˈʌŋkl/

Ordinal numbers

first /fərst/
second /ˈsɛkənd/
third /θərd/
fifth /fɪfθ/
eighth /eɪtθ/
ninth /naɪnθ/
twelfth /twɛlfθ/
twentieth /ˈtwɛntiəθ/
twenty-first /ˌtwɛnti ˈfərst/

Other nouns

ball /bɔl/
boy /bɔɪ/
car /kɑr/
category /ˈkæt̬əgɔri/
channel /ˈtʃænl/
class /klæs/
computer lab /kəmˈpyut̬ər ˌlæb/
expert /ˈɛkspərt/
final /ˈfaɪnl/
geography /dʒiˈɑgrəfi/
history /ˈhɪstəri/
moment /ˈmoʊmənt/
movie /ˈmuvi/
passion /ˈpæʃn/
people /ˈpipl/
quiz show /ˈkwɪz ˌʃoʊ/
sport /spɔrt/
star /stɑr/
test /tɛst/

Verbs

happen /ˈhæpən/
meet /mit/
say /seɪ/

Adjectives

funny /ˈfʌni/
happy /ˈhæpi/
late /leɪt/
popular /ˈpɑpyələr/
strange /streɪndʒ/

Review A

Nouns

celebration /ˌsɛləˈbreɪʃn/
kangaroo /ˌkæŋgəˈru/
koala /koʊˈɑlə/
thing /θɪŋ/
time capsule /ˈtaɪm ˌkæpsl/
writer /ˈraɪt̬ər/

Adjectives

crazy (about) /ˈkreɪzi (əˌbaʊt)/
half /hæf/
important /ɪmˈpɔrtnt/
interested /ˈɪntrəstəd/
special /ˈspɛʃl/
terrible /ˈtɛrəbl/

Adverb

again /əˈgɛn/

Unit 3

House and furniture

apartment /əˈpɑrtmənt/
armchair /ˈɑrmtʃɛr/
backyard /ˌbækˈyɑrd/
bathroom /ˈbæθrum/
bathtub /ˈbæθtʌb/
bed /bɛd/
bedroom /ˈbɛdrum/
bookcase /ˈbʊkkeɪs/
cabinet /ˈkæbənət/
couch /kaʊtʃ/
cushion /ˈkʊʃn/
dining room /ˈdaɪnɪŋ ˌrum/
dresser /ˈdrɛsər/
floor /flɔr/
fridge /frɪdʒ/
hallway /ˈhɔlweɪ/
kitchen /ˈkɪtʃən/
lamp /læmp/
living room /ˈlɪvɪŋ ˌrum/
mirror /ˈmɪrər/
painting /ˈpeɪntɪŋ/
poster /ˈpoʊstər/
shelf / shelves /ʃɛlf, ʃɛlvz/
shower /ˈʃaʊər/
sink /sɪŋk/
stairs /stɛrz/
stove /stoʊv/
table /ˈteɪbl/
toilet /ˈtɔɪlət/
wall /wɔl/
wardrobe /ˈwɔrdroʊb/
washing machine /ˈwɑːʃɪŋ məˌʃiːn/
window /ˈwɪndoʊ/

Prepositions of place

across from /əˈkrɔs frəm/
behind /bɪˈhaɪnd/
between /bɪˈtwin/
in /ɪn/
in front of /ˌɪn ˈfrʌnt əv/
near /nɪr/
next to /ˈnɛkst tə/
on /ɑn/
under /ˈʌndər/

Other nouns

baby /ˈbeɪbi/
boomerang /ˈbuməˌræŋ/
building /ˈbɪldɪŋ/
child / children /tʃaɪld, ˈtʃɪldrən/
clothes /kloʊz/
collection /kəˈlɛkʃn/
comic book /ˈkɑmɪk ˌbʊk/
concert /ˈkɑnsərt/
elevator /ˈɛləˌveɪt̬ər/
exercise /ˈɛksərˌsaɪz/
fun /fʌn/
game /geɪm/
girl /gərl/
letter /ˈlɛt̬ər/
mess /mɛs/
minute /ˈmɪnət/
ocean /ˈoʊʃn/
one thousand /ˌwʌn ˈθaʊznd/
person /ˈpərsn/
remote control /rɪˌmoʊt kənˈtroʊl/
sandwich /ˈsænwɪtʃ/
seashell /ˈsiʃɛl/
second /ˈsɛkənd/
step /stɛp/
woman / women /ˈwʊmən, ˈwɪmən/

Verb

arrive /əˈraɪv/

Adjectives

best /bɛst/
bright /braɪt/
correct /kəˈrɛkt/

difficult /ˈdɪfɪˌkʌlt/
horrible /ˈhɔrəbl/
incorrect /ˌɪnkəˈrɛkt/
neat /nit/
other /ˈʌðər/
small /smɔl/
tall /tɔl/
upset /ʌpˈsɛt/
welcome /ˈwɛlkəm/

Adverbs

downstairs /ˌdaʊnˈstɛrz/
soon /sun/
there /ðɛr/
tonight /təˈnaɪt/
upstairs /ˌʌpˈstɛrz/

Unit 4

My things

bike /baɪk/
camera /ˈkæmrə/
cell phone /ˈsɛl ˌfoʊn/
game console /ˈɡeɪm ˌkɑnsoʊl/
guitar /ɡɪˈtɑr/
MP3 player /ˌɛm pi ˈθri ˌpleɪər/
planner /ˈplænər/
skateboard /ˈskeɪtbɔrd/
soccer ball /ˈsɑkər ˌbɔl/
sunglasses /ˈsʌnˌɡlæsəz/
tablet /ˈtæblət/

Other nouns

activity /ækˈtɪvət̬i/
application form /ˌæpləˈkeɪʃn ˌfɔrm/
bag /bæɡ/
cent /sɛnt/
change /tʃeɪndʒ/
club /klʌb/
coach /koʊtʃ/
Computer Science /kəmˈpyut̬ər ˌsaɪəns/
course /kɔrs/
dollar /ˈdɑlər/
football /ˈfʊtbɔl/
French /frɛntʃ/
garage /ɡəˈrɑʒ/
language /ˈlæŋɡwɪdʒ/
member /ˈmɛmbər/
musical instrument /ˌmyuzɪkl ˈɪnstrəmənt/
piano /piˈænoʊ/
playlist /ˈpleɪlɪst/
problem /ˈprɑbləm/
receipt /rɪˈsit/
scout /skaʊt/
skater /ˈskeɪt̬ər/
technology /tɛkˈnɑlədʒi/
trophy /ˈtroʊfi/
video /ˈvɪdiˌoʊ/
watch /wɑtʃ/

Verbs

click /klɪk/
come in /ˌkʌm ˈɪn/
do /du/
enter /ˈɛntər/
take /teɪk/

Adjectives

different /ˈdɪfrənt/
expensive /ɪkˈspɛnsɪv/
impossible /ɪmˈpɑsəbl/
jealous /ˈdʒɛləs/
outdoor /ˈaʊtdɔr/
perfect /ˈpərfɪkt/
stupid /ˈstupəd/

Adverbs

really /ˈrili/
tomorrow /təˈmɑroʊ/

Review B

Nouns

beanbag /ˈbinbæɡ/
idea /aɪˈdiə/
pool table /ˈpul ˌteɪbl/
popcorn maker /ˈpɑpkɔrn ˌmeɪkər/
screen /skrin/
sports equipment /ˈspɔrts ɪˌkwɪpmənt/
stuff /stʌf/

Verbs

cook /kʊk/
get /ɡɛt/
hear /hɪr/
imagine /ɪˈmædʒən/
send /sɛnd/
think /θɪŋk/
want /wɑnt/

Adjectives

colorful /ˈkʌlərfl/
involved /ɪnˈvɑlvd/
massive /ˈmæsɪv/
modern /ˈmɑdərn/

Unit 5

Daily routines

chat online /ˌtʃæt ˌɑnˈlaɪn/
do my homework /ˌdu ˌmaɪ ˈhoʊmwərk/
finish school /ˌfɪnɪʃ ˈskul/
get dressed /ˌɡɛt ˈdrɛst/
get home /ˌɡɛt ˈhoʊm/
get up /ˌɡɛt̬ ˈʌp/
go to bed /ˌɡoʊ t̬ə ˈbɛd/
have breakfast /ˌhæv ˈbrɛkfəst/
have dinner /ˌhæv ˈdɪnər/
have lunch /ˌhæv ˈlʌntʃ/
start school /ˌstɑrt ˈskul/
take a shower /ˌteɪk ə ˈʃaʊər/
watch TV /ˌwɑtʃ ˌti ˈvi/
use the computer /ˌyuz ðə kəmˈpyut̬ər/

Nouns

bus /bʌs/
dance move /ˈdæns ˌmuv/
Drama /ˈdrɑmə/
hour /ˈaʊər/
park /pɑrk/
period /ˈpɪriəd/
photography /fəˈtɑɡrəfi/
schedule /ˈskɛdʒul/
Science /ˈsaɪəns/
snack /snæk/

Other verbs

bring /brɪŋ/
clean (up) /ˌklin (ˈʌp)/
come /kʌm/
go /ɡoʊ/
hate /heɪt/
help /hɛlp/
kiss /kɪs/
know /noʊ/
learn /lərn/
like /laɪk/
live /lɪv/
make /meɪk/
play /pleɪ/
practice /ˈpræktəs/
prefer /prɪˈfər/
speak /spik/
stop /stɑp/
study /ˈstʌdi/
teach /titʃ/
visit /ˈvɪzət/
wear /wɛr/
work /wərk/

Adjectives

bored /bɔrd/
busy /ˈbɪzi/
classical /ˈklæsɪkl/
creative /kriˈeɪt̬ɪv/
exciting /ɪkˈsaɪt̬ɪŋ/
hungry /ˈhʌŋɡri/
long /lɔŋ/
own /oʊn/
personal /ˈpərsənl/
sorry /ˈsɑri/
tired /ˈtaɪərd/
worried /ˈwərid/

Adverbs

after that /ˌæftər ˈðæt/
always /ˈɔlweɪz/
instead /ɪnˈstɛd/
never /ˈnɛvər/
often /ˈɔfn/
outside /ˌaʊtˈsaɪd/
probably /ˈprɑbəbli/
rarely /ˈrɛrli/
sometimes /ˈsʌmtaɪmz/
then /ðɛn/
usually /ˈyuʒuəli/

Unit 6

Food and drink

apple /ˈæpl/
banana /bəˈnænə/
bread /brɛd/
cake /keɪk/
carrots /ˈkærəts/
cheese /tʃiz/
chicken /ˈtʃɪkən/
chocolate /ˈtʃɑklət/
corn /kɔrn/
dairy products /ˈdɛri ˌprɑdʌkts/
drink /drɪŋk/
eggs /ɛɡz/
fish /fɪʃ/
fries /fraɪz/
fruit /frut/
grapes /ɡreɪps/
ham /hæm/
ice cream /ˈaɪs ˌkrim/
meat /mit/
milk /mɪlk/
orange juice /ˈɔrɪndʒ ˌdʒus/
pastry /ˈpeɪstri/

peach /pitʃ/
pear /pɛr/
peas /piz/
potato chips /pə'teɪt̬oʊ ˌtʃɪps/
potatoes /pə'teɪt̬oʊz/
salad /'sæləd/
salmon /'sæmən/
shrimp /ʃrɪmp/
soda /'soʊdə/
sugar /'ʃʊgər/
tomatoes /tə'meɪt̬oʊz/
tuna /'tunə/
vegetables /'vɛdʒtəblz/
water /'wɔt̬ər/

Other nouns

camping /'kæmpɪŋ/
center /'sɛntər/
combination /ˌkɑmbə'neɪʃn/
filling /'fɪlɪŋ/
fire /'faɪər/
flavor /'fleɪvər/
German /'dʒərmən/
ingredients /ɪn'gridiənts/
invention /ɪn'vɛnʃn/
menu /'mɛnyu/
mystery /'mɪstəri/
recipe /'rɛsəpi/
restaurant /'rɛstəˌrɑnt/
vegetarian /ˌvɛdʒə'tɛriən/
world /wərld/

Verbs

buy /baɪ/
call /kɔl/
can't stand /ˌkænt 'stænd/
defend /dɪ'fɛnd/
eat /it/
enjoy /ɪn'dʒɔɪ/
hope /hoʊp/
keep /kip/
swim /swɪm/
taste /teɪst/

Adjectives

angry /'æŋgri/
common /'kɑmən/
delicious /dɪ'lɪʃəs/
dried /draɪd/
Italian /ɪ'tælyən/
native /'neɪt̬ɪv/
normal /'nɔrml/
right /raɪt/
typical /'tɪpɪkl/
unusual /ʌn'yuʒuəl/

Adverbs

also /'ɔlsoʊ/
finally /'faɪnəli/
once /wʌns/
only /'oʊnli/
surprisingly /sər'praɪzɪŋli/
twice /twaɪs/

Review C

Nouns

glass /glæs/
lemon /'lɛmən/
mint /mɪnt/
movie theater /'muvi ˌθiət̬ər/
store /stɔr/
strawberry /'strɔˌbɛri/
supermarket /'supərˌmɑrkət/
vanilla /və'nɪlə/

Verbs

carry /'kæri/
hurry /'həri/
include /ɪn'klud/
walk /wɔk/

Unit 7

Sports

baseball /'beɪsbɔl/
basketball /'bæskətˌbɔl/
biking /'baɪkɪŋ/
field hockey /'fild ˌhɑki/
gymnastics /dʒɪm'næstɪks/
karate /kə'rɑt̬i/
skiing /'skiɪŋ/
soccer /'sɑkər/
swimming /'swɪmɪŋ/
tennis /'tɛnəs/
track and field /ˌtræk ən 'fild/
volleyball /'vɑliˌbɔl/

Other nouns

Arabic /'ærəbɪk/
captain /'kæptən/
charity /'tʃærət̬i/
contest /'kɑntɛst/
cookie /'kʊki/
costume /'kɑstum/
curry /'kəri/
driver /'draɪvər/
end /ɛnd/
fashion /'fæʃn/
meal /mil/
money /'mʌni/
party /'pɑrt̬i/
performance /pər'fɔrməns/
poem /'poʊəm/
specialty /'spɛʃəlti/
street fair /'strit ˌfɛr/
talent /'tælənt/
theme /θim/
track /træk/
workshop /'wərkʃɑp/

Verbs

can /kæn/
count /kaʊnt/
draw /drɔ/
drive /draɪv/
forget /fər'gɛt/
join /dʒɔɪn/
paint /peɪnt/
prepare /prɪ'pɛr/
remember /rɪ'mɛmbər/
ride /raɪd/
run /rʌn/
sell /sɛl/
show /ʃoʊ/
sing /sɪŋ/
ski /ski/
touch /tʌtʃ/

Adjectives

amazing /ə'meɪzɪŋ/
artistic /ɑr'tɪstɪk/
awful /'ɔfl/
careful /'kɛrfl/
easy /'izi/
local /'loʊkl/
new /nu/
safe /seɪf/
shy /ʃaɪ/
slow /sloʊ/

Adverbs

early /'ərli/
fast /fæst/
hard /hɑrd/
pretty /'prɪt̬i/

Unit 8

Clothes

baseball hat /'beɪsbɔl ˌhæt/
boots /buts/
coat /koʊt/
dress /drɛs/
hat /hæt/
hoodie /'hʊdi/
jacket /'dʒækət/
jeans /dʒinz/
leggings /'lɛgɪŋz/
pants /pænts/
scarf /skɑrf/
shirt /ʃərt/
shoes /ʃuz/
shorts /ʃɔrts/
skirt /skərt/
sneakers /'snikərz/
sweater /'swɛt̬ər/
T-shirt /'ti ˌʃərt/
top /tɑp/

Other nouns

champion /'tʃæmpiən/
fitting rooms /'fɪtɪŋ ˌrumz/
luck /lʌk/
percentage /pər'sɛntɪdʒ/
personality /ˌpərsə'nælət̬i/
rule /rul/
size /saɪz/
uniform /'yunəˌfɔrm/
winner /'wɪnər/

Verbs

believe /bɪ'liv/
choose /tʃuz/
guess /gɛs/
hold /hoʊld/
leave /liv/
shop /ʃɑp/
stand /stænd/
try (sthg) on /ˌtraɪ … 'ɑn/
win /wɪn/

Adjectives

better /'bɛt̬ər/
dark /dɑrk/
denim /'dɛnəm/
excited /ɪk'saɪt̬əd/
large /lɑrdʒ/
medium /'midiəm/
nervous /'nərvəs/
poor /pʊr/

rich /rɪtʃ/
short /ʃɔrt/

Adverbs

just /dʒʌst/
loudly /ˈlaʊdli/
too /tu/

Review D

Nouns

athlete /ˈæθlit/
beach /bitʃ/
beginning /bɪˈɡɪnɪŋ/
ceremony /ˈsɛrəˌmoʊni/
designer /dɪˈzaɪnər/
event /ɪˈvɛnt/
million /ˈmɪlyən/
race /reɪs/
reason /ˈrizn/
training /ˈtreɪnɪŋ/
turn /tərn/
warm-up /ˈwɔrm ˌʌp/

Verbs

cost /kɔst/
design /dɪˈzaɪn/
hit /hɪt/
laugh /læf/
need /nid/
represent /ˌrɛprɪˈzɛnt/
smile /smaɪl/
spend /spɛnd/

Adjectives

cold /koʊld/
future /ˈfyutʃər/
quiet /ˈkwaɪət/
warm /wɔrm/

Adverb

possibly /ˈpɑsəbli/

Culture 1–4

Nouns

area /ˈɛriə/
bottle /ˈbɑt̬l/
century /ˈsɛntʃəri/
childhood /ˈtʃaɪldhʊd/
culture /ˈkʌltʃər/
diaper /ˈdaɪpər/
difference /ˈdɪfrəns/
education /ˌɛdʒəˈkeɪʃn/
England /ˈɪŋɡlənd/
example /ɪɡˈzæmpl/
follower /ˈfɑloʊər/
form /fɔrm/
gadget /ˈɡædʒət/
goal /ɡoʊl/
image /ˈɪmɪdʒ/
influence /ˈɪnfluəns/
instant /ˈɪnstənt/
Ireland /ˈaɪərlənd/
life /laɪf/
lifestyle /ˈlaɪfstal/
loaf / loaves /loʊf, loʊvz/
mother /ˈmʌðər/
movement /ˈmuvmənt/
museum /myuˈziəm/
north /nɔrθ/
origin /ˈɔrədʒən/
pair /pɛr/
past /pæst/
public /ˈpʌblɪk/
seat /sit/
set /sɛt/
stroller /ˈstroʊlər/
Sweden /ˈswidn/
the Netherlands /ðə ˈnɛðərləndz/
toy /tɔɪ/
use /yus/

Verbs

knock /nɑk/
move /muv/

Adjectives

African-American /ˌæfrɪkən əˈmɛrɪkən/
Afro-Caribbean /ˌæfroʊ ˌkærəˈbiən, kəˈrɪbiən/
ancient /ˈeɪnʃənt/
another /əˈnʌðər/
boring /ˈbɔrɪŋ/
each /itʃ/
fascinating /ˈfæsəˌneɪt̬ɪŋ/
Irish /ˈaɪrɪʃ/
necessary /ˈnɛsəˌsɛri/
old /oʊld/
royal /ˈrɔɪəl/
separate /ˈsɛprət/
simple /ˈsɪmpl/
true /tru/

Adverbs

actually /ˈæktʃuəli/
nearly /ˈnɪrli/
perhaps /pərˈhæps/
traditional /trəˈdɪʃənl/

Culture 5–8

Nouns

accident /ˈæksədənt/
article /ˈɑrt̬ɪkl/
billion /ˈbɪlyən/
break /breɪk/
burger /ˈbərɡər/
committee /kəˈmɪt̬i/
daughter /ˈdɔt̬ər/
effect /ɪˈfɛkt/
high school /ˈhaɪ ˌskul/
item /ˈaɪt̬əm/
job /dʒɑb/
mall /mɔl/
middle school /ˈmɪdl ˌskul/
opportunity /ˌɑpərˈtunət̬i/
organization /ˌɔrɡənəˈzeɪʃn/
planet /ˈplænət/
sale /seɪl/
sprint /sprɪnt/
teenager /ˈtinˌeɪdʒər/
type /taɪp/
view /vyu/
way /weɪ/

Verbs

become /bɪˈkʌm/
change /tʃeɪndʒ/
continue /kənˈtɪnyu/
mean /min/
take part /ˌteɪk ˈpɑrt/
try /traɪ/

Adjectives

aged /eɪdʒd/
cheap /tʃip/
free /fri/
main /meɪn/
Paralympic /ˌpærəˈlɪmpɪk/
sunny /ˈsʌni/
top /tɑp/
unpopular /ʌnˈpɑpyələr/

Adverbs

exactly /ɪɡˈzæktli/
hopefully /ˈhoʊpfəli/
maybe /ˈmeɪbi/

CLIL Extra A–D

Nouns

art gallery /ˈɑrt ˌɡæləri/
artist /ˈɑrt̬ɪst/
Central America /ˌsɛntrəl əˈmɛrɪkə/
cloud /klaʊd/
crater /ˈkreɪt̬ər/
Europe /ˈyʊrəp/
exhibition /ˌɛksəˈbɪʃn/
experience /ɪkˈspɪriəns/
farm /fɑrm/
gas /ɡæs/
grandchildren /ˈɡrænˌtʃɪldrən/
independence /ˌɪndɪˈpɛndəns/
link /lɪŋk/
Mars /mɑrz/
mountain /ˈmaʊntn/
musician /myuˈzɪʃn/
Pacific Ocean /pəˌsɪfɪk ˈoʊʃn/
poetry /ˈpoʊətri/
report /rɪˈpɔrt/
rest /rɛst/
ring /rɪŋ/
rock /rɑk/
scientist /ˈsaɪəntɪst/
solution /səˈluʃn/
South America /ˌsaʊθ əˈmɛrɪkə/
Venus /ˈvinəs/
volcano /vɑlˈkeɪnoʊ/

Verbs

be born /ˌbi ˈbɔrn/
break /breɪk/
create /kriˈeɪt/
feel /fil/
grow /ɡroʊ/

Adjectives

active /ˈæktɪv/
dangerous /ˈdeɪndʒərəs/
dormant /ˈdɔrmənt/
extinct /ɪkˈstɪŋkt/
hot /hɑt/
ideal /aɪˈdiəl/
inactive /ɪnˈæktɪv/
real /ril/
unique /yuˈnik/

Adverbs

quickly /ˈkwɪkli/
still /stɪl/

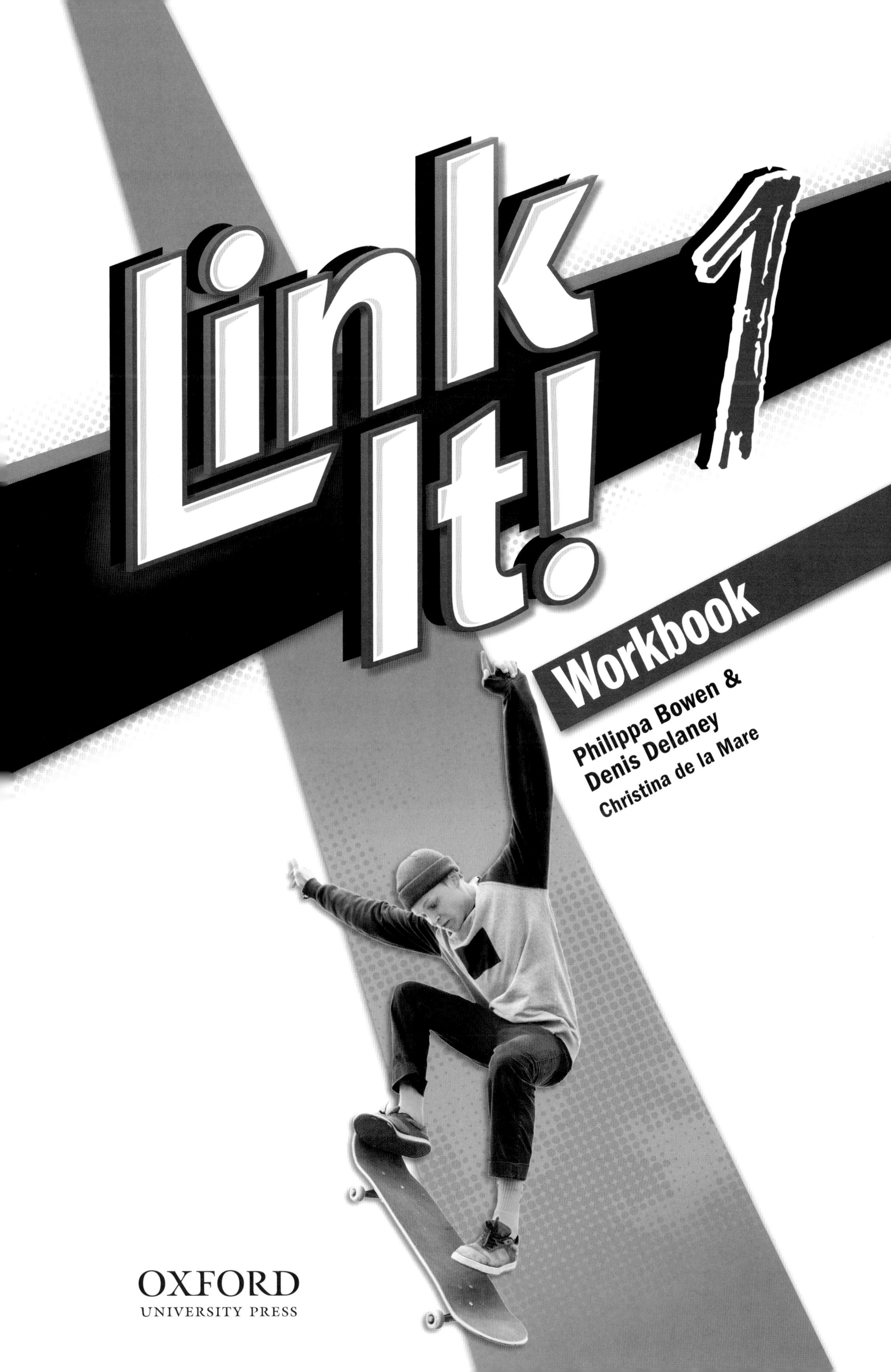
Link It! 1
Workbook
Philippa Bowen &
Denis Delaney
Christina de la Mare
OXFORD
UNIVERSITY PRESS

1 Grammar rules

Subject pronouns p.13

Singular	Plural
I	we
you	you
he / she / it	they

1 We always write *I* with a capital letter.

I am Blanca and I am from Spain.

2 We use *you* for singular and plural.

You are a new student.

You are new students.

3 We use *he* for a boy or a man.

Mr. Petrov is Russian. He is the Science teacher.

4 We use *she* for a girl or a woman.

Claire is Australian. She is my friend.

5 We use *it* for a thing or an animal.

It is a rabbit.

It is a pencil.

6 We can use *he* or *she* to talk about pets.

He's my dog, Rudy. She's my cat, Minnie.

7 The third person plural is *they*. We use it for the plural for people, animals, and things.

They are friends.

They are big dogs.

They are books.

Look!

In English, it is essential to use subject pronouns.

*Gabriel is my friend. **He** is very nice.*

NOT ~~*Gabriel is my friend. Is very nice.*~~

Possessive adjectives p.13

Singular	Plural
my	our
your	your
his / her / its	their

1 Possessive adjectives are the same for singular and plural nouns.

my pen my pens

2 We use *his* to show that a person or thing belongs to a boy or a man.

This is Michael. His mom is a teacher.

His backpack is green.

3 We use *her* to show that a person or thing belongs to a girl or a woman.

This is Jen. Her dad is tall.

Her eraser is in her pencil case.

4 We use *its* to show that something or a person belongs to a thing, place, or animal.

That is my house. Its door is red.

5 We can use *his* or *her* for pets.

That guinea pig is brown. His name is Spot.

This guinea pig is white and black. Her name is Daisy.

6 We use *your* with singular and plural nouns.

Isabella is your new teacher.

Your friends are in the classroom.

7 In English, there is never a definite article before the possessive adjective.

My car is red.

NOT ~~The my car is red~~.

be: Simple present p.16

Affirmative

Full form	Short form
I **am** Daniela.	I**'m** Daniela.
You **are** Jaime.	You**'re** Jaime.
He **is** a teacher.	He**'s** a teacher.
She **is** Chinese.	She**'s** Chinese.
It **is** a nice name.	It**'s** a nice name.
We **are** late.	We**'re** late.
You **are** students.	You**'re** students.
They **are** friends.	They**'re** friends.

1 We normally use short forms in conversation or in informal messages to friends.

Mark! You're late for school. The teacher's angry!

2 We use full forms when we write formal messages or emails.

Dear Mrs. Ross,

I am very sorry that I am not at school today–I am sick.

3 We can use the short form of *be* after a noun. We don't write the short form with plural nouns.

My dogs are black.

NOT ~~My dog're black.~~

Look!

We use the verb **be** to talk about age.

*I **am** 12. He **is** 14.*

NOT ~~*I have 12. He has 14.*~~

Look!

The short form of ***it is*** = ***it's***.

*That is my house. **It's** yellow.*

The possessive adjective for ***it*** = ***its***. There is always a noun after ***its***.

*That is my house. **Its** door is green.*

Word list

Review the vocabulary. Write your own study notes or translation for each word

Countries

Australia __________
Brazil __________
Canada __________
Chile __________
China __________
Japan __________
Mexico __________
Portugal __________
Spain __________
Turkey __________
the U.K. __________
the U.S. __________

Nationalities

American __________
Australian __________
Brazilian __________
British __________
Canadian __________
Chilean __________
Chinese __________
Japanese __________
Mexican __________
Portuguese __________
Spanish __________
Turkish __________

Check it out!

arguments __________
bring it on __________
Chill out __________
competition __________
Don't worry __________
gymnast __________
I'm nervous. __________
in real life __________
reality drama __________
talented __________
TV show __________
You're late! __________

Real English

Hey. __________
Hello / Hi! __________
Good morning. __________
Good afternoon. __________
Good evening. __________
How are you? __________
I'm very well __________
I'm fine. __________
I'm good, thanks. __________
I'm not bad, thanks. __________
Goodbye. __________
Goodnight. __________
Bye. / Bye then. __________
See you later! __________
See you on Monday. __________
Have a good day. __________
Have a nice weekend. __________

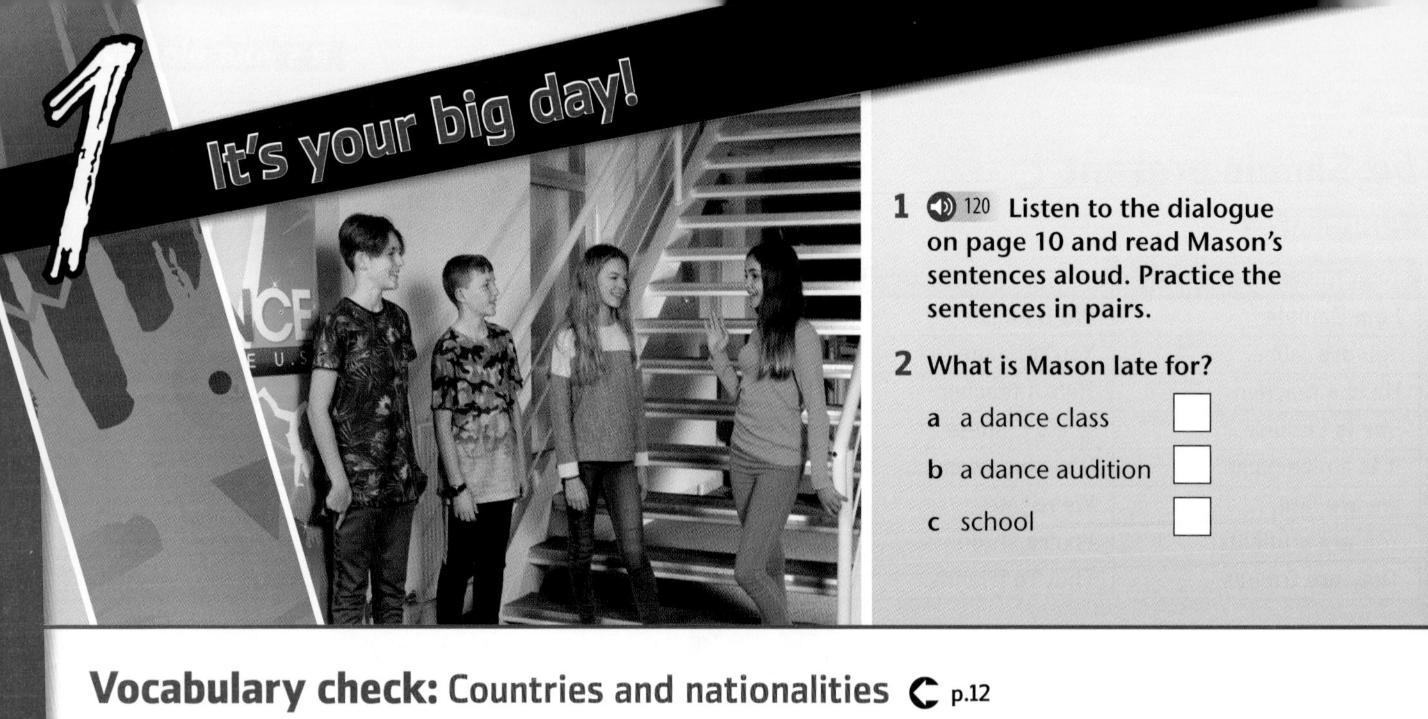

1 120 Listen to the dialogue on page 10 and read Mason's sentences aloud. Practice the sentences in pairs.

2 What is Mason late for?

a a dance class ☐
b a dance audition ☐
c school ☐

Vocabulary check: Countries and nationalities p.12

3 Look at the pictures of the famous people and the countries they come from. Complete the sentences for each one.

Japan | 1 the U.K. | 2 Spain | 3 Brazil | 4 Mexico | 5 Australia

He's Japanese. He's from Japan.

1 She's __________ . She's from __________ .
2 He's __________ . He's from __________ .
3 She's __________ . She's from __________ .
4 He's __________ . He's from __________ .
5 He's __________ . He's from __________ .

Grammar: Subject pronouns p.13

4 Complete the sentences with the correct subject pronouns.

Hugo is from La Paz. He's Bolivian.

1 David and Charlotte are students at Park High School. ______'re in 9th grade.
2 Look! It's Steve Aoki. ______'s a famous DJ.
3 Micaela is my friend. ______'s nice.
4 Patrick and ___ are Canadian. We're from Winnipeg.
5 *Deadpool* is my favorite movie. _____'s fantastic.
6 Joey and I are friends. ______ 're in the same dance class.

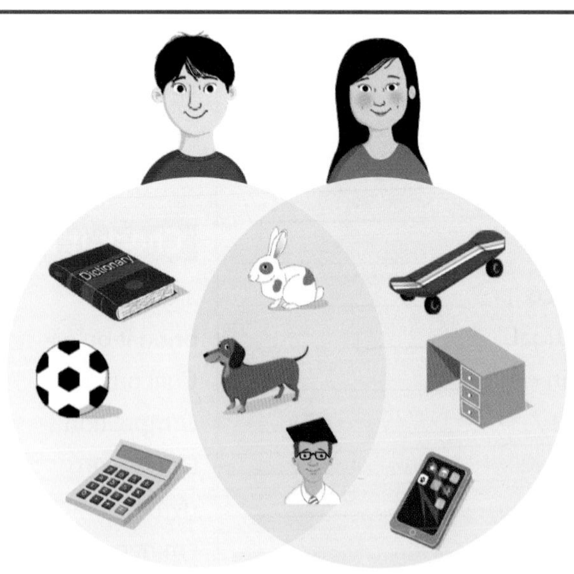

Possessive adjectives p.13

5 Match the subject pronouns 1–8 with the possessive adjectives a–h.

1 I d	5 it ____	a her	e their
2 you ____	6 we ____	b our	f your
3 he ____	7 you ____	c your	g his
4 she ____	8 they ____	d ~~my~~	h its

6 Look at the diagram. Complete the sentences with *his*, *her*, or *their*.

It's his dictionary.

1 It's _______ skateboard.
2 It's _______ rabbit.
3 It's _______ calculator.
4 It's _______ desk.
5 It's _______ dog.
6 It's _______ ball.
7 It's _______ cell phone.
8 He's _______ teacher.

7 Complete the sentences with the words in the box.

her ~~your~~ its their his your our

Kelly, what's <u>your</u> cell phone number?

1 He's my friend. ______ name is George.
2 We're with ______ mom and dad.
3 Alfie and Ruby have Art class together. Mr. Watson is ______ Art teacher.
4 Cartagena de Indias is a big city in Colombia. It's famous for ______ beautiful buildings.
5 John and Liam, close ______ books!
6 She's my Math teacher. ______ name is Miss Wood.

8 Complete the text with the correct possessive adjectives.

My name's Bianca. I'm American, but <u>my</u> dad is Brazilian. [1]______ name is Cássio. He's from São Paulo, in Brazil. My mom is British. [2]______ name is Alison.

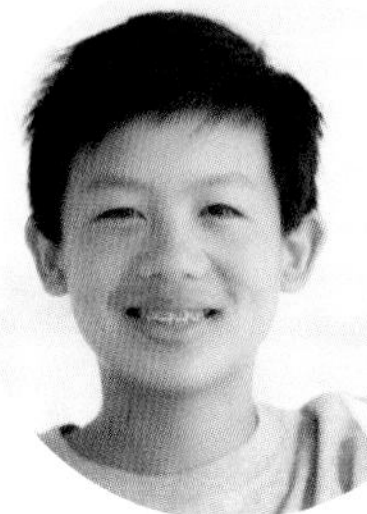

I'm a student at Greenwood Junior High. [3]______ best friends are in my class. [4]______ names are Andrei and Sabina. We're fans of the Red Sox baseball team, and [5]______ favorite player is J. D. Martinez.

be: Simple present affirmative p.16

9 Choose the correct alternatives.

I (am) / is 12 years old.

1 He **is** / **are** my dad.
2 You **are** / **am** late!
3 Mike and Lewis **is** / **are** American.
4 Ben and I **am** / **are** from London.
5 João **are** / **is** a popular name in Brazil.
6 You and Cooper **are** / **is** in the same class.

10 Complete the sentences with the short forms of *am*, *is*, or *are*.

Lucy is 14 and she<u>'s</u> Canadian.

1 I ______ 13 years old today.
2 She ______ my mom.
3 It ______ my favorite song.
4 We ______ students.
5 Mr. Bau is the Geography teacher. He ______ a great teacher.
6 They ______ from South Africa.

11 Look at the chart and complete the text about Jason with the correct forms of the verb *be*.

Name	Jason	Daniela
Age	13 years old	12 years old
City	Lincoln	Wisconsin
Nationality	American and Polish	Spanish and American
School	Roosevelt High School	Westvale Junior High
Friends	Seth and Quinn	Nathan and Linda
Grade	8th	7th

His name<u>'s</u> Jason. He [1]_____ 13 years old. Jason [2]_____ from Lincoln. His family [3]_____ American and Polish. He [4]_____ a student at Roosevelt High School. It [5]_____ a big school. Seth and Quinn [6]_____ his friends. They [7]_____ in 8th grade.

12 Use the information about Daniela in the chart in exercise 11 to write a paragraph. Use the short form of *be* if possible.

<u>Her name is Daniela. She's …</u>

Round-up

1 Choose the correct alternatives.

Hello! (My) / I name is Jasmine. I [1] **am** / **is** 12 years old and [2]**my** / **I'm** from Richmond, Virginia. A lot of people in my city [3] **are** / **is** fans of the Washington Nationals baseball team. My dad and I [4] **are** / **'s** big fans, too.

In the picture, I'm with [5]**my** / **our** best friends, Marney and Chrissie. [6]**You're** / **We're** students at Westport High School. Marney and I [7]**we are** / **are** in 7th grade. [8]**Our** / **Their** favorite teacher is Miss Walker. She [9]**'re** / **'s** our English teacher. Chrissie is in 8th grade. [10]**She's** / **He's** 13 years old. Music is [11]**my** / **the** passion. My favorite pop band is *Little Mix*.

Greetings p.14

1 **Complete the chart with the expressions in the box.**

~~Goodbye.~~ Bye. ~~Hello.~~ Hey. Goodnight. Good evening.
How are you? See you later. Hi. Have a good day! Good morning.

Real English

When you meet someone	When you leave someone
Hello.	Goodbye.
1 ______	6 ______
2 ______	7 ______
3 ______	8 ______
4 ______	9 ______
5 ______	

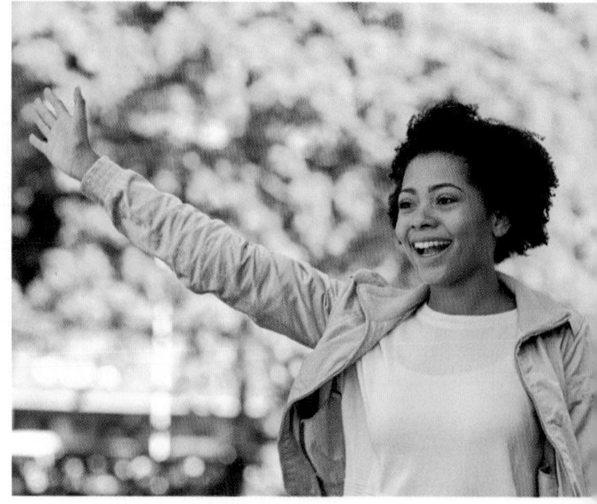

2 121 **Listen again to the dialogues on page 14 and complete them.**

1

Dominic Hey, Arianna!
Arianna Hi, Dominic.
Dominic How are you, Arianna?
Arianna [1] ______, thanks. And you?
Dominic Not bad, thanks.
Later ...
Dominic [2] ______ then. See you later!
Arianna Bye. [3] ______ !

2

Mrs. Bauer [4] ______, Arianna.
Arianna Hello, Mrs. Bauer.
Mrs. Bauer [5] ______ ?
Arianna I'm fine, thanks. And you?
Mrs. Bauer I'm very well, [6] ______ .
Later ...
Mrs. Bauer Goodbye, Arianna. [7] ______
Arianna Thanks. [8] ______ .
See you on Monday.

3 122 **Choose the correct alternatives to complete the mini-dialogues. Then listen and check.**

Jayden Good afternoon.
Emily ______
a Hello. **b** See you.

1 **Willow** Bye.
Declan ______
a See you later. **b** And you?

2 **Xander** Have a nice weekend.
Andres ______
a Not bad, thanks. **b** See you on Monday.

3 **Mr. Wilks** How are you?
Kaiden ______
a Good morning. **b** I'm fine, thanks.

4 **Write two conversations: (1) between Mrs. Lennox and her student, Sean, and (2) between friends Liam and Ava. Use the phrases in exercise 1 to help you.**

Extra listening

Listening strategy

When you listen, don't try to understand every word. Focus on the information you need for the task. If you can't answer a question, don't panic. Keep listening and try to answer the next one.

1 123 **Listen to Kayla talking about her school. The underlined information is incorrect. Write the correct word.**

Kayla is a teacher at Fairbanks High School.
student

1 Her school is 18 years old. ______
2 She's in 7th grade. ______
3 Miwa is her mom. ______
4 Miwa is Japanese. ______
5 Kayla's favorite subject is Science. ______
6 Her History teacher is American. ______
7 Her favorite school day is Friday. ______
8 Kayla is in the school music club. ______

Reading and writing competences p.18

Carson Peters

About me

Name: Carson
Age: [1] ______ Parents' names: [5] ______
City: [2] ______ Favorite singer: [6] ______
School: [3] ______ Favorite song: [7] ______
Grade: [4] ______ Favorite actor: [8] ______

Hi, I'm Carson. I'm 13 years old, and I'm from Rochester, New York–not New York City, but New York State! It's a city in the west of the state, near Lake Ontario.

I'm a student at Middleton Junior High. It's a big school with over 1,000 students. My friends, TJ and Jonah, are students at Middleton, too. We're in 8th grade.

What else? I'm half American and half Australian. My mom is from Perth, in Australia. Her name's Holly. My dad, Bradley, is American.

I'm crazy about music. My favorite singer is Drake. He's my hero! He's awesome. His song *Nice for What* is my favorite song. My sister, Aimee, is 17, and she's in a band. Its name is Blue Dawn. They're very good.

My other hobbies are movies and video games. My favorite actor is Michael B. Jordan. He's a big star in Hollywood now. He's in the movie *Black Panther.*

Javier, Spain
3 friends are online
Silvia, Portugal
Andres, Chile
Brody, Canada
Carson and Javier, you're now friends!

Check it out!

Find these words and phrases and check their meaning.

state half He's awesome.
What else? I'm crazy about

Reading

1 124 **Read and listen** **Complete the *About me* box using the information in Carson's profile.**

2 **Comprehension** **Read the profile again. Match the sentence halves.**

1 Rochester is d
2 Carson's school ____
3 His friends ____
4 His mom ____
5 His dad ____
6 Drake ____
7 His sister's band ____
8 His favorite actor ____

a is in *Black Panther.*
b is his hero.
c is called Blue Dawn.
d ~~near Lake Ontario.~~
e is American.
f is big.
g is Australian.
h are TJ and Jonah.

Writing

3 **Write three true sentences and three false sentences about Carson. Use the sentences in exercise 2 and the information in the *About me* box.**

4 **Complete the *About me* box with information about a friend.**

About me

Name: ______ Parents' names: ______
Age: ______ Favorite singer: ______
City: ______
School: ______ Favorite song: ______
Grade: ______ Favorite actor: ______

5 **Use the information in exercise 4 to write a text about your friend.**

Writing check

We use capital letters for the subject pronoun *I*, names, countries, and nationalities.

*I'm from **B**razil. **I**'m **B**razilian.*

Did you use capital letters correctly?

2 Grammar rules

be: Simple present

Negative p.23

Full form	Short form
I **am not** hungry.	I**'m not** hungry.
You **are not** the teacher.	You **aren't** the teacher.
He / She **is not** in the classroom.	He / She **isn't** in the classroom.
It **is not** her planner.	It **isn't** her planner.
We / You / They **are not** tired.	We / You / They **aren't** tired.

1 We make the negative simple present of *be* with:

Subject	*am* + *are* *is*	+ *not*

2 We add *-n't* to *is* and *are* to make the negative short forms.

are + not = aren't

You **aren't** Mexican.

is + not = isn't

It **isn't** Saturday.

3 The short form of *I am not* is *I'm not*.

I'm **not** tired. NOT ~~I amn't tired.~~

4 We usually use short forms in conversation or when we write to friends.

Interrogative and short answers p.23

Interrogative	Short answers	
	Affirmative	Negative
Am I late?	**Yes**, you **are**.	**No**, you **aren't**.
Are you Spanish?	**Yes**, I **am**.	**No**, I**'m not**.
Is he / **she** 13?	**Yes**, he / she **is**.	**No**, he / she **isn't**.
Is it your book?	**Yes**, it **is**.	**No**, it **isn't**.
Are we / **you** / **they** early?	**Yes**, we / you / they **are**.	**No**, we / you / they **aren't**.

1 We put *am*, *are*, or *is* before the subject to make a question.

Am *Are* *Is*	+ subject	+ *?*

Are you American? NOT ~~You are American?~~

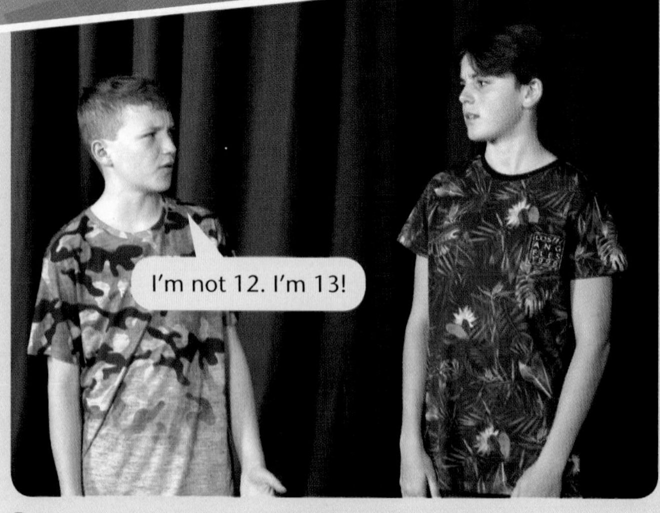

2 In English, we normally answer questions with a short answer.

Is it interesting? Yes, it is. No, it isn't.

3 We form short affirmative answers with:

Yes,	+ subject	+ *am / are / is.*

We form short negative answers with:

No,	+ subject	+ *'m not / aren't / isn't.*

4 We usually use the short form in negative answers.

Are you hungry? No, I'm **not**.

Am I late? No, you **aren't**.

Is it Monday? No, it **isn't**.

5 We never use the short form of *be* in short affirmative answers.

Are you hungry? Yes, I **am**. NOT ~~Yes, I'm.~~

Am I late? Yes, you **are**. NOT ~~Yes, you're.~~

Is it Monday? Yes, it **is**. NOT ~~Yes, it's.~~

Question words + *be* p.26

Question word	Verb	Subject
Who	are	you?
What	is	it?
Where	am	I?
When	is	your birthday?
Which	is	your book?
How old	are	you?

1 We put the question word before *be*.

Question word	+ *am* + *are* + *is*	+ subject?

Where **is** your school? NOT ~~Where your school is?~~

2 We can use the short form of *is* with question words. We do this when we talk and write to friends.

Who's your teacher? What's his name?

When's your birthday? Where's Jo?

What are your names?

NOT ~~What're your names?~~

3 We use full sentences to answer questions that start with a question word. We can't use short answers.

Where are you from? I'm from Sydney.

Demonstratives

this, that, these, those

p.26

Singular	Plural
This is a pencil.	**These** are pencils.
That is a bag.	**Those** are bags.

1 We use *this* and *these* for people and things that are near to us.

2 We use *that* and *those* for people and things that are not near to us.

3 We can use the short form of *is* with *that* (*that's*), but we can't use short forms with *this*, *these*, or *those*.

That's my teacher.

This is my mom. NOT ~~This's my mom.~~

These are my pictures. NOT ~~These're my pictures.~~

Those are my friends. NOT ~~Those're my friends.~~

4 We use *this*, *that*, *these*, and *those* before the verb *be* or before a noun.

This is my sister.

That girl is Mexican.

5 We use *this*, *that*, *these*, and *those* to introduce and identify people.

This is my friend Michael.

Who is that in the classroom?

That's my English teacher.

Word list

Review the vocabulary. Write your own study notes or translation for each word.

Family

aunt ______

brother ______

cousin ______

dad ______

grandma ______

grandpa ______

grandparents ______

mom ______

parents ______

sister ______

uncle ______

Check it out!

Are you serious?

______

Good luck. ______

He's into ______

historical figure ______

No way! ______

prize ______

She's crazy about

______

Sorry ______

team ______

traveling ______

vacation ______

You're a star ______

Real English

What's the date today?

______

It's May 2nd. ______

When's your birthday?

______

It's on March 28th.

______

It's in March. ______

1 🔊 125 **Listen to the dialogue on page 20 and read the judge's sentences aloud. Practice the sentences in pairs.**

2 **Check (✓) the correct sentence.**

a The judge thinks Mason is very serious. ☐
b The judge thinks Mason isn't very good. ☐
c The judge thinks Mason is a star. ☐

Vocabulary check: Family p.22

3 **Complete the crossword with the family words.**

Across →

4 Archie is my dad. His dad is my ...
6 My mom's mom and dad are my ...
10 Aunt Esme's son, Salva, isn't my brother. He's my ...
11 Heather and Salva are ... and sister.

↓ Down

1 Poppy and Carter are my ... and grandpa.
2 Carter is my dad's ...
3 Hallie is my mom. Hallie and Dylan are brother and ...
5 Mom and Dad are my ...
7 They're Uncle Rory and ... Phoebe.
8 My dad's ... is Grandma Poppy.
9 Dylan is my ...

Grammar: *be*: Simple present p.23

Negative

4 **Choose the correct alternatives.**

She **is not** / **are not** my mom.
1 Tom and Nick **is not** / **are not** brothers.
2 I **am not** / **are not** from Turkey.
3 The backpack **is not** / **are not** cheap.
4 Elliot and I **am not** / **are not** in 9th grade.
5 My parents **is not** / **are not** Russian.
6 Mr. Jackson **is not** / **are not** our teacher.

5 **Rewrite the sentences in exercise 4. Use the short form of the negative.**

She isn't my mom.

Interrogative and short answers

6 **Match the questions and answers.**

1 Is it Thursday today? e
2 Are you Mr. Jones? ____
3 Am I in your class? ____
4 Is Ángel from Mexico? ____
5 Are the boys here? ____
6 Is she your mom? ____

a No, he isn't.
b Yes, you are.
c Yes, she is.
d No, they aren't.
e ~~No, it isn't.~~
f Yes, I am.

7 **Use the prompts to write questions. Then write affirmative (✓) or negative (✗) short answers.**

your dog / big? (✗) Is your dog big? No, it isn't.
1 it / cold today? (✓)
2 your little brother / 6? (✗)
3 you and David / Chilean? (✓)
4 the girls / in Canada? (✗)

Question words + *be* p.26

8 **Choose the correct alternatives.**

When / (Where) are the students?

1 **What** / **Who** is your mom?
2 **What** / **Who** is your name?
3 **How old** / **When** are you?
4 **When** / **Which** is your brother's birthday?
5 **What** / **Which** girl is your sister–Lexi or Rose?

9 **Complete the questions with the words in the box.**

Which What How old ~~When~~ Who Where

When is our Math test? Is it on Monday?

1 __________ is your little sister? Is she 3?
2 __________ is he? Is he your uncle?
3 __________ is your favorite class–Art or Math?
4 __________ is my pen? It isn't in my backpack.
5 __________ is *apple*? It's a fruit.

10 **Use the prompts to write questions. Then write your own answers.**

What / your name / ?
What's your name? My name is Juliano.

1 how old / you / ?
2 when / your birthday / ?
3 which / day of the week / your favorite / ?
4 what / your favorite school subjects / ?

Demonstratives p.26

this, that, these, those

11 **Complete the chart with *this, that, these,* and *those.***

	Singular	Plural
near	1 __________	3 __________
far	2 __________	4 __________

12 **Complete the sentences with *this, that, these,* or *those.***

This is the American flag.

1 ________ are my cats.

2 ________ is the Sydney Opera House.

3 ________ are my shoes!

Round-up

1 **Read the interview and choose the correct alternatives.**

Let's talk: a special interview

Isaac Today, we are with a new student in our school, Naiara Salles. Hi, Naiara. (Where) / **Who** are you from?
Naiara I'm from Brazil.
Isaac [1] **Are** / **Is** it your first time in the U.S.?
Naiara Yes, it [2] **is** / **isn't**.
Isaac Is it difficult to be far from home?
Naiara No, it [3] **aren't** / **isn't** difficult. The people are great!
Isaac [4] **When** / **Who** are you here with?
Naiara I'm here with my mom and brother. But my dad and sister [5] **aren't** / **isn't** here right now. They're in Brazil. Look, this is a picture of them.
Isaac That's a great picture!

Naiara It's an old picture! Look, [6] **this** / **those** is my brother, Rafael. Here, he's about 8, I think. He's 21 now. [7] **These** / **This** is my sister, Lucia. She's 18, but she's probably only 5 in the picture. And [8] **that** / **those** are my parents, Patrícia and Luis. And, of course, [9] **these** / **this** are my grandparents, Vito and Marcela.
Isaac [10] **How old** / **What** are you, Naiara?
Naiara I'm 13.
Isaac [11] **When** / **Which** are your favorite subjects?
Naiara Art and Music!
Isaac That's awesome! Naiara, welcome to our school!

2 **Correct the false statements about Naiara and her family.**

Naiara is Portuguese.
Naiara isn't Portuguese. She's Brazilian.

1 It's her second time in the U.S.
2 Her mom and brother are in Brazil.
3 Her sister is 21.
4 Naiara is 12.
5 Her favorite subjects are Math and History.

Dates and special days p.24

1 Write the ordinal numbers in words.

6th sixth

1 12th ____________
2 30th ____________
3 13th ____________
4 2nd ____________
5 25th ____________
6 1st ____________
7 8th ____________
8 3rd ____________

2 Complete the sentences with the dates. Use the months in the box.

~~August~~ May September June October

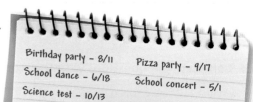

Birthday party – 8/11
Pizza party – 9/17
School dance – 6/18
School concert – 5/1
Science test – 10/13

The birthday party is on August 11th.

The school dance is on 1 ________________.

The Science test is on 2 ________________.

The pizza party is on 3 ________________.

The school concert is on 4 ________________.

3 126 Listen again to the dialogues on page 24. Complete the missing dates.

1

Dominic Hey, Arianna!
Arianna Hey!
Dominic It's February 2nd. Happy Groundhog Day!
Arianna It's not Groundhog Day today!
Dominic What?!
Arianna Look! It's 1 ________________ today!

2

Dominic What's the date today?
Arianna It's 2 ________________. My birthday's in August.
Dominic Oh! When's your birthday?
Arianna It's on 3 ________________.

4 Use the prompts to write a short dialogue.

You what / date / today / ?
What's the date today?
Jack it / August 28th
1 ________________________________
You when / your birthday / ?
2 ________________________________
Jack it / September / 18th
3 ________________________________
You how old / you / ?
4 ________________________________
Jack I / 14
5 ________________________________

Extra listening

Listening strategy

When you do a listening exercise with answer options, look carefully at the options before you listen, and think how they sound.

1 127 Listen to Logan in an interview for a TV quiz show. Choose the correct alternatives.

Name:	Logan **Smith** / **(Williams)**
Age:	1 **17** / **18**
Birthday:	October 2 **21st** / **23rd**
Family:	mom, dad, and two 3 **sisters** / **brothers**
Favorite sport:	4 **basketball** / **soccer**
Favorite singer:	5 **Sam Smith** / **Sean Paul**
Favorite actor:	6 **Emma Stone** / **Emma Watson**

Reading and writing competences

p.28

STAR FOCUS:

ZENDAYA COLEMAN

Who is Zendaya?
Zendaya is a famous American actor and singer. Her full name is Zendaya Maree Stoermer Coleman! She's from Oakland, California.

What is she famous for?
She's in the movies *Spider-Man: Homecoming* and *The Greatest Showman*. She's also famous as Rocky Blue in the *Shake It Up* TV show, and as K.C. Cooper in *K.C. Undercover*. Oh, and her music album, *Zendaya*, is great, too!

Is Zendaya from a big family?
Yes, she is. Zendaya is one of six brothers and sisters. She's also an aunt!

Is her family famous, too?
No, her family isn't famous. Her mom and dad are teachers.

What are her passions?
Well, Zendaya is into singing, dancing, and fashion. She's interested in the countries her parents are from. Her dad is African-American, and her mom is Scottish and German!

Check it out!

Find these words and phrases and check their meaning.

famous   is into   Scottish
passions   fashion   German

Reading

1 128 **Read and listen** **Check (✓) the correct sentences.**

a Zendaya is a singer and actor. ☐
b Zendaya isn't famous. ☐
c Zendaya is in movies and TV shows. ☐

2 **Comprehension** **Read the text about Zendaya and answer the questions.**

Where is Zendaya from?
She's from Oakland, California.

1 Which movies is she in?
2 What is the name of her album?
3 Is Zendaya's family a big or small family?
4 What are her mom and dad's jobs?
5 What nationalities are her parents?

Writing

3 **Use the prompts to write questions. Then use the information in the profile about Ross Lynch to write answers.**

who / Ross Lynch?
Who is Ross Lynch? He's a famous American actor and singer.

1 where / he from?
2 what / his full name?
3 what / he famous for?
4 he / from a big family?
5 who / famous in his family?
6 what / his interests?

ROSS LYNCH: American actor and singer

From Littleton, Colorado
Full name Ross Shor Lynch
Famous for his roles in TV show *Austin and Ally* (Austin Moon), TV movie *Teen Beach Movie* (Brady), Netflix series *The Chilling Adventures of Sabrina* (Harvey). He is also in two bands.
Family sister (x1): Rydel, brothers (x3): Riker, Rocky, Ryland; cousins are Derek and Julianna Hough (famous actors)
Music Ross, his brothers, and his sister are in a band, R5. Ross and his brother, Rocky, are in a band, The Driver Era.
Passions hockey, airplanes, and skateboarding

4 **Write a *Star Focus* article like the one about Zendaya Coleman. Write about Ross Lynch. Use the notes and your answers from exercise 3 to help you.**

Star focus: Ross Lynch
Who is Ross Lynch?
Ross Lynch is a famous American actor and singer.

Writing check

Did you use commas? We use commas to divide things in a list.

His brothers' names are Riker, Rocky, and Ryland.

3 Grammar rules

Prepositions of place p.37

We use prepositions of place to say where we can find a person, place, or thing.

in

on

under

behind

next to

near

in front of

across from

between

Plural nouns

Regular plurals p.37

Most nouns	+ *-s*	table–table**s** chair–chair**s**
Nouns ending in *-s, -x, -ss, -sh, -ch, -o*	+ *-es*	bus–bus**es** box–box**es** sandwich–sandwich**es** hero–hero**es**
Nouns ending in consonant + *-y*	*y* + *-ies*	family–famil**ies** nationality–nationalit**ies**
Nouns ending in vowel + *-y*	+ *-s*	boy–boy**s** day–day**s**
Nouns ending in *f* or *fe*	*f* + *-ves*	half–hal**ves** life–li**ves**

Irregular plurals p.37

Some nouns have an irregular plural form:

man → men
woman → women
child → children
person → people
fish → fish
foot → feet
mouse → mice

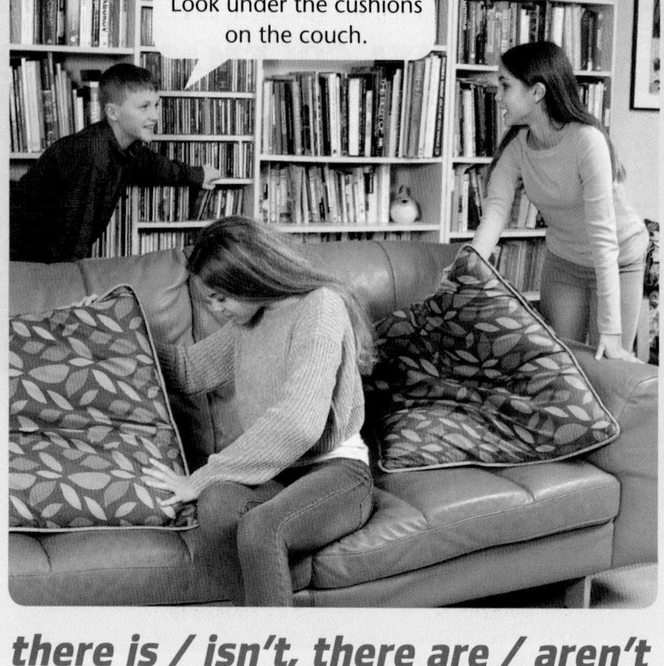
Look under the cushions on the couch.

there is / isn't, there are / aren't

Affirmative and negative p.40

	Singular	Plural
Affirmative	**There is (There's)**	**There are**
Negative	**There is not (There isn't)**	**There are not (There aren't)**

1. **We don't have a short form for *There are*.**
2. **We put *a* or *an* after *There's* or *There isn't*. We use *an* when the noun starts with a vowel.**
   There's a sandwich on the bed.
   There isn't an apple on the table.
3. **After *There are*, we put *some* or a number.**
   There are some books on the shelf, and there are three books on the desk.
4. **After *There aren't*, we put *any* or a number.**
   There aren't three apples; there are only two.
   There aren't any bananas.
5. **When we make a list of things, we use *There is* when the first noun is singular.**
   There is a couch and two armchairs.
   NOT ~~There are a couch and two armchairs.~~
6. **When the first noun in a list is plural, we use *There are*.**
   There are four chairs and a table.
   NOT ~~There is four chairs and a table.~~

Is there ...? / Are there ...?

Interrogative and short answers p.40

	Singular	Plural
Interrogative	**Is there** a desk?	**Are there** any desks?
Short answers	✓ Yes, **there is**. ✗ No, **there isn't**.	✓ Yes, **there are**. ✗ No, **there aren't**.

1 We make questions like this:

Is there	+ *a / an*	+ singular noun	+ ?

Is there a clock in your classroom?

or

Are there	+ *any* / a number	+ plural noun	+ ?

Are there any shelves in your bedroom?

Are there two windows in your bedroom?

2 In affirmative short answers, we don't use short forms.

Is there a clock in your classroom?

Yes, there is. NOT ~~Yes, there's.~~

3 We can only use short forms in negative short answers.

No, there isn't. No, there aren't.

some / any p.40

1 We use *some* and *any* before plural nouns when we don't know the exact number of things.

2 We use *some* in affirmative sentences.

There are some pens on the desk.

3 We use *any* in negative sentences and questions.

There aren't any books on the shelf.

Are there any books on the shelf?

they're / their / there p.40

In English, the words *they're*, *their*, and *there* sound the same, but they have different meanings.

they're	**They're** brothers.
their	**Their** house is big.
there	**There** is a chair in the garden.

Word list

Review the vocabulary. Write your own study notes or translation for each word.

Rooms in the house

backyard ______
bathroom ______
bedroom ______
dining room ______
hallway ______
kitchen ______
living room ______
stairs ______

Furniture

armchair ______
bathtub ______
bed ______
bookcase ______
cabinet ______
chair ______
couch ______
desk ______
dresser ______
fridge ______
lamp ______
mirror ______
painting ______
poster ______
shelf ______
shower ______
sink ______
stove ______
table ______
toilet ______
wardrobe ______
washing machine
______

Check it out!

a mess ______
bright ______
characters ______
Cheer up ______
Come on ______
Here it is! ______
Leave me alone ______
neat ______
share ______
sleep ______
space ______

Real English

How many hotels are there?
______
There's one hotel.
______
How many elevators are there?
______
There are 73.
______

3 Are there any movie channels on your TV?

1 🔊 129 Listen to the dialogue on page 34 and read Jacob's sentences aloud. Practice the sentences in pairs.

2 🔊 129 Listen again. Where is Mason?

____

Vocabulary check: House and furniture p.36

3 Complete the names of the furniture in the rooms.

Living room	Bedroom	Kitchen	Bathroom
c o u c h	[5]b ___ ___	[10]c ___ ___ i n ___ t	[15]b ___ ___ h ___ u b
[1]p a ___ n t ___ ___ g	[6]w ___ r ___ r o ___ e	[11]s t ___ v ___	[16]s h ___ ___ ___ r
[2]a ___ m c ___ a ___ r	[7]d ___ s ___	[12]f ___ ___ d g ___	[17]t ___ ___ ___ e t
[3]l ___ ___ p	[8]s ___ e ___ f	[13]t ___ b ___ e	[18]s ___ ___ k
[4]b o ___ k ___ a ___ e	[9]d r ___ ___ s ___ r	[14]w ___ s ___ i n g m a ___ ___ i n e	[19]m ___ ___ r ___ r

Grammar: Prepositions of place p.37

4 Complete the sentences with the prepositions of place in the box.

~~in~~ on between next to under across from in front of behind

1

2

3

4

5

The dog is _in_ the bath.

1 The sink is ___________ the shower and the bath.

2 Jason is ___________ Katie.

3 The mouse is ___________ the chair. The woman is ___________ the chair.

4 Gemma is ___________ Kyle, and Kyle is ___________ Gemma.

5 The hotel is ___________ a bank.

Plural nouns p.37

5 Write the plural form of the regular nouns in the correct columns in the chart.

~~book~~ class shelf story couch window family hero nationality stove

Plural nouns	
+ -*s*	+ -*es*
books 1 ________ 2 ________	6 ________ 7 ________ 8 ________
~~*y*~~ + -*ies*	~~*f*~~ + -*ves*
3 ________ 4 ________ 5 ________	9 ________

6 Match the irregular nouns to their plural forms.

1 child _c_ — a people
2 man ____ — b fish
3 mouse ____ — ~~c children~~
4 foot ____ — d feet
5 fish ____ — e men
6 person ____ — f women
7 woman ____ — g mice

there is / isn't, there are / aren't p.40

Affirmative and negative

7 Complete the sentences with *There's* / *There are* (✓) or *There isn't* / *There aren't* (✗).

(✓) There's a TV in my bedroom.

(✗) There aren't two bathrooms in my house.

1 (✓) ____________ a pencil case on the desk.

2 (✗) ____________ two lamps in the living room.

3 (✓) ____________ three paintings on the wall.

4 (✗) ____________ a lamp behind the armchair.

5 (✓) ____________ 26 students in my class.

Is there ...? / Are there ...? p.40

Interrogative and short answers

8 Complete the mini-dialogues with *is* / *isn't* and *are* / *aren't*.

A Is there a book on the desk?
B Yes, there is.

1 A ________ there two beds in your bedroom?
B Yes, there ________ .

2 A ________ there a computer in your classroom?
B No, there ________ .

3 A ________ there five people in your family?
B No, there ________ .

some / any p.40

9 Choose the correct alternatives.

Are there **some** / **(any)** DVDs in the box?

1 There are **some** / **any** books on the shelves.

2 There aren't **some** / **any** people on the bus.

3 Are there **some** / **any** pencils in your pencil case?

4 Are there **some** / **any** English students in your class?

10 Use the prompts to make affirmative (✓) and negative (✗) sentences or questions (?) with the correct form of *There are* ... and *some* / *any*.

books on the table (✓)
There are some books on the table.

1 posters in your bedroom (?)

2 new songs on my playlist (✓)

3 famous people in my town (✗)

4 computers in your school (?)

they're / their / there p.40

11 Match the sentences halves.

1 There
2 Their
3 They're
4 Under the desk, there

a brothers.
b dad is my uncle.
c 's a backpack.
d are ten questions on the test.

Round-up

1 Choose the correct alternatives.

I live **(in)** / **near** a house with my parents and two brothers. We have lots of rooms inside the house–we have three bedrooms, a [1] **backyard** / **living room**, a dining room, a bathroom, and a kitchen. In the dining room, [2] **there** / **their** is a massive table–big enough for ten [3] **people** / **persons**–and [4] **a** / **an** old painting. There [5] **aren't** / **isn't** a TV. My parents have one bedroom, and my brothers and I are in the two other rooms. [6] **There** / **They're** pretty small. My room is nice–there's a desk [7] **across from** / **under** my bed, and lots of [8] **shelfs** / **shelves**. But my brothers' room isn't nice. [9] **Their** / **They're** room is terrible! There [10] **are** / **is** clothes, books, and pizza boxes [11] **in** / **on** the floor. And there aren't [12] **any** / **some** posters. In my room, [13] **there are** / **they're** lots of posters [14] **on** / **in front of** my walls!

In the kitchen, there [15] **is** / **are** a stove, [16] **any** / **some** cabinets, a fridge, and [17] **a bathtub** / **a sink**. And [18] **in** / **across from** our living room, there's a TV, a [19] **bookcase** / **washing machine**, and two big couches, but there aren't [20] **any** / **some** armchairs.

Quantity p.38

1 **Write the numbers in words.**

115	one hundred fifteen	3 446	______
1 137	______	4 867	______
2 283	______	5 1,000	______

2 130 **Listen again to the dialogue between the Quizmaster (QM) and Dominic on page 38 and complete it.**

QM Welcome, Dominic. Your topic is the Empire State Building, right? Are you ready for your first question?
Dominic Hi! Yes, I'm ready!
QM How many floors are there in the Empire State Building?
Dominic There are 103 floors.
QM Correct. How tall is the building?
Dominic It is [1]______ meters tall.
QM How many [2]______ are in the building?
Dominic There are 6,514 windows.
QM [3]______ hotels are there?
Dominic [4]______ one hotel.
QM Sorry, that isn't correct. There aren't [5]______ hotels. OK, next question: how many steps [6]______ ?
Dominic There are 1,872 steps.
QM How many elevators are there?
Dominic There are [7]______ elevators.
QM Our time is up! Thanks for joining us, Dominic ...

3 **Complete the sentences with the words in the box.**

There aren't There's ~~How many~~ There are

Real English

You hear	You answer
How many books are there on the desk?	[1]______ one book on the desk.
	[2]______ four books on the desk.
	[3]______ any books on the desk.

4 **Look at the information about South Central Junior High School. Use this information to write a dialogue. Use the dialogue in exercise 2 to help you.**

South Central Junior High	
Number of students	963
Number of teachers	67
Classrooms	45
Windows	115
Music rooms	2
Computer science laboratories	4
Gym	1
Theater	0

A How many students are there at South Central Junior High?

B There are 963 students.

Extra listening

Listening strategy

In a listening activity with multiple-choice answers, you sometimes hear more than one of the answer options. It can be confusing, but only one option is correct. If possible, listen twice to check your answers.

1 131 **Listen to five people talking about their houses or apartments. Check (✓) the correct answer.**

1 How many rooms are there in the apartment?

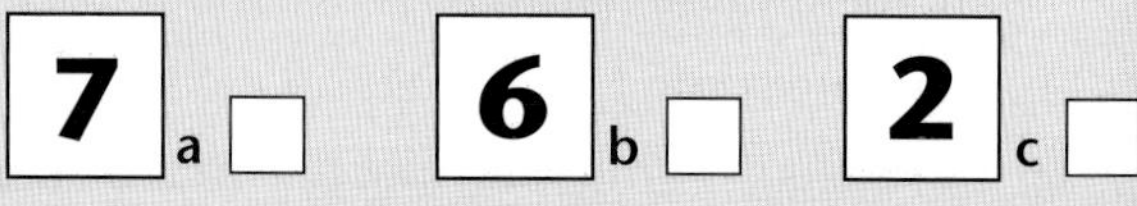

2 Where's the bathroom?

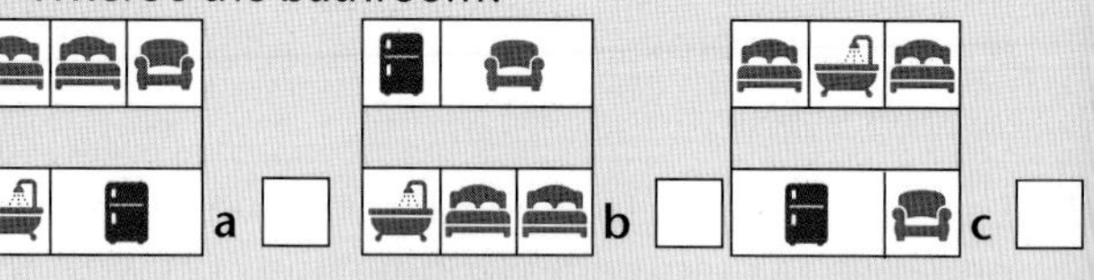

3 What's in the bathroom?

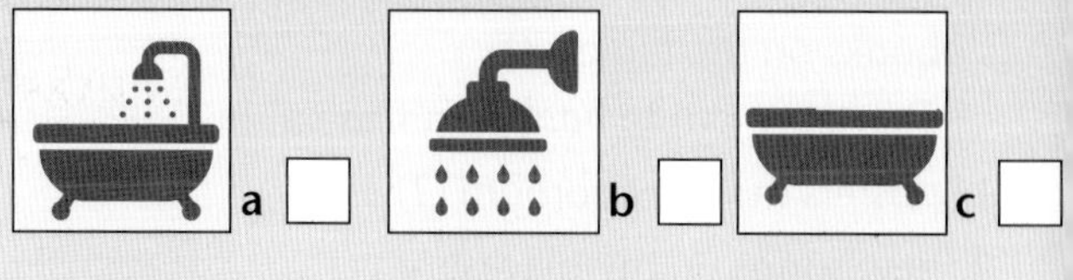

4 How many TVs are there in the apartment?

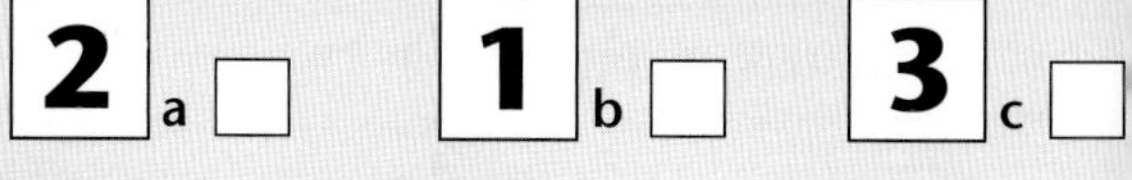

5 What's his favorite room?

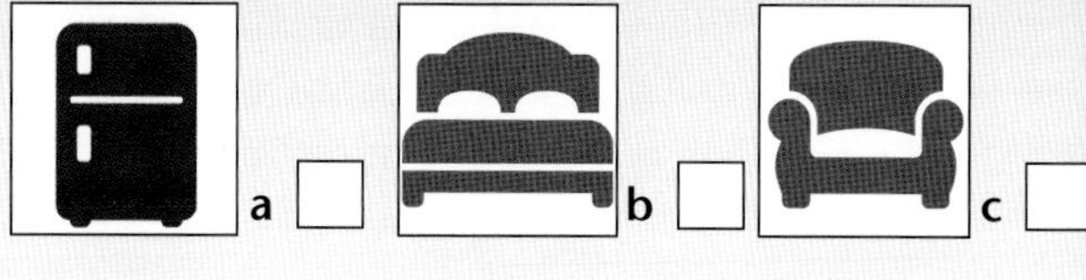

Reading and writing competences p.42

Welcome to **TRAVELER'S REST YOUTH HOSTEL** ★★★ 8.9

Traveler's Rest Youth Hostel is in Oregon, near the city of Portland. The hostel is a beautiful, old house. It's perfect for families and small groups.

There are twelve bedrooms with four or six beds. The rooms are big and bright. There are lockers for your possessions next to the beds. There's a sink and a mirror in every room. There aren't bedrooms with private bathrooms, but there are four big communal bathrooms, with showers and toilets, near the bedrooms.

There's a kitchen with a fridge, a stove, and a microwave. Across from the kitchen, there's a large dining room. Near the dining room, there's a small café. It's open from 8 a.m. to 6 p.m. and it has a lot of drinks and sandwiches.

There are some cool things to do in the hostel, too! There's a TV room with a game console and some video games. Wi-Fi is free in the hostel. There's a living room with a bookcase with some great books.

Are you musical? There's a music room with a piano and a guitar. Do you want to relax? Come outside—there's a beautiful backyard with tables and chairs behind the house.

QUICK FACTS

Name: Traveler's Rest Youth Hostel

Location: 1 ______

Number of bedrooms: 2 ______

Furniture in bedrooms: 3 ______

______

Other rooms:

4 ______

______

Amenities

Wi-Fi: 5 **Free / $2 per hour**

TV: 6 **Yes / No** TV in bedrooms: 7 **Yes / No**

Backyard: 8 **Yes / No**

Food and drink available: 9 **Yes / No**

Check it out!

Find these words and phrases and check their meaning.

bright	communal	things to do
lockers	drinks	free

Reading

1 132 **Read and listen** **Complete the *Quick facts* section of the website with information about the hostel.**

2 Imagine you are on a school trip to Oregon and you are staying at Traveler's Rest Youth Hostel with your classmates. Answer the questions.

Where is the hostel?

It's in Oregon, near Portland.

1 How many beds are in your bedroom?
2 Who are you in the bedroom with?
3 What's in the bedroom?
4 Where is the bathroom?
5 What other rooms are there in the hostel?
6 What's your favorite room in the hostel?

Writing

3 Now write a message to a friend telling him / her about your stay at Traveler's Rest Youth Hostel. Use your answers from exercise 2 to help you.

Hi! 🙂 I'm in Oregon on a school trip. It's great! Mrs. Jones is with our class. We're at the Traveler's Rest Youth Hostel near Portland. I'm in a bedroom with …

Writing check

We use *there's* with a singular noun.
We use *there are* with plural nouns.

Did you use *there is* and *there are* correctly?

4 Grammar rules

have: Simple present

Affirmative p.47

Affirmative		
I	**have**	a tablet.
You	**have**	a planner.
He	**has**	a pen.
She	**has**	a camera.
It	**has**	a ball.
We	**have**	our books.
You	**have**	homework.
They	**have**	their bags.

1 We make affirmative sentences with *have* with:

Subject	+ *have* / *has*

2 We use *have* to talk about:

- possessions

  I **have** a computer.

  He **has** a cell phone.
- family, friends, and other relationships

  I **have** a sister.

  She **has** a friend from China.
- descriptions of people, animals, and objects

  I **have** blue eyes.

  My cell phone **has** a really cool camera.

3 We use *has* with *he*, *she*, and *it*. For all other subjects, we use *have*.

He / She / It **has** a camera.

I / You / We / They **have** a planner.

Look!

We don't use *have* to talk about age. Instead, we use the verb *be*.

*I **am** 13 years old.*

NOT ~~I have 13 years old.~~

Negative p.47

Full form	Short form
I **do not have** a tablet.	I **don't have** a tablet.
You **do not have** a planner.	You **don't have** a planner.
He **does not have** a pen.	He **doesn't have** a pen.
She **does not have** a camera.	She **doesn't have** a camera.
It **does not have** a ball.	It **doesn't have** a ball.
We **do not have** our books.	We **don't have** our books.
You **do not have** homework.	You **don't have** homework.
They **do not have** their bags.	They **don't have** their bags.

1 We make the negative form of *have* with:

Subject	+ *do not* / *don't*	*have*
	+ *does not* / *doesn't*	

2 We use *does not* with the third person singular (*he*, *she*, *it*). We use *do not* with all other subjects.

She **does not have** her planner.

It **does not have** a camera.

You **do not have** a bag.

They **do not have** sunglasses.

3 The short form of *do not* is *don't*, and the short form of *does not* is *doesn't*.

We **don't have** the bags.

He **doesn't have** his game console.

4 We use short forms more often than full forms.

Look!

To make negative sentences with the verb *have*, we always put *have* after *does* and *don't*. In negative sentences, *have* doesn't change in the third person singular.

*He **doesn't have** a notebook.*

NOT ~~He doesn't has a notebook.~~

have: Simple present
Interrogative and short answers p.50

Interrogative	Short answers	
	Affirmative	Negative
Do I **have** the bags?	**Yes**, you **do**.	**No**, you **don't**.
Do you **have** sisters?	**Yes**, I **do**.	**No**, I **don't**.
Does he **have** a pen?	**Yes**, he **does**.	**No**, he **doesn't**.
Does she **have** a tablet?	**Yes**, she **does**.	**No**, she **doesn't**.
Does it **have** the ball?	**Yes**, it **does**.	**No**, it **doesn't**.
Do we **have** Math?	**Yes**, you **do**.	**No**, you **don't**.
Do you **have** a dog?	**Yes**, we **do**.	**No**, we **don't**.
Do they **have** English?	**Yes**, they **do**.	**No**, they **don't**.

1 We make questions with ***have*** in the simple present with:

Do / Does	+ subject	+ ***have***	+ *?*

2 We make affirmative short answers with:

Yes,	+ subject	+ ***do / does.***

3 We make negative short answers with:

No,	+ subject	+ ***don't / doesn't.***

The possessive *'s* p.50

1 We use the possessive *'s* to talk about possessions or family and relationships.

That is Fábio's ball.

That is Silvia's pencil.

Eduarda is Adriano's sister.

2 We use *'s* with singular nouns.

The **dog's** bed is in the kitchen.

3 With plural nouns ending in *-s*, we add an apostrophe (').

The **boys'** bags are here.

4 With singular nouns ending in *-s*, and with names of people that end with the letter *-s*, we add *'s*.

Douglas's cat

5 When we talk about something that belongs to two or more people, we use *'s* after the last person.

Ana and **Lucila's** bedroom is green.

Word list

Review the vocabulary. Write your own study notes or translation for each word.

My things

bike ____________
camera ____________
game console ____________
guitar ____________
phone ____________
planner ____________
skateboard ____________
soccer ball ____________
sunglasses ____________
tablet ____________

Check it out!

Bring it on! ____________
Deal with it! ____________
Don't ask me! ____________
fun ____________
I'm really bad at
____
I'm really into
____
learn ____________
Liar! ____________
Not now. ____________
penfriend ____________
What's up? ____________

Real English

How much is this ..., please?
____
It's ... ____________
It's nice. I'll take it.
____
OK, that's ... ____________
Here you are.
____
Thank you. Here's your change, and here's your receipt.
____
Thank you. Goodbye.
____
How much is this ..., please?
____
That's expensive! No, thank you.
____
No problem. Goodbye.
____

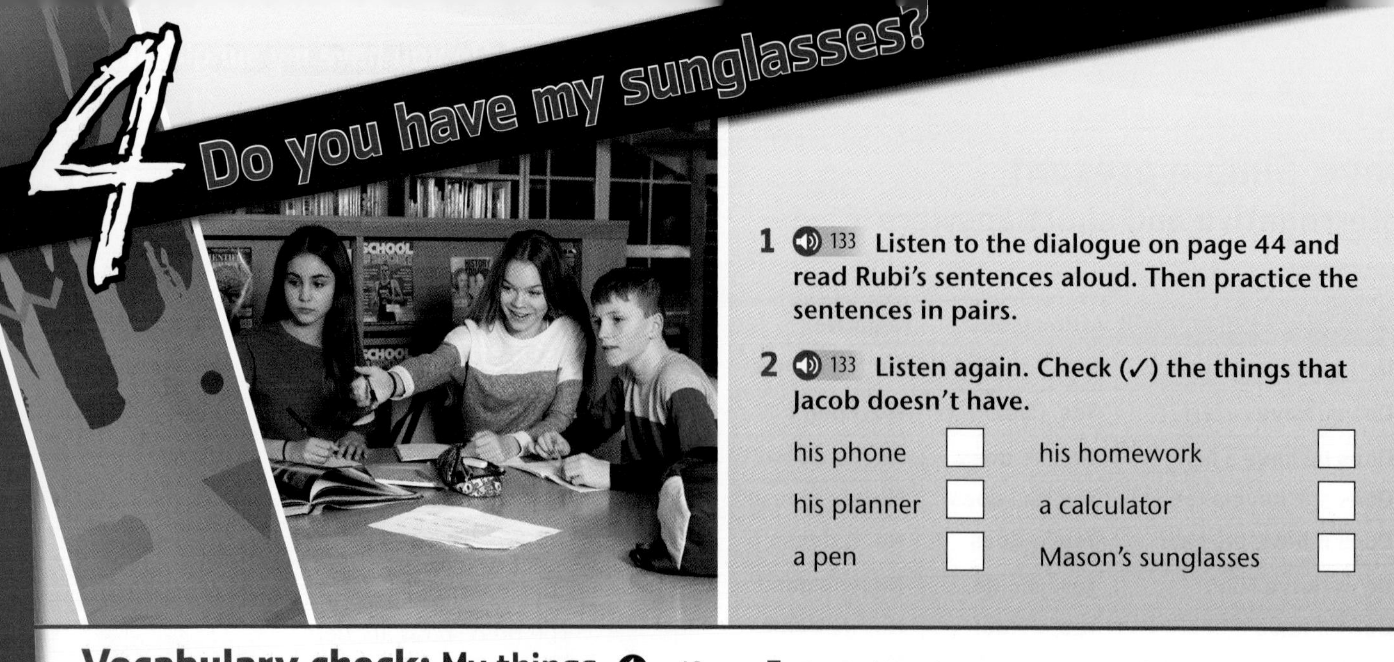
4
Do you have my sunglasses?

1 🔊 133 Listen to the dialogue on page 44 and read Rubi's sentences aloud. Then practice the sentences in pairs.

2 🔊 133 Listen again. Check (✓) the things that Jacob doesn't have.

his phone	☐	his homework	☐
his planner	☐	a calculator	☐
a pen	☐	Mason's sunglasses	☐

Vocabulary check: My things p.46

3 Find nine more possessions in the wordsearch.

~~sunglasses~~ camera game console phone bike
guitar tablet planner soccer ball skateboard

S	U	N	G	L	A	S	S	E	S	A
T	A	B	A	G	A	D	I	A	K	Q
N	C	A	M	E	R	A	F	X	A	W
P	V	I	E	P	V	D	Q	A	T	E
H	D	E	C	E	W	B	I	K	E	Y
O	W	V	O	D	T	A	V	T	B	D
N	P	J	N	S	M	A	G	L	O	P
E	E	B	S	A	Q	E	D	W	A	E
W	V	D	O	G	U	I	T	A	R	V
T	A	B	L	E	T	W	E	Q	D	T
E	T	A	E	C	D	V	B	D	W	P
A	B	W	E	P	L	A	N	N	E	R
S	O	C	C	E	R	B	A	L	L	Y

Grammar: *have:* Simple present p.47

Affirmative

4 Choose the correct alternatives.

He **have** / (**has**) a new tablet.

1 They **have** / **has** a famous brother.
2 Holly **has** / **have** a red bike.
3 Mark **have** / **has** a big bedroom.
4 I **have** / **has** three pets.
5 Sophie **have** / **has** blond hair.
6 You **has** / **have** a good camera.

5 Complete the sentences with *have* or *has* and the objects in the pictures.

1 2 3 4 5

I have homework.
1 Dad ______________________.
2 Charlie ______________________.
3 The boys ______________________.
4 I ________________.
5 You __________________.

Negative

6 Complete the chart with the full forms and short forms.

	Full form	Short form
I	do not have	don't have
you	1 ____________	don't have
he / she / it	does not have	2 ____________
we / you / they	3 ____________	don't have

7 Rewrite the sentences in the negative form. Use short forms.

Evandro has red hair.
Evandro doesn't have red hair.

1 Sarah has a Chilean cousin.
2 We have Science now.
3 I have a desk in my bedroom.
4 The book has pictures.

8 **Complete the text with the affirmative or negative form of the verb *have*.**

My name's Grace. I have three sisters, but I [1] ________ a brother. We live in New Orleans. It's very nice. My favorite animals are dogs, but we [2] ________ a dog because our house [3] ________ a backyard. We [4] ________ a cat called Kitty. She's black and she [5] ________ green eyes.

have: Simple present p.50

Interrogative and short answers

9 **Choose the correct alternatives.**

Does your house have a backyard?

a Yes, I do. (b) Yes, it does.

1 Do you have Wi-Fi at school?

a Yes, he does. b Yes, we do.

2 Does Carmen have a brother?

a No, she doesn't. b No, he doesn't.

3 Do you have a passport?

a No, I don't. b No, it doesn't.

4 Do the girls have their planners?

a No, we don't. b No, they don't.

10 **Look at the chart. Use the prompts to write questions and short answers with *have*.**

	skateboard	guitar	camera
Jorge	✓	✗	✗
Ellie	✗	✓	✓
Bruno	✓	✗	✗
Sofia	✗	✗	✓

Bruno / a camera?
Does Bruno have a camera? No, he doesn't.

1 Ellie / a guitar?

2 Sofia / a skateboard?

3 Jorge / a camera?

4 the girls / cameras?

5 the boys / guitars?

The possessive *'s* p.50

11 **Underline the possessive *'s* in the sentences.**

My friend's dog's very cute!

1 What's the woman's last name?

2 Josh's skateboard's in the backyard.

3 The children's homework's in the classroom.

4 That's Noah's camera.

Round-up

1 **Swap Shop is a website for people to swap one thing for other things. Complete the sentences with the correct form of *have*.**

Swap Shop

HOME | ABOUT US | SWAPS | NEWS

1 My offer

I have a cell phone. It's three years old. It [1] ________ (✗) the original box, but it [2] ________ (✓) the instruction book and it's in good condition. It [3] ________ (✗) a great camera, too.

I want ...

[4] ________ you [5] ________ an old skateboard? BELLE, 13

2 My offer

I [6] ________ (✓) a guitar. I [7] ________ (✗) the case for it, but I [8] ________ (✓) five music books with guitar lessons. One book [9] ________ (✓) my teacher's writing in it, but they're all in good condition.

I want ...

[10] ________ you [11] ________ an old MP3 player or a bike? MARLEY, 13

2 **Rewrite the sentences using the possessive *'s*.**

Belle has a cell phone. It's black.
Belle's cell phone is black.

1 Belle doesn't have a new cell phone.
________ isn't new.

2 Marley has a guitar, but not its case.
________ doesn't have a case.

3 Belle has a great camera on her cell phone.
The camera on ________ is great.

4 Belle and Marley have old things.
________ are old.

3 **Use the prompts to write questions. Then answer the questions.**

How old / be / Belle's cell phone?
How old is Belle's cell phone?
It's three years old.

1 What book / Belle / have?

2 What / Belle's cell phone / have / on it?

3 How many music books / Marley / have?

4 What / one of the books / have / in it?

Prices and paying for things p.48

1 **Complete the chart with the expressions in the box.**

~~It's $15.50.~~ No problem. here's your receipt. It's expensive! I'll take it.

Real English

You say	You hear
How much is this / that (bag)?	It's $15.50.
It's nice. [1] ________	OK, that's $15.50.
Here you are. Here's $20.	Thank you. Here's your change and [2] ________.
[3] ________ No, thanks.	[4] ________

2 134 **Listen again to the dialogues on page 48 and complete them.**

1

Arianna Excuse me. How much is this bag, please?
Assistant It's $13.49.
Arianna [1] ________. I'll take it.
Assistant OK, that's $13.49, then.
Arianna Here [2] ________.
Assistant Thank you. Here's 51 cents [3] ________, and here's your [4] ________.
Arianna [5] ________. Goodbye.

2

Dominic [6] ________. How much is this game, [7] ________?
Assistant It's $30.99.
Dominic Oh, that's expensive! [8] ________, thank you.
Assistant No problem. Goodbye.
Dominic [9] ________!

3 **Complete the dialogues.**

1

You Excuse me. How much is this lamp, please?
Assistant It's $19.99.
You It's nice. [1] ________ it.
Assistant OK, that's $19.99, please.
You [2] ________ $20.00.
Assistant Thank you. Here's your receipt and 1 cent change.
You [3] ________ you.

2

You Excuse me. [4] ________ is this clock, please?
Assistant It's $49.00.
You It's expensive. [5] ________ thank you.
Assistant No problem. Goodbye.
You [6] ________

3

You Excuse me. [7] ________ is that poster, please?
Assistant That poster? It's $12.50.
You It's nice. I'll take it.
Assistant OK, that's $12.50, please.
You [8] ________ you are.
Assistant Thank you. Here's your [9] ________ and 50 cents [10] ________.
You Thank you.

Extra listening

Listening strategy

Sometimes in a multiple-choice activity, you have to choose the correct picture. Before listening, look carefully at the pictures. What can you see? Write words next to the pictures to help you.

1 135 **Listen to three short conversations. There is a question for each conversation. Check (✓) the correct answer.**

1 Which birthday present is perfect for Zac?

a ☐ b ☐ c ☐

2 How many brothers and sisters does Amy have?

a ☐ b ☐ c ☐

3 Which are Brianna's pets?

a ☐ b ☐ c ☐

Reading and writing competences

p.52

WHAT DO YOU HAVE IN YOUR BACKPACK?

What do you have in your school backpack? Do you have just school things, or do you have other things, too? These are the things in Cole's backpack. Do you have the same things?

What do I have in my backpack? *Cole Jackson (12)*

1 School things

I have my books for Science, French, English, Art, and Music. I don't have my Math books because we don't have Math at school today (that's good!). I have my pencil case and my planner, too. My planner has a picture of my dog, Rocky, on the front. It's cool!

2 My phone

I have my phone, but it doesn't have any credit … that's typical! It's Mom's old phone. It's OK, but you can't get on the Internet. Mom has an expensive smartphone now!

3 A video game

Umm … this isn't for school. It's for my friend, Fletcher. It's Fletcher's game– he has hundreds of great video games. I have a game console at home, but I don't have any good games.

4 MP3 player

This is my favorite thing! I'm really into music, and my MP3 player has a lot of songs and videos. My favorite singers are Tinie Tempah and Labrinth. I have all their songs.

5 Money

Wow! I have $3.26 in my backpack. (That's a nice surprise!) I have money for some candy after school!

6 A burrito

Hmm … What's this? Oh … there's an old burrito in my backpack, too. (That isn't a nice surprise!)

Check it out!

Find these words and phrases and check their meaning.

just	on the front	all
the same	a lot of	after

Reading

1 136 **Read and listen** Are the things in Cole's backpack only for school?

____

____

2 **Comprehension** Answer the questions.

1 What school things does Cole have in his backpack?
2 What does his planner have on the front?
3 What problem does Cole have with his phone?
4 Who is Fletcher?
5 What's Cole's favorite thing?
6 Who are Cole's favorite singers?
7 How much money does Cole have in his backpack?
8 What horrible thing is there in Cole's backpack?

Writing

3 Write a paragraph about the things in your backpack. Use Cole's text to help you.

What do I have in my backpack?
1 School things: I have my books for …

Writing check

We use *and* and *but* to connect two sentences.

*I have my pencil case **and** my planner, too.*
*I have a game console, **but** I don't have any good games.*

Did you connect your sentences with *and* and *but*?

5 Grammar rules

Simple present

Affirmative p.61

Affirmative		
I	**love**	pasta.
You	**live**	in Idaho.
He	**speaks**	Portuguese.
She	**goes**	on vacation.
It	**starts**	at 8:30 a.m.
We	**run**	in the park.
You	**study**	English.
They	**make**	cake.

1 **We make affirmative sentences in the simple present with:**

I / You / We / They	+ base form	
He / She / It	+ base form	+ *s*

2 **We use the simple present to talk about:**

- daily routines

  I **get up** at seven o'clock in the morning.
- habits and things that happen often

  She **plays** tennis every weekend.

  They **watch** TV every night.
- facts and permanent situations

  They **work** in Los Angeles.

  He **lives** in Canada.
- timetables

  The English class **starts** at ten o'clock.

Spelling variations p.61

1 **We make the third person singular with the base form of the verb + *-s*.**

like + -s   She likes baseball.

2 **We use the base form of the verb + *-es* when the verb ends in *-ch*, *-s*, *-sh*, *-x*, *-z*, or *-o*.**

He watches TV.

She does her homework.

The movie finishes soon.

3 **When the verb ends in a consonant + *-y*, we change the *-y* to *-i* and add *-es*.**

He studies History.   It flies.

4 **When the verb ends in a vowel + *-y*, we add *-s*.**

He plays tennis after school.

She stays home on Sundays.

Pronunciation

1 **We add an *-s* or *-es* to make the third person singular form. There are three ways to say the *-s* or *-es*: /s/, /z/, and /ɪz/.**

2 **When the verb ends in a hard consonant sound, we pronounce the ending /s/.**

likes → /laɪks/

makes → /meɪks/

3 **When the verb ends in a vowel or a soft consonant sound, we pronounce the ending /z/.**

goes → /goʊz/

reads → /riːdz/

4 **When the verb ends in a consonant + *-es*, we pronounce the ending /ɪz/.**

watches → /wɑːtʃɪz/

uses → /juːzɪz/

Practice

137 **Listen to the verbs in the box. Write them in the correct column. Then listen again and repeat.**

has ~~cooks~~ relaxes sleeps travels comes writes washes dances

/s/	/z/	/ɪz/
cooks	3 ______	6 ______
1 ______	4 ______	7 ______
2 ______	5 ______	8 ______

Prepositions of time

at, in, on p.64

1 We use *at* with times and the word *night*.

at four o'clock

at 8:30 p.m.

at night

2 We use *in* for parts of the day, months, seasons, and years.

in the morning in March

in the spring in 2025

3 We use *on* with days of the week, dates, special days, and the word *weekend*.

on Monday(s) on July 12th

on my birthday

on the weekend / on weekends

4 We sometimes use the expressions *in the morning*, *in the afternoon*, *in the evening*, and *at night* with times so it is clear which part of the day we are talking about.

3:00 a.m. = It's three o'clock **in the morning**.

3:00 p.m. = It's three o'clock **in the afternoon**.

Adverbs of frequency p.64

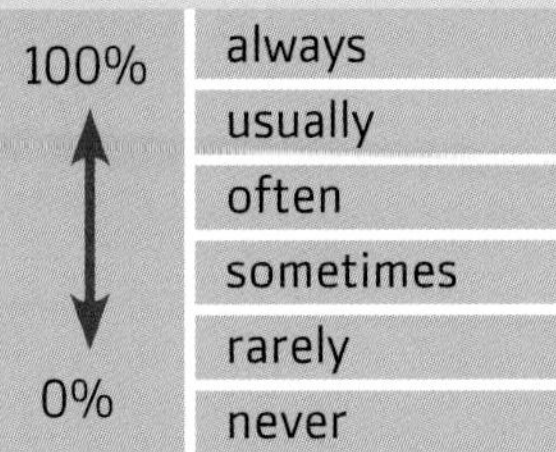

1 We use adverbs of frequency to say how often something happens.

2 We usually put adverbs of frequency between the subject and the verb.

I **often** go to the movies.

NOT ~~I go often to the movies.~~

We **usually** get home at four o'clock.

NOT ~~We get usually home at four o'clock.~~

3 With the verb *be*, we put the adverb of frequency after the verb.

He's **never** at home. They're **often** late.

Look!

In English, we do not use the double negative. We use ***never*** with the affirmative form of the verb.

*My dad **never watches** TV.*

NOT ~~*My dad doesn't never watch TV.*~~

Word list

Review the vocabulary. Write your own study notes or translation for each word.

Daily routines

- do (my) homework
- finish school
- get dressed
- get home
- get up
- go to bed
- have breakfast
- have dinner
- have lunch
- start school
- take a shower
- watch TV

Check it out!

- cafeteria
- call out
- class roster
- cute
- homeroom
- I feel bad
- I'm very busy.
- move around
- period
- Really?
- What a surprise!
- You're crazy!

Real English

- What do you want to do?
- Let's play / watch / go ...
- Do you want to play / watch / go ...?
- OK, cool!
- OK, great!
- OK, that's a good idea!
- No, let's ... instead.
- No, I'm sorry, but I'm busy.
- Sorry, I'm tired.
- Sorry, I have homework.

5 I get up at six o'clock

1 138 **Listen to the dialogue on page 58 and read Jacob's sentences aloud. Practice the sentences in pairs.**

2 Check (✓) the days the dance teacher comes to the studio.

Monday ☐ Friday ☐
Tuesday ☐ Saturday ☐
Wednesday ☐ Sunday ☐
Thursday ☐

Vocabulary check: Daily routines p.60

3 Complete the mind map with the words in the box to make expressions about daily routines.

dressed up ~~breakfast~~ a shower home lunch dinner to school to bed my homework TV the bus

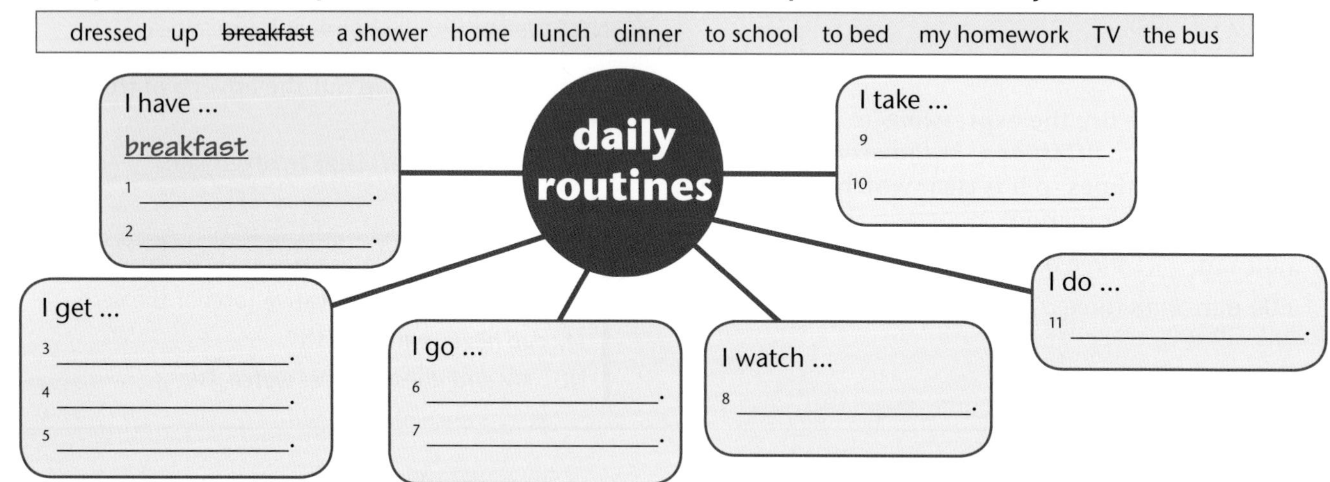

Grammar: Simple present p.61

Affirmative

4 Choose the correct alternatives.

I (**get up**) / **gets up** at 7 a.m.
1 We **live** / **lives** in a big house.
2 He **listen** / **listens** to music on his cell phone.
3 You **goes** / **go** to work at 8 a.m.
4 The movie **starts** / **start** at 8 p.m.
5 My grandparents **play** / **plays** video games!
6 My mom **sing** / **sings** in the shower. She's awful!

5 Complete the sentences with the correct form of the verbs in the box.

play read sleep ~~use~~ visit

I *use* the computer in the evenings.
1 Patrick ______ books on Saturday mornings.
2 We ______ our grandma every Sunday.
3 You and Geraldo ______ video games in the afternoon.
4 At night, our dog ______ in the kitchen.

Spelling variations

6 Look at the three verbs. Check (✓) the verb that has a different spelling rule in the third person singular.

	play	☐	enjoy	☐	study	✓
1	live	☐	do	☐	eat	☐
2	clean	☐	listen	☐	have	☐
3	speak	☐	watch	☐	wash	☐
4	finish	☐	start	☐	like	☐
5	read	☐	walk	☐	kiss	☐
6	fly	☐	practice	☐	cry	☐
7	go	☐	get	☐	do	☐

Prepositions of time: *at, in, on* p.64

7 Complete the chart with the words in the box.

Mondays night ~~October~~ five o'clock summer the weekend

Prepositions		
in	*on*	*at*
the morning	March 5th	6:30
October	2 ______	4 ______
1 ______	3 ______	5 ______

Adverbs of frequency p.64

8 Write the adverbs of frequency in the correct order.

sometimes never rarely ~~always~~ usually often

100%	80%	60%
always	1 ______	2 ______

50%	20%	0%
3 ______	4 ______	5 ______

9 Rewrite the sentences with the adverbs of frequency in parentheses.

I get up at 8 a.m. on Saturday morning. (never)
I never get up at 8 a.m. on Saturday morning.

1 We watch TV after dinner. (always)
2 Juliana and Ivete are late for school. (rarely)
3 We play baseball on the weekend. (often)
4 My bedroom is clean. (never)
5 Nilton has lunch at school. (usually)

10 Complete the text with the adverbs of frequency and the correct form of the verbs in parentheses.

I *usually get up* (usually / get up) at 9 a.m. on Saturdays. I 1______ (always / be) happy on the weekend because there's no school! After breakfast, I 2______ (always / go) to the park with our dog, Rusty. My sister, Rachel, 3______ (never / get up) before 11 a.m., and she 4______ (rarely / have) breakfast. She 5______ (usually / watch) TV in the living room and she 6______ (rarely / go out) with her friends. They 7______ (always / be) in her bedroom, but she 8______ (never / clean) it.

Round-up

1 Answer the questions. Do you have a busy and very active lifestyle (*busy bee*) or a slow and relaxed lifestyle (*cool cat*)?

Are you a "busy bee" or a "cool cat"?

1 **I get up before 9 a.m. on the weekend.**
a never b sometimes c always

2 **I play sports.**
a rarely b sometimes c often

3 **I watch TV all day on the weekend.**
a often b sometimes c rarely

4 **I love playing video games in my room.**
a often b sometimes c never

5 **I walk to school.**
a never b sometimes c always

6 **I clean my bedroom.**
a never b sometimes c always

Calculate your score!
a = 1 point **b** = 2 points **c** = 3 points
My score is: ___
1–6 You're a cool cat!
7–12 You have a good balance!
13–18 You're a busy bee!

Check it out!
Find these words and phrases and check their meaning.
busy bee cool cat balance

2 Read the text in exercise 10 again and answer the question.

Is Rachel a busy bee or a cool cat?

She's a ______.

3 Write sentences comparing yourself to Rachel.

I sometimes get up before 9 a.m. on the weekend, but Rachel never gets up before 9 a.m.

Rachel rarely leaves the house, because she is with her friends at home. I usually go out to meet my friends.

Asking for and making suggestions p.62

1 Complete the mind map with the expressions in the box.

~~Let's play a video game~~ watch TV instead OK, great a good idea cool have music club

What do you want to do?

Let's play a video game.

1 ____________.
That's 2 ____________.
OK, 3 ____________!

No, let's 4 ____________.
No, I'm sorry,
I 5 ____________.

2 139 Listen again to the dialogues on page 62 and complete them.

1
Arianna I'm bored. What do you want to do?
Dominic Let's play *Super Mario*.
Arianna 1 ____________. I love that game.

2
Arianna What 2 ____________?
Dominic Let's do our homework.
Arianna Oh ... OK, but 3 ____________ a snack first?
Dominic OK, 4 ____________. I'm hungry!

3
Arianna I'm bored. 5 ____________?
Dominic Let's watch TV.
Arianna Mmm ... 6 ____________ any good shows on TV. 7 ____________ to the movies instead.
Dominic Cool. I want 8 ____________ the new Star Wars movie.

3 Write three dialogues. Use the prompts and the expressions in exercise 1 to help you.

1 Tom is bored. Laura has an idea. Tom agrees.
Tom I'm bored. What do you want to do?
Laura Oh! I have an idea. Let's walk to town ...

2 Dylan is bored and asks for an idea. Alice has an idea, but Dylan says no. Dylan suggests another activity. Alice thinks it is a good idea.

3 Nicola wants to do something, and she asks Lina for an idea. Nicola says no to Lina's idea and says why. Lina has another idea, but Nicola says no. Lina asks Nicola for an idea. Nicola suggests an activity. Lina thinks it is a good idea.

Extra listening

Listening strategy

When you have to correct underlined words in a listening activity, look carefully at the incorrect words. Think about the alternative that you will possibly hear. This will help you identify the information you need during the listening activity.

1 140 Listen to Amelia talking about babysitting for her aunt and uncle. The underlined information is incorrect. Write the correct word.

Amelia's aunt and uncle go to a restaurant on Friday evenings. *the movies*

1 She goes to their house at seven o'clock. ______
2 She has lunch with her aunt and uncle. ______
3 Noah is 6 years old. ______
4 Noah is usually good. ______
5 Before dinner, they often play games. ______
6 At 7:30 p.m., Noah takes a shower ______.
7 Noah's favorite song is *Creature Teacher*. ______
8 Noah goes to bed at 8.00 p.m. on Fridays. ______
9 When Noah goes to bed, Amelia usually reads her text messages or watches TV. ______
10 Her aunt and uncle get home at 11.00 p.m. ______

Reading and writing competences p.66

What are your favorite ways to **relax?**

Young people are often very busy–they go to school, they do their homework, they play sports, they're on school teams or go to after-school clubs, or they play musical instruments. It's great to be busy and to learn new things, but it's also very important to unwind. So, we have a question for you! What are your favorite ways to relax?

"After dinner, I usually finish my homework, and then I go to my bedroom to chill out. I often listen to music, or I read books. I have a notebook and I write or draw in it every day. I play the guitar and I sometimes write songs. I like to be creative." **Alyssa, 13**

"In the summer, I usually go skateboarding with my friends. There's a skatepark near my house. On the weekend, I play soccer in the backyard with my dad, or we sometimes go to the movies. When we finish school on Fridays, I always go to my friend Jamie's house. We play video games, or we watch our favorite Netflix series. I have dinner at his house. We usually have pizza–my favorite!" **Felipe, 13**

"When I get home from school, I usually relax for an hour. I check Snapchat and Instagram, and then I read any messages I have from my friends and chat with them online. Then I often go for a walk with our dog, Koji. We usually go to the park, and he plays with other dogs. It's fun and relaxing. Sometimes I call my best friend, too." **Tomomi, 15**

Check it out!

Find these words and phrases and check their meaning.

unwind	chill out	go skateboarding
so	draw	skatepark

Reading

1 141 **Read and listen** **Match the names with the people's favorite ways to relax. Write *A* (Alyssa), *F* (Felipe), or *T* (Tomomi).**

listen to music A
1 read books ____
2 watch Netflix series ____
3 message friends ____
4 go for a walk ____
5 play the guitar ____
6 write songs ____
7 go to a skatepark ____
8 go to the movies ____
9 go online ____
10 write in a notebook ____
11 play soccer ____
12 play video games ____
13 call her best friend ____
14 go to a friend's house ____

2 **Comprehension** **Read the article again and choose the correct sequencing words.**

Alyssa finishes her homework (after) / **before** she has dinner.
1 Alyssa reads books or listens to music **then** / **when** she goes to her bedroom.
2 Felipe goes to his friend's house **after** / **before** school on Fridays.
3 Tomomi checks Snapchat and Instagram **after** / **before** she gets home from school.
4 Tomomi relaxes at home, **after** / **then** she takes her dog for a walk.
5 **Before** / **When** she takes her dog for a walk, she goes to the park.

Writing

3 **Write a short text for the website about your three favorite ways to relax. Use the reading text and exercise 2 to help you.**

Writing check

We use sequencing words to order events. How many sequencing words are there in your text?

*I listen to music **before** I go to bed.*

***After** dinner, I play video games.*

*I have a snack, and **then** I watch TV.*

*I do my homework, and **after that**, I hang out with my friends.*

6 Grammar rules

Simple present

Negative p.71

What do you call cheese that isn't your cheese?
I don't know.

Full form	Short form
I **do not play** soccer.	I **don't play** soccer.
You **do not like** corn.	You **don't like** corn.
He **does not study** Music.	He **doesn't study** Music.
She **does not eat** ice cream.	She **doesn't eat** ice cream.
It **does not open** at 8 a.m.	It **doesn't open** at 8 a.m.
We **do not live** in the U.S.	We **don't live** in the U.S.
You **do not write** letters.	You **don't write** letters.
They **do not drink** soda.	They **don't drink** soda.

1 We make the negative form of the simple present with:

Subject	+ *do not* (*don't*)	+ base form
	+ *does not* (*doesn't*)	

2 We usually use the short forms (***don't*** and ***doesn't***). We don't often use the full forms.

We **don't** play tennis at school.

My sister **doesn't** like eggs.

3 We use ***doesn't*** with the third person singular (***he***, ***she***, ***it***).

She **doesn't** like Math.

My grandpa **doesn't** play video games.

4 We use ***don't*** with all other persons.

I **don't** eat tomatoes.

You **don't** live near here.

We **don't** have Math on Mondays.

They **don't** teach at our school.

Look!

We do not add ***-s*** to the negative form of the verb in the third person singular.

He ***doesn't*** *play baseball.*

NOT ~~He doesn't plays baseball.~~

Interrogative and short answers p.71

Interrogative	Short answers	
	Affirmative	Negative
Do I **work**?	**Yes**, you **do**.	**No**, you **don't**.
Do you **like** ham?	**Yes**, I **do**.	**No**, I **don't**.
Does he / she **like** gym class?	**Yes**, he / she **does**.	**No**, he / she **doesn't**.
Does it **open** at 9 a.m.?	**Yes**, it **does**.	**No**, it **doesn't**.
Do we / you / they **have** homework?	**Yes**, we / you / they **do**.	**No**, we / you / they **don't**.

1 We make the interrogative form of the simple present with:

Do / Does	+ subject	+ base form	+ *?*

2 We often answer questions with short answers. We make affirmative short answers with:

Yes,	+ subject	+ *do / does.*

3 We make negative short answers with:

No,	+ subject	+ *don't / doesn't.*

4 We usually use short forms in negative short answers.

Question words + simple present

p.74

Question word	Simple present
What	do you study at school?
When	do they have dinner?
Where	does Katie live?
What time	does she get up?

We make questions with the simple present and question words:

Question word	+ *do / does*	+ subject	+ base form	+ *?*

What does she study on Mondays?

What time does she get up?

When do her lessons start?

How often ...? p.74

Questions with *How often ...?*	Answers with expressions of frequency
How often do you eat salmon?	I eat it **once a week**.
How often does she play tennis?	She plays it **every day**.
How often does he eat meat?	He eats it **twice a day**.
How often do we have Math?	We have it **four times a week**!

1 **We make questions with *How often* and the simple present with:**

How often	+ *do* / *does*	+ subject	+ base form	+ ?

How often do you eat eggs?

How often does he buy fish?

2 **When we answer questions with *How often*, we can use the following expressions of frequency:**

every	+ *hour*, *day*, *week*, etc.
once / *twice*	+ *an hour*, *a day*, *a week*, etc.
three / *four times*	+ *an hour*, *a day*, *a week*, etc.

Object pronouns p.74

Subject pronouns	Object pronouns
I	**me**
you	**you**
he / she / it	**him** / **her** / **it**
we	**us**
you	**you**
they	**them**

1 **We use both subject and object pronouns to substitute nouns.**

John / He goes to that school.

I hate peas. I hate them.

Sally Adams teaches English. I like her.

2 **We put subject pronouns before a verb.**

We get up at 7:30 a.m.

She studies Art on Fridays.

3 **We put object pronouns after a verb or after a preposition.**

A I like the band 30 Seconds to Mars.

B I like them, too.

A I have music lessons with Sara.

B I have music lessons with her, too.

Word list

Review the vocabulary. Write your own study notes or translation for each word.

Food and drink

apple ______

bread ______

carrots ______

cheese ______

chicken ______

corn ______

eggs ______

fries ______

grapes ______

ham ______

ice cream ______

milk ______

orange juice ______

peach ______

pear ______

peas ______

potato chips ______

potatoes ______

salad ______

salmon ______

soda ______

tomatoes ______

tuna ______

water ______

Check it out!

annoying ______

awful ______

beef ______

graham cracker ______

he's a real show-off

______

I can't stand him.

______

jelly ______

marshmallow ______

peanut butter ______

salty ______

Shut up! ______

So what? ______

sweet ______

Real English

Do you like ...? ______

Yes, I do. / No, I don't.

______

What do you think about ...?

______

I like ______

I like ... a lot / very much.

______

I really like ... ______

I love ... ______

I don't like ... very much.

______

I don't like ... at all.

______

I can't stand ... ______

6 You don't know him

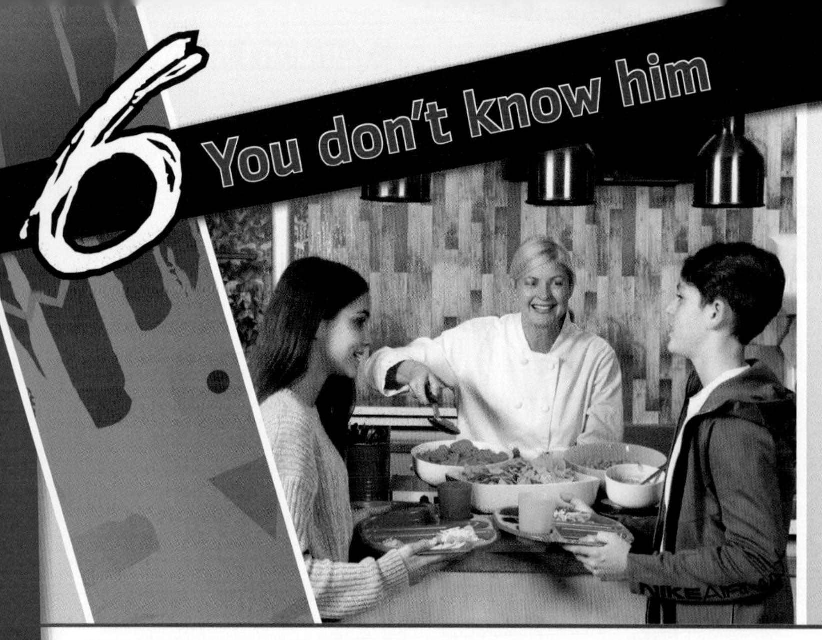

1 🔊 142 **Listen to the dialogue on page 68 and read Mason's sentences aloud. Practice reading the sentences in pairs.**

2 Check (✓) the food Mason chooses.

nachos ☐ carrots ☐
salad ☐ corn ☐
cheese ☐ tomatoes ☐

Vocabulary check: Food and drink p.70

3 Complete the crossword.

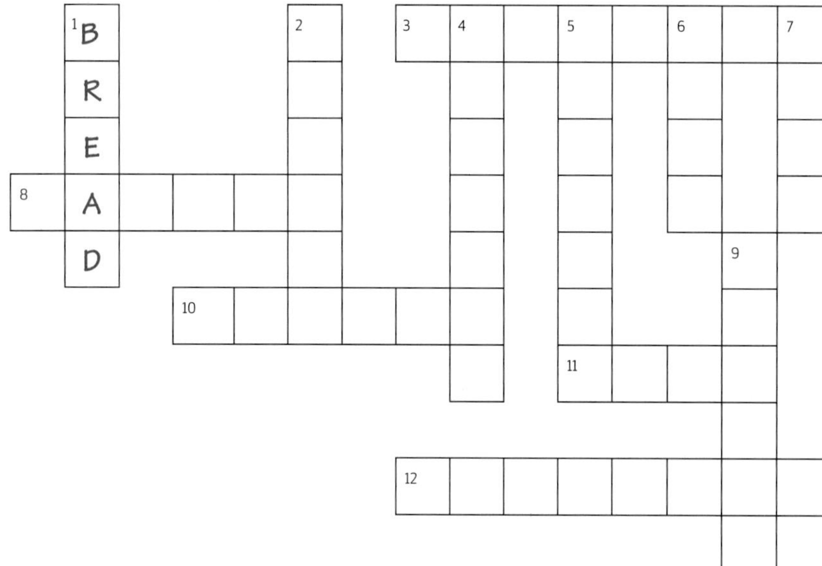

Across

3 a cold dessert
8 a type of fish
10 a yellow dairy product–good for sandwiches
11 a drink with bubbles, for example, cola
12 red and often in salads

Down

1 important for sandwiches
2 a color and type of juice
4 a bird and a type of meat
5 vegetables that are orange
6 ingredients for omelettes
7 a drink and a dairy product
9 small purple or green fruit

Grammar: Simple present p.71

Negative

4 Choose the correct alternatives.

Grandma **don't** / **(doesn't)** eat cheese.

1 Ellie and Matt **don't** / **doesn't** watch Netflix together.
2 Thomas doesn't **like** / **likes** fries.
3 We **don't** / **doesn't** have Gym class on Wednesdays.
4 My dad doesn't **come** / **comes** from the U.K.
5 Mr. Williams **don't** / **doesn't** teach Spanish.

5 Complete the sentences with the negative form of the verbs in parentheses.

I *don't get dressed* before breakfast. (get dressed)

1 My sister ________________ coffee. (drink)
2 We ________________ tennis in the winter. (play)
3 Samuel ________________ eggs. (like)
4 Our cat ________________ tuna. (eat)
5 The children ____________ to bed late. (go)

Interrogative and short answers

6 Match the questions and answers.

1 Do you like peas? *c*
2 Does the dog eat meat? ____
3 Does Ines live here? ____
4 Do you and Diego cook? ____
5 Do Jo and Caz bake? ____

a No, they don't.
b Yes, we do.
c ~~Yes, I do.~~
d Yes, it does.
e No, she doesn't.

7 Use the prompts to write questions. Then look at the fact file and answer the questions.

JUNIOR BAKING CHAMPIONSHIP WINNER!

Name	Linsey Lam
From	New Jersey, U.S.
Favorite dish	cake
Likes	baking, making YouTube videos, her dog
Prize	$25,000

Linsey / come from the U.S.?
Does Linsey come from the U.S.?
Yes, she does.

1 she / live in New York City?
2 she / bake cakes?
3 she / make videos / for YouTube?
4 winners of the show / get $50,000?

Question words + simple present p.74

8 Choose the correct alternatives.

When / (Where) do you live?

1 **What time** / **How** does your school finish?
2 **When** / **What** do you do after school?
3 **Where** / **Who** does your best friend live?
4 **When** / **What** do you speak English?
5 **What** / **How** do you say "Thanks" in Spanish?

How often ...? p.74

9 Complete the questions with *How often do* / *How often does*. Complete the answers with the time expressions in the box.

twice a month every day once a year ~~three times a day~~ four times a year once a week

How often does Sarah drink coffee?
She drinks it three times a day.
(8 a.m., 2 p.m., 7 p.m.)

1 ______ they go to the movies?
They go ______ . (2x per month)

2 ______ you take a shower?
I take a shower ______ .
(9 p.m. Monday–Sunday)

3 ______ you visit your grandparents?
We visit them ______ . (on Sundays)

4 ______ he visit his grandparents?
He visits them ______ . (4x per year)

5 ______ they have parties?
They have them ______ .
(every August 15th)

Object pronouns p.74

10 Choose the correct alternatives.

I love cola. I drink **him** / (**it**) every day.

1 I live near Katie. I often see **her** / **it**.
2 Ava is Mario's girlfriend. She likes **her** / **him**.
3 We like Josh, but he doesn't like **them** / **us**.
4 I know those boys. I play soccer with **it** / **them**.
5 You can't hear me, but I can hear **them** / **you**!

Round-up

1 Look at the information about the food that Jordan likes and doesn't like. Use the prompts to write questions.

(how often / you / eat / vegetables) How often do you eat vegetables? Never! I don't like them!
(how often / you / eat / meat) 1 ______ ? Every day. I love it.
(what snack / you / prefer) 2 ______ ? Ice cream or pizza.
(which sandwich / you / like) 3 ______ ? A chicken and ham sandwich.
(which / meat dish / you love) 4 ______ ? A cheeseburger.
(what food / you / eat / at a barbecue) 5 ______ ? Chicken and bread.

2 Complete the text about Jordan with the words in the box. Use exercise 1 to help you.

ham them ~~like~~ ice cream meat it chicken doesn't them

Jordan doesn't like vegetables, and he never eats 1______ . Meat is his favorite food, and he eats 2______ every day.
His favorite snacks are 3______ and pizza. He 4______ eat cheese sandwiches–he only likes chicken and 5______ sandwiches. His favorite 6______ dish is a cheeseburger. He loves 7______ and bread, too, and he always eats 8______ at barbecues.

3 Answer the questions in exercise 1 for yourself.

Likes and dislikes p.72

1 Write the phrases in the correct order.

I can't stand … I don't like … at all. I don't like … very much. I like … ~~I love …~~ I really like … I like … a lot / very much.

😀😀😀😀 I love …
😀😀😀 1 ____
😀😀 2 ____
😀 3 ____
☹ 4 ____
☹☹ 5 ____
☹☹☹ 6 ____

2 Read the mini-dialogues and complete the sentences. Use the symbols and exercise 1 to help you.

1 A Do you like chocolate?
B [1]____, I do. I [2]____ like it. 😀😀😀

2 A [3]____ do you think [4]____ Maluma?
B I [5]____ like him very much. ☹

3 A Do you like peas?
B No, I can't [6]____. ☹☹☹

4 A What do you [7]____ Cardi B's new song?
B I [8]____ it. 😀

3 143 Listen to the dialogues on page 72 again and complete them.

1

Arianna What's on the menu today?
Dominic It's chicken with potatoes and carrots. Do [1]____?
Arianna Yes, I do. [2]____. What about you?
Dominic I like it a lot, but [3]____!
Arianna Oh, I really like them!

2

Arianna Do you like Katy Perry?
Dominic No, [4]____. What about you?
Arianna I really like her! Her new album's great!
Dominic [5]____ Justin Bieber?
Arianna He's fantastic! I love him!
Dominic Really? [6]____!

4 Put the words in the correct order to make questions.

1 Do / you / **Monday mornings** / like / ?

____

2 the / you / think / What / about / do / **Deadpool movies** / ?

____

3 **Drake** / think / you / do / What / about / ?

____

4 like / Do / **salmon** / you / ?

____

5 Write a questionnaire. Use the questions in exercise 4. Replace the words in **bold** with your own ideas.

6 Write your own answers to the questions in your questionnaire from exercise 5. Then write the answers for two other people.

Extra listening

Listening strategy

Don't panic if you don't understand everything the first time you listen. Try to get a general idea of the content, and then concentrate on details the second time you listen.

1 144 Listen to four students talking about the food they like and don't like. Match the names in the box with the pictures.

Bethany Tyler Jackson ~~Lucia~~

1 Lucia
2 ____
3 ____
4 ____

Reading and writing competences p.76

Do you like meat? Do you like music? Do you like barbecues? YES?

Then the Blues and Bones Festival is perfect for you! The Blues and Bones Festival takes place every summer in Idaho and California. The festival has music, competitions, and, of course, great food!

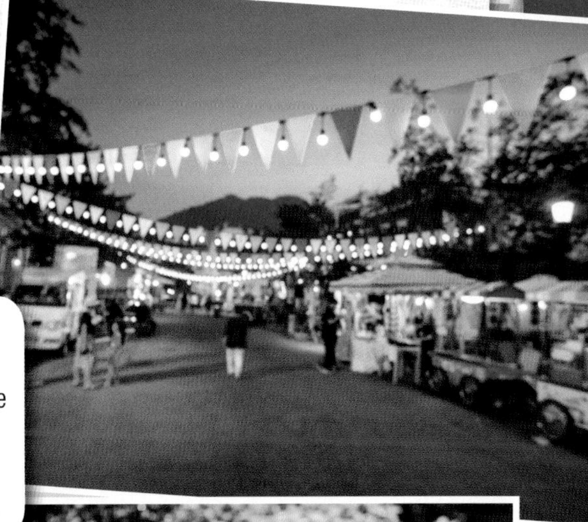

My family and I go to Blues and Bones every year. We love it, especially Dad. Dad is a good cook and he makes great barbecue. He doesn't usually cook vegetables, but his spicy chicken is great! There's a competition at the festival, too, when all the people at the festival vote for the best barbecue stall there! Mom and I don't eat a lot when we're there. We prefer to listen to the music. Lots of blues bands play at the festival, and some of them are really good! ***Ava Miles***

I usually go to the Blues and Bones Festival with my family. I don't like blues music, so I don't listen to the bands. Instead, I go to all the barbecue stalls and try the food! Mom and Dad stay near the stage, and they listen to the music for hours! The food at Blues and Bones is incredible! There's every type of meat you can imagine, but there are vegetables and salads, too. My favorite thing to eat is the sausages–I love them! ***Ryan Wilton***

Check it out!

Find these words and phrases and check their meaning.

barbecues takes place spicy stage

Reading

1 145 **Read and listen** **Choose the correct alternatives.**

1 **Ava's / Ryan's** favorite thing about the festival is the food.

2 **Ava's / Ryan's** favorite thing about the festival is the music.

2 **Comprehension** **Answer the questions.**

When does the Blues and Bones festival take place?

It takes place every summer.

1 Where does the festival take place?

2 What does the festival have?

3 How often does Ava and her family go to the festival?

4 Who chooses the best barbecue stall in the competition?

5 Who does Ryan go to the festival with?

6 What do his parents do at the festival?

7 What does he think about the food at the festival?

Writing

3 **Complete the questionnaire with true answers.**

1 How often do you have a barbecue or a picnic?

____

2 Where do you eat? ______________________

3 Who do you eat outside with?

____

4 What do you usually eat?

____

5 What do you think about barbecues and picnics?

I love them. ☐ I like them. ☐ I can't stand them. ☐

4 **Write a short paragraph about when and where you have barbecues and picnics. Use your answers from exercise 3.**

My family and I sometimes have a barbecue. We have a barbecue or a picnic about five times a …

Writing check

We use *so* to show the consequence of something.

She doesn't like rock music, ***so*** *she doesn't watch the bands.*

Are there examples of *so* in your text?

7 Grammar rules

can (ability)

Affirmative and negative p.85

Affirmative	
I **can** dance.	It **can** fly.
You **can** sing.	We **can** play tennis.
He **can** do karate.	You **can** cook.
She **can** ski.	They **can** speak English.

Negative	
Full forms	**Short forms**
I **cannot** dance.	I **can't** dance.
You **cannot** sing.	You **can't** sing.
He **cannot** do karate.	He **can't** do karate.
She **cannot** ski.	She **can't** ski.
It **cannot** fly.	It **can't** fly.
We **cannot** play tennis.	We **can't** play tennis.
You **cannot** cook.	You **can't** cook.
They **cannot** speak English.	They **can't** speak English.

1 We form affirmative sentences with *can* with:

Subject	+ *can / can't*	+ base form

2 We only use one form for all persons.

I can dance. He can dance. We can dance.

3 We do not add an *-s* to *can* with *he*, *she*, and *it*.

He can ski. NOT ~~He cans ski.~~

4 After *can*, we put another verb in the base form.

I can run. She can swim.

5 The negative form of *can* is *cannot* (*can* + *not*). In conversation and in informal writing, we usually use the short form, *can't*.

He cannot play tennis. = He can't play tennis.

Look!

We never use *don't / doesn't* in negative sentences with *can*.

We can't swim. NOT ~~*We don't can swim.*~~

Can I do karate?
No, you can't.

Interrogative and short answers p.85

Interrogative	Short answers	
	Affirmative	**Negative**
Can I **dance**?	**Yes**, you **can**.	**No**, you **can't**.
Can you **swim**?	**Yes**, I **can**.	**No**, I **can't**.
Can he **cook**?	**Yes**, he **can**.	**No**, he **can't**.
Can she **draw**?	**Yes**, she **can**.	**No**, she **can't**.
Can it **fly**?	**Yes**, it **can**.	**No**, it **can't**.
Can we **act**?	**Yes**, you **can**.	**No**, you **can't**.
Can you **paint**?	**Yes**, we **can**.	**No**, we **can't**.
Can they **sing**?	**Yes**, they **can**.	**No**, they **can't**.

1 We form questions with *can* in the same way for all persons. We make questions with *can* like this:

Can	+ subject	+ base form	+ ?

Can you use a computer?

Can she send a text message?

2 We make affirmative short answers with:

Yes,	+ subject	+ *can.*

Can you swim? — Yes, I can.

Can Paul ski? — Yes, he can.

3 We make negative short answers with:

No,	+ subject	+ *can't.*

Can you ski? — No, I can't.

Can Carla dance? — No, she can't.

4 We never use *do*, *don't*, *does*, or *doesn't* in questions and short answers with *can*.

Imperatives p.88

Affirmative	Negative
Listen!	Don't listen!
Look!	Don't look!
Start!	Don't start!

1 We use the imperative form when we want someone to do (or not to do) something.

Open your book. Don't open your book.

2 There is only one form of the imperative for singular and plural.

Come here, John! Come here, boys!

3 The imperative is the same as the base form of the verb.

4 We make the negative with ***don't*** + base form.

Don't go!

5 With the imperative of ***be***, we always use an adjective.

Be quiet! Don't be sad.

6 We never use subject pronouns with imperatives.

Look! NOT ~~You look!~~

Why? / Because ... p.88

Why is a question word. We use it to ask about reasons for something. We use because to express the reason for something.

Why do you get up early?

Because school starts at 8 a.m.

Adverbs of manner

Regular adverbs p.88

Adjective		Adverb
slow	+ *-ly*	**slowly**
easy	*-y* → *-i* + *-ly*	**easily**
fantastic	+ *-ally*	**fantastically**

1 We use adverbs of manner to say how we do something. They give extra information or meaning about the verb.

Laura plays the guitar badly.

2 Adverbs of manner always come after a verb or after an object.

Subject	+ verb	(+ object)	+ adverb of manner

Maria talks to him quietly.

Irregular adverbs p.88

Adjective	Adverb
good	well
early	early
late	late
fast	fast
hard	hard

There are some irregular adverbs. There are no rules, so you have to learn them.

Tina plays baseball well.

NOT ~~Tina plays baseball goodly.~~

Word list

Review the vocabulary. Write your own study notes or translation for each word.

Sports

do gymnastics ____
do karate ____
do track and field
____
go biking ____
go skiing ____
go swimming ____
play baseball ____
play basketball ____
play field hockey
____
play soccer ____
play tennis ____
play volleyball ____

Check it out!

arts and crafts ____
bake a cake ____
champions ____
design ____
Don't be stupid.
____
exhibition ____
I guess ____
Like what? ____
make fun of ____
miss ____
take part ____
town ____
training ____

Real English

Can you ... well? ____
Yes, I can. / No, I can't.
____
How well can you ...?
____
I can ... very well. ____
I can ... well. ____
I can ... pretty well.
____
I'm great at ... ____
I'm good at ... ____
I can't ... very well. ____
I can't ... at all. ____
I'm not very good at ... ____
I'm awful at ... ____

7 You can talk to girls!

1 146 **Listen to the dialogue on page 82 and read Jacob's sentences aloud. Practice the sentences in pairs.**

2 **Complete the sentence with three things Jacob can't do but Mason can do.**

Jacob can't [1] ________________ ,
[2] ________________ , or [3] ________________ .

Vocabulary check: Sports p.84

3 **Complete the chart.**

Sports you play with a ball	Sports you play without a ball
play s *o c c e* r	[6] go b _ _ _ _ g
[1] play b _ _ _ _ _ _ _ _ l	[7] go s _ _ _ _ _ _ _ g
[2] play f _ _ _ _ _ _ _ _ _ y	[8] go s _ _ _ _ g
[3] play b _ _ _ _ _ _ l	[9] do t _ _ _ k _ _ d f _ _ _ d
[4] play v _ _ _ _ _ _ _ _ l	[10] do g _ _ _ _ _ _ _ _ s
[5] play t _ _ _ _ s	[11] do k _ _ _ _ e

4 **Choose the correct alternative.**

We use the verb *play* for sports **with** / **without** a ball.

Grammar: *can* (ability) p.85

Affirmative and negative

	dance	swim	play field hockey	speak Spanish	sing	play the piano
me	👍	👎	👎	👎	👎	👍
you	👍	👎	👎	👍	👎	👎
Pedro	👎	👎	👍	👎	👍	👍
Nina	👎	👎	👍	👍	👎	👍
we	👍	👎	👍	👍	👎	👍
the boys	👍	👍	👎	👎	👎	👎

5 **Look at the chart and choose the correct alternatives.**

I (**can**) / **can't** dance.

1 You **can** / **can't** swim.
2 Pedro **can** / **can't** play field hockey.
3 We **can** / **can't** speak Spanish.
4 The boys **can** / **can't** play the piano.

6 **Use the prompts to write questions. Then look again at the chart in exercise 5 and write short answers.**

Nina / sing / ?
Can Nina sing? No, she can't.

1 Nina / speak Spanish / ?
2 Nina and Pedro / dance / ?
3 Pedro / swim / ?

Interrogative and short answers

7 **Choose the correct alternatives.**

1 A (**Can you**) / **You can** play volleyball?
B Yes, [1] **I am** / **I can**. I'm very good at it.

2 A My brother's in a rock band.
B Wow! [2] **Do he can** / **Can he** sing?
A No, he [3] **can't** / **not can**. He plays the guitar.

3 A Can you and Rob [4] **play** / **plays** volleyball?
B [5] **No, we do** / **Yes, we can**, but we [6] **can't** / **not** play basketball.

Imperatives p.88

8 **Complete the chart with the correct form of the imperative.**

Affirmative	Negative
Go!	Don't go!
Open it!	1 ______
2 ______	Don't close it!
Sit down!	3 ______
4 ______	Don't stand up!

9 **Complete the school rules with the verbs in the box. Use the affirmative or negative form of the imperative.**

use ~~listen~~ say run be close

SCHOOL RULES

Listen to the teachers.

1 ______ cell phones in class.

2 ______ "please" and "thank you."

3 ______ the windows and doors after classes.

4 ______ late.

5 Walk. ______ !

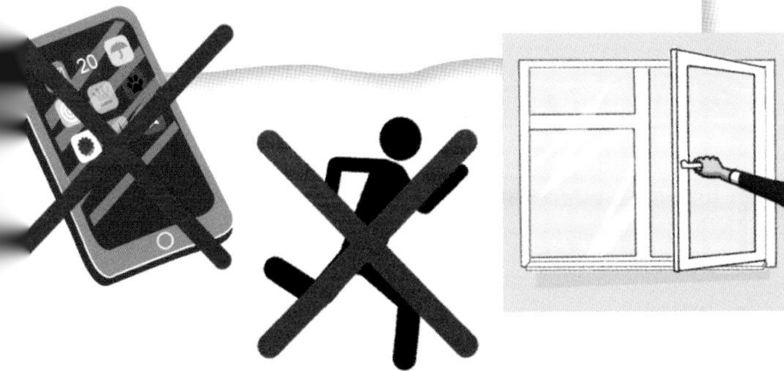

Why...? / Because ... p.88

10 **Match the questions and answers.**

1 Why are you happy today? d
2 Why do you go to music lessons? ____
3 Why do you like Justin Bieber? ____
4 Why does Eurico like Saturdays? ____

a Because I want to be in a band.
b Because he doesn't go to school on Saturdays.
c Because he can sing and dance well.
~~d Because it's my birthday.~~

Adverbs of manner p.88

11 **Choose the correct adjective for the sentences. Then complete the sentences with the corresponding adverb.**

Sarah sings beautifully. (**beautiful** / **lucky**)

1 I go to bed ______ on school nights. (**early** / **easy**)
2 Our team never wins because we play ______. (**lucky** / **bad**)
3 He's great at tennis. He wins his games ______. (**easy** / **hard**)
4 Please repeat the question ______. (**happy** / **slow**)
5 He isn't a very good student. He doesn't study ______. (**slow** / **hard**)
6 James speaks French very ______. (**good** / **late**)

Round-up

1 **Read the text and choose the correct alternatives.**

Star Turn

Star Turn is a new TV show. Every week, famous people learn to do new things on the show. This week, our star is Cooper Brown. He's a famous baseball player, but he has a secret passion. He wants to be a rock star!

Star Turn **Why** / **Because** are you on *Star Turn*?
Cooper [1] **Why** / **Because** I want to be a rock star!
Star Turn [2] **Can you** / **Do you can** sing or play an instrument?
Cooper No, I [3] **can't** / **can**, but I want to learn.
Star Turn [4] **Can** / **Are** you dance?
Cooper I can dance [5] **badly** / **bad**!
Star Turn You [6] **can't** / **can don't** sing, play an instrument, or dance! One week isn't very long to be a rock star!
Cooper Yes, but I can work [7] **hard** / **good**. I'm an athlete. I [8] **early get up** / **get up early**, and I train [9] **hardly** / **hard**.
Star Turn [10] **Don't** / **Not to** miss *Star Turn*! [11] **Watch** / **To watch** the show on Tuesdays at 8 p.m. on TV4.

Ability p.86

1 Complete the mind map with the expressions in the box.

I can't pretty well at all ~~Can you~~ I can really How well

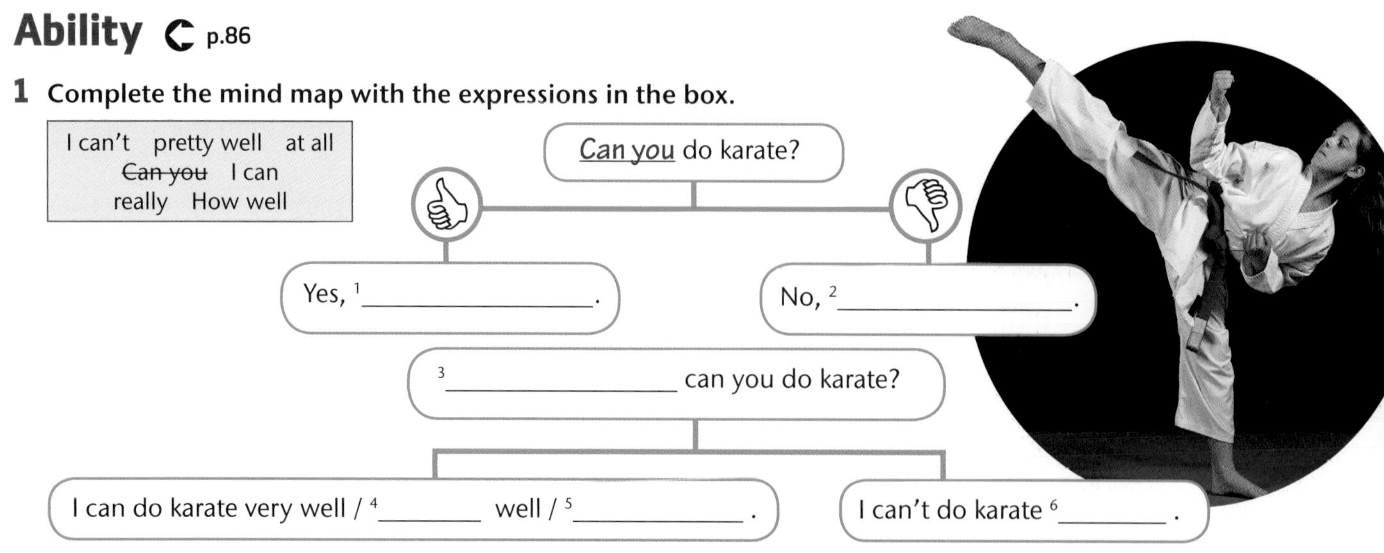

Can you do karate?
Yes, 1 ___.
No, 2 ___.
3 ___ can you do karate?
I can do karate very well / 4 ___ well / 5 ___.
I can't do karate 6 ___.

2 147 Listen to the dialogues on page 86 again and complete them.

1

Arianna How well can you swim, Dominic?
Dominic I can swim 1 ___.
Arianna What other sports can you play?
Dominic I can play basketball, and 2 ___, too. I'm 3 ___ at it, but I love it.
Arianna What about soccer?
Dominic I can't play soccer 4 ___. I'm awful at it! Can you?
Arianna Yes, I can.
Dominic Can you 5 ___?
Arianna Yes, I can. I'm on the school team.

2

Dominic Can you sing?
Arianna Yes, I can. I can sing 6 ___. I'm in a band.
Dominic Oh, really? Can you play a musical instrument?
Arianna Yes, I can play 7 ___.
Dominic 8 ___ can you play the piano?
Arianna I'm pretty good at it.
Dominic 9 ___ read music?
Arianna 10 ___, but not very well. It's really difficult!

3 Imagine you are joining the Get Active Sports Center in Chicago. Your new sports coach is asking you some questions. Give personal answers.

Coach What's your name?
You 1 ___
Coach How old are you?
You 2 ___
Coach We have tennis, volleyball, and basketball in this sports center. How well can you play those sports?
You 3 ___
Coach How well can you swim?
You 4 ___
Coach We have swimming classes on Saturday morning. Do you want to go to swimming classes?
You 5 ___

Extra listening

Listening strategy

Keep calm if you can't answer a question during a listening exercise. Leave that question and listen for the answer to the next question.

1 148 Georgia is helping her friend Miguel to choose an after-school club. Listen and choose the correct alternatives.

Miguel can't sing (well) / **at all**.

1 He can play the **guitar** / **piano**.
2 He **can** / **can't** dance.
3 There **are some** / **aren't any** sports clubs.
4 Miguel can't play soccer **very well** / **at all**.
5 Miguel can swim **well** / **really well**.
6 The swimming club is on Wednesday **afternoons** / **evenings**.
7 Miguel finishes school at **two** / **three** o'clock on Wednesdays.
8 The contact number is **319-555-0317** / **315-555-0357**.

Reading and writing competences p.90

THREE TALENTED TEENS!

They go to school, they do their homework, they play sports, and they have fun with their friends. But these teenagers aren't ordinary! They can do extraordinary things. Meet three teenagers with incredible talents.

Belén Fernandez is 13 years old, and she's a genius with numbers. She can add, subtract, and multiply very big numbers incredibly fast. Belén is in 8th grade, but for her Math class, she goes to a local college. The students in her class are 18 years old!

How many musical instruments can you play? One? Two? **Jayden Nowak** can play over 20 musical instruments! Jayden is 13 years old, and he lives in San Diego, in the U.S. He doesn't come from a musical family. His parents can't play any musical instruments. Jayden has a website with songs and videos. He has over 20,000 online fans.

Caio Duarte is 15 years old, and he can play soccer and swim really well. He's on the Brazilian under-17s soccer team, and he's a national swimming champion. Caio trains very hard. In his free time, he's always at his local soccer club, or at the swimming pool. Caio wants to study Sports Science in college.

Check it out!

Find these words and check their meaning.

talented add multiply local
genius subtract trains

Reading

1 149 **Read and listen** **Answer the questions.**

1 What extraordinary thing can Belén do?
2 How old is Belén and how old are the students in her Math class?
3 How many musical instruments can Jayden play?
4 Which sports can Caio do really well?
5 What does Caio want to study in college?

Writing

2 Choose the correct alternatives.

What are / ('s) your name?
1 How old **are** / **have** you?
2 Where **can** / **do** you live?
3 Which sports **can** / **are** you play?
4 How well **does** / **can** you sing and dance?
5 What **is** / **does** your special talent?
6 How many online fans **can** / **do** you have?

3 Imagine you are talking to Rachel, a talented teen. Use the questions in exercise 2 and the information in the fact file to write a dialogue.

Name	Rachel
Age	13
City	Michigan
Sports	plays volleyball (well), swims (pretty well)
Music	sings (pretty well), dances (well)
Special talent	cooks really well, her YouTube food channel has over 200,000 online fans.

You What's your name?
Rachel My name is Rachel.

Writing check

Don't forget that the verb form in the question can help you to choose the correct verb form in the answer.

Are *you musical?*	*Yes, I* ***am***.
How well ***can*** *you* ***sing***?	*I* ***can sing*** *pretty well.*
How often ***do*** *you* ***dance***?	*I* ***dance*** *every day.*

Look at your text again and see if the verbs in the answers match the verb forms in the questions.

8 Grammar rules

Present progressive

Affirmative p95

He's dancing really well!

Full form	Short form
I **am wearing** shorts.	I**'m wearing** shorts.
You **are talking**.	You**'re talking**.
He **is singing**.	He**'s singing**.
She **is playing**.	She**'s playing**.
It **is working**.	It**'s working**.
We **are cooking**.	We**'re cooking**.
You **are eating**.	You**'re eating**.
They **are acting**.	They**'re acting**.

1 **We make the present progressive with:**

Subject	+ *am / is / are*	+ base form	+ *-ing*

2 **We usually use the short forms of the verb *be* when we talk or write to friends. We use full forms in formal writing.**

3 **We use the present progressive:**

– to describe something that is happening now

He's watching TV right now.

– to describe pictures or drawings

In this picture, I'm playing tennis with my cousin Hannah.

4 **We often use the following expressions with the present progressive: *now*, *today*, *right now*.**

Look!

There are some verbs that we can't use in the present progressive. For example: *be*, *hate*, *like*, *love*, *prefer*, *want*.

*I **love** this movie.*

NOT ~~I'm loving this movie~~.

Spelling variations p.95

1 **For most verbs, we add *-ing* to the base form.**

play + *-ing* = ***playing***

walk + *-ing* = ***walking***

2 **There are some spelling variations:**

– For verbs ending in a consonant plus *-e*, we remove the *-e* and add *-ing*.

have → ***having***

– For short verbs ending in a vowel plus a consonant, we double the final consonant and add *-ing*.

sit → ***sitting***

Negative p.95

Full form	Short form
I **am not playing**.	I**'m not playing**.
You **are not looking**.	You **aren't looking**.
He **is not talking**.	He **isn't talking**.
She **is not studying**.	She **isn't studying**.
It **is not working**.	It **isn't working**.
We **are not acting**.	We **aren't acting**.
You **are not listening**.	You **aren't listening**.
They **are not writing**.	They **aren't writing**.

1 **We make the negative form of the present progressive with:**

Subject	+ *am / is / are*	+ *not*	+ base form	+ *-ing*

2 **We usually use the negative short forms of the verb *be* in conversation or when we write to friends. We use full forms in formal writing.**

Present progressive

Interrogative and short answers p.98

Interrogative	Short answers	
	Affirmative	Negative
Am I **playing**?	**Yes,** you **are**.	**No,** you **aren't**.
Are you **working**?	**Yes,** I **am**.	**No,** I**'m not**.
Is he **listening**?	**Yes,** he **is**.	**No,** he **isn't**.
Is she **talking**?	**Yes,** she **is**.	**No,** she **isn't**.
Is it **raining**?	**Yes,** it **is**.	**No,** it **isn't**.
Are we **studying**?	**Yes,** you **are**.	**No,** you **aren't**.
Are you **watching**?	**Yes,** we **are**.	**No,** we **aren't**.
Are they **singing**?	**Yes,** they **are**.	**No,** they **aren't**.

1 We make present progressive questions with:

Am / Is / Are	+ subject	+ base form	+ *-ing*	+ *?*

2 We make short answers with:

Yes,	+ subject	+ *am / is / are.*
No,	+ subject	+ *'m not / isn't / aren't.*

3 In short answers, we only use the verb *be*.
We do not repeat the verb in the *-ing* form.

Is she listening to music?

Yes, she is. NOT ~~Yes, she is listening.~~

No, she isn't. NOT ~~No, she isn't listening.~~

4 We only contract negative short answers.
We do not contract affirmative short answers.

Are they going to school?

Yes, they are. NOT ~~Yes, they're.~~

No, they aren't.

Question words + present progressive p.98

Question word	Present progressive
Where	are you go**ing**?
What	are you do**ing**?
Who	are you call**ing**?
Why	are you leav**ing**?

When we make questions with the present progressive and question words, we put the question word before the form of *be* (*am* / *is* / *are*).

Word list

Review the vocabulary. Write your own study notes or translation for each word.

Clothes

baseball hat ______

boots ______
coat ______
dress ______
hat ______
hoodie ______
jacket ______
leggings ______
pants ______
scarf ______
shirt ______
shoes ______
shorts ______
skirt ______
sneakers ______
sweater ______
top ______
T-shirt ______

Check it out!

Are you kidding? ______

Come on ______
concentrate ______
equal ______
he looks great! ______

polo shirt ______
schoolyard ______
strict ______
That's so cute! ______

tie ______
Way to go! ______

Real English

Can I help you? ______
Yes, please. ______
No, thanks. I'm just looking. ______

How much is this ...? ______
How much are these ...? ______
It's / They're dollars. ______

Can I try it / them on? ______
Yes, of course. ______
What size are you? ______
I'm a small / medium / large. ______

Where are the fitting rooms? ______

The fitting rooms are over there. ______

Is it OK? ______
Yes, it is. I'll take it. ______
No, they're too big / small. ______

Thanks anyway. ______

8 The music's starting!

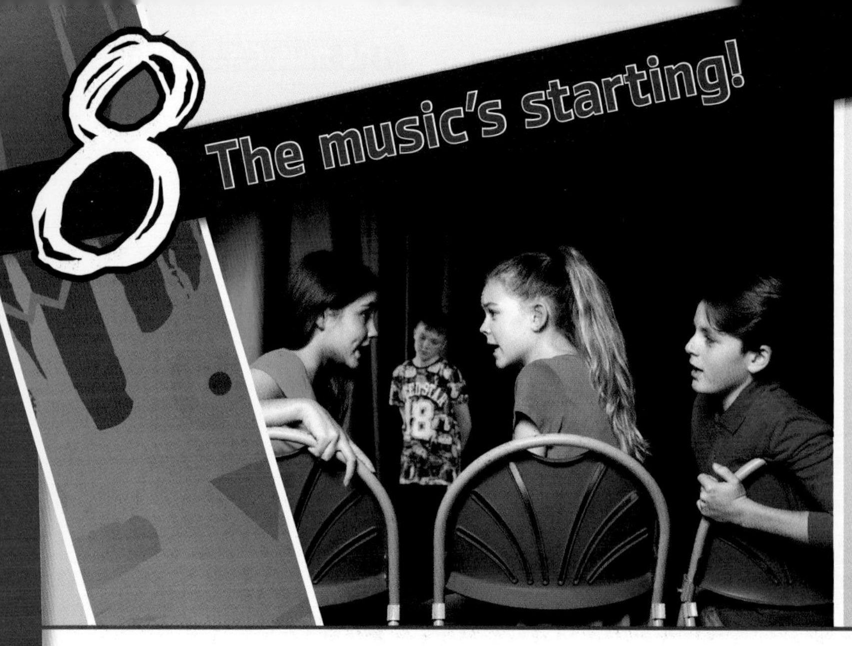

1 150 **Listen to the dialogue on page 92 and read Mason's sentences aloud. Then practice the sentences in pairs.**

2 Check (✓) the correct answer.

Is Mason happy for Jacob?

Yes, he is. ☐ No, he isn't. ☐

Vocabulary check: Clothes p.94

3 Complete the words in the mind map.

clothes

Head and shoulders
b a s e b a l l h a t
[1] s c _ _ _

Body
T-shirt jacket coat top
[7] s w _ _ _ _ _
[8] s h _ _ _
[9] h o _ _ _ _
[10] d _ _ _ _

Legs
leggings
[2] p _ _ _ _
[3] s _ _ _ _ _
[4] s _ _ _ _

Feet
boots
[5] s _ _ _ _
[6] s n _ _ _ _ _ _

Grammar: Present progressive p.95

Affirmative

4 Complete the sentences with the words in the box.

going eating ~~reading~~ doing wearing playing

I'm *reading* a book.

1 You're _________ a cool jacket!
2 The boys are _________ tennis.
3 We're _________ our homework.
4 Amy is _________ an apple.
5 I'm _________ to bed.

5 Use the prompts to write affirmative sentences with the present progressive. Use short forms.

Our teacher / speak English
Our teacher's speaking English.

1 Jamie / buy some jeans
2 I / help Dad in the kitchen
3 We / wait for the bus
4 Gemma / sing in the shower
5 They / drink some soda

Spelling variations

6 How do you write the *-ing* form of these verbs? Write *R* (regular) or *SV* (spelling variation). Then write the *-ing* form.

	teach	*teaching*	*R*
	write	*writing*	*SV*
1	use	______	___
2	say	______	___
3	get	______	___
4	study	______	___
5	start	______	___
6	run	______	___
7	walk	______	___
8	make	______	___
9	open	______	___
10	stop	______	___

Negative

7 Match the sentence halves.

1 Jack isn't using d
2 Ellen isn't tidying ____
3 We aren't having ____
4 I'm not winning ____
5 You aren't going ____

a to the park.
b this video game.
c her room.
~~d the computer.~~
e lunch.

8 Look at the picture. Then use the prompts in the picture to write affirmative and negative sentences.

The students / walk to school
The students aren't walking to school.
1 They / sit / in a park
2 They / study
3 The girl / listen / to music
4 She / eat / an ice cream
5 The boy / chat / to the girl
6 He / look / at his cell phone

Present progressive p.98

Interrogative and short answers

9 Complete the questions and short answers. Use the present progressive of the verb in parentheses.

Are you leaving? (leave)
No, I'm not.
1 _______ Tina _________ on my jacket? (sit)
Yes, _________ .
2 _______ I _________ well? (sing)
Yes, _________ .
3 _______ they _________ lunch? (have)
No, ___________ .
4 _______ the concert ___________ ? (start)
Yes, _______ .
5 _____ you and Ellie ___________ for clothes? (shop)
No, ___________ .

Question words + present progressive p.98

10 Choose the correct alternatives.

(Who) / What is Jamie talking to?
1 **Who** / **Why** is Olivia studying?
2 **Where** / **What** are the boys doing?
3 **What** / **How** are you feeling?
4 **Where** / **Who** is Tom going?

Round-up

1 Complete Rosie's planner entry with the present progressive form of the verbs in parentheses. Use short forms where possible.

Rosie's planner

School trip to Cape Cod (day three)

We 're sitting (sit) in a beach café! I [1] ___________ (eat) an ice cream. ☺ Liam, Amy, and I [2] _______________ (watch) our friends. Danny is on the beach–he [3] ___________ (wear) a yellow baseball hat. It looks cool! Marco is in the ocean, but he [4] _______________ (not swim). He [5] ___________ (have) a surfing lesson. He [6] _______________ (not do) very well!

2 Write questions for answers 1–4. Use the underlined words to help you, and use *how*, *what*, *where*, and *who*.

What's Rosie eating?
Rosie is eating an ice cream.
1 ______________________?
They're watching their friends.
2 ______________________?
Danny is wearing a yellow baseball hat.
3 ______________________
______________________?
Marco is having his surfing lesson in the ocean.
4 ______________________?
He isn't doing very well.

Shopping for clothes p.96

1 Complete the chart with the questions in the box.

Is it OK? ~~Can I help you?~~ Where are the fitting rooms? How much is this T-shirt? Can I try it on? What size are you?

Real English

Store assistant	Customer
Can I help you?	3 ______
1 ______	4 ______
2 ______	5 ______

2 Choose the correct alternatives.

Can I help you?
(a) Yes, please.
b Yes, of course.

1 Can I help you?
a No, thanks. I'm just looking.
b No, thanks. I'm a small.

2 How much is this jacket?
a They're $25.99.
b It's $25.99.

3 Can I try it on?
a No, thanks.
b Yes, of course.

4 What size are you?
a I'm a medium.
b I'm just looking.

5 Where are the fitting rooms?
a They're too big.
b They're over there.

6 Is it OK?
a Yes, it is. I'll take it.
b Yes, it is. I'll leave it.

3 151 Put the sentences in the correct order to make dialogues. Then listen and check.

1 ____ Can I help you?
2 No, thanks. I'm just looking.

2 ____ Can I try it on?
1 Excuse me. How much is this top, please?
____ I'm a medium.
____ Yes, it is. I'll take it.
____ It's $19.99.
____ Here you are. The fitting rooms are over there.
____ Is it OK?
____ Yes, of course. What size are you?
____ OK, come with me.

3 ____ Where are the fitting rooms?
____ Yes, please. How much are these jeans?
____ They're $39.99.
____ No, they aren't. They're too big. Thanks anyway.
____ Can I try them on?
____ Are they OK?
1 Can I help you?
____ Yes, of course.
____ Thank you.
____ They're over there.

4 Read the prompts and write two conversations.

1 You like some shorts in a store, and you ask the price. They're $19.50. You try them on, but they're too big, and you don't buy them.

2 You like a jacket in the store, and you ask the price. It's $34.99. You want to try it on and the assistant asks what size you are. You're a medium. The jacket is OK, and you buy it.

Extra listening

Listening strategy

When you have completed a listening task, listen again carefully to check you have given the correct answers.

1 152 Ethan and Hailey meet outside a movie theater in a big mall. They plan to watch a movie with friends. Listen to their conversation and match the people 1–6 to the activities a–f.

1 Hailey *b*
2 Isabel ____
3 Jess ____
4 David ____
5 Jason ____
6 Ethan ____

a is buying the movie tickets.
~~b is waiting for Isabel.~~
c is looking at some clothes.
d is trying on some pants.
e is going to the bathroom.
f is making a phone call.

Reading and writing competences p.100

An email from Central Park

Hi, Lewis!

Greetings from New York City! I'm writing to you from Central Park. It's a cool park on Fifth Avenue. I'm sending you a picture of it. I hope you can open it.

It's lunchtime right now, so the park is full of people. Some people are having lunch, and others are riding bikes or running. A man near us is doing yoga, and some people are sunbathing.

Mom and I are sitting near the Lake, one of the biggest lakes in the park, and we're eating bagels–a type of sandwich. I'm watching the boats on the lake and the people in them. Some of the people aren't rowing the boats very well and the boats are going in circles!

Dad isn't here right now. He's visiting an art museum. It's near the park. Dad wants to visit every museum in New York City, but there are over a hundred ...

Are you having a good vacation? I hope you aren't studying!

See you at school, Tadeu

Check it out!

Find these words and phrases and check their meaning.

full of — lake — circles

sunbathing — boats

Reading

1 153 **Read and listen** **Check (✓) the things that Tadeu talks about in his email.**

- ☐ bagels
- ☐ a park
- ☐ what he is drinking
- ☐ an email
- ☐ a taxi
- ☐ museums
- ☐ sports

2 **Comprehension** **Answer the questions.**

Where is Tadeu writing the email from?

He's writing the email from Central Park.

1 Why is the park full of people right now?

2 What are the people in the park doing?

3 Where are Tadeu and his mom sitting?

4 What's Tadeu doing?

5 What kind of museum is Tadeu's dad visiting?

3 **Read Tadeu's email again and underline the uses of the present progressive.**

Writing

4 **Imagine you are on vacation. Write an email to a friend. Use the email in exercise 1 as a model. Include the following information:**

- where you are
- what you're doing
- what you're wearing
- what your friend is doing
- what the other people in the park are doing

Writing check

We use adjectives to describe people, things, and attractions. We can put the adjective after *be* or before a noun.

*It's **cold**!* *It's a **cool** park!*

Are there examples of adjectives in your email?

Great Clarendon Street, Oxford, OX2 6DP, United Kingdom

Oxford University Press is a department of the University of Oxford. It furthers the University's objective of excellence in research, scholarship, and education by publishing worldwide. Oxford is a registered trade mark of Oxford University Press in the UK and in certain other countries

First published in 2019
2023 2022 2021
10 9 8 7 6 5

ISBN: 978 0 19 482398 2 Student Book and Workbook
ISBN: 978 0 19 482406 4 Student Access Card
ISBN: 978 0 19 482448 4 Pack

Printed in China

This book is printed on paper from certified and well-managed sources

ACKNOWLEDGEMENTS

Back cover photograph: Oxford University Press building/David Fisher

Cover photographs reproduced with permission from: Getty Images (camping/Hero Images) & Shutterstock (Tokyo/ESB Professional), (skateboarder/yanik88).

Back cover photograph: Oxford University Press building/David Fisher.

Commissioned photography by: Graham Alder/MM Studios pp.10, 11, 19(ex5), 20, 21, 22(this is me), 34, 35, 44, 45, 58, 59, 68, 69, 82, 83, 92, 93, W4, W8, W10, W14, W16, W20, W22, W26, W28, W32, W34, W38, W39, W44, W46

Illustrations by: Adam Linely/Beehive Illustration pp.12 (ex1), 119; Addy Rivera Sonda/Astound US pp.9, 30, 54, 94, W47; Ebony Glenn/The Bright Agency pp.46; Ellie O'Shea/Advocate Art pp.26(ex5), 60, 61, 97, 121; Emily Balsley/The Bright Agency pp.7 (ex23), 70, 102; Emma Trithart/The Bright Agency pp.4, 36, W24, W36; Erika Meza/The Bright Agency pp.26, 37, W14; Gareth Llewhellin/The Bright Agency pp. W16, W29, W49; Geraldine Rodriguez/The Bright Agency pp.8; Lisa Hunt/The Bright Agency pp.43(ex3.4), W4, W41; Mark Duffin pp.84, 104; Martin Sanders/Beehive Illustration pp.115; Mark Ruffle pp. W9; Matthew Robson/NB Illustration pp.6, 47, 99

Video stills by: Oxford University Press pp.14, 24, 31, 38, 48, 55, 62, 72, 79, 86, 96, 103

The publisher would like to thank the following for permission to reproduce photographs: Alamy Stock Photo pp.42 (Marvel comics/Classic image), 56 (Popcorn maker/Shawn Hempel), 80 (Chocolate/fStop images), 109 (Magic lantern projector/John Henshall), 112 (Petrucio Ferreira/Avpics), 113 (Second hand market/Rachel Torres), W42 (Card payment/Blue Jeans Images); Getty Images pp.22 (Graduate/cornstock), 28 (Male student/Monkeybusinessimages), 28 (senior man/Jose Luis Pelaez Inc), 28 (teen girl/Bounce), 28 (middle aged man/Gary John Norman), 46 (shop assistant with cap/Westend61), 49 (Girl shopping/Tetra images), 49 (Diary/Patrycja Polechonska/EyeEm), 52 (Teenage girl/DGLimages), 52 (DJ/Rawpixel), 66 (Girl standing on road/Harpazo_hope), 66 (Teacher/Colorblind images), 86 (School boy/Wavebreakmedia), 86 (Smiling girl/Daisy-daisy), 91 (Boy looking at camera/kate_sept2004), 101 (group of teens/Caiaimage/Robert Daly), 102 (Tennis/Swell media), 113 (Vintage store/Trevoe Williams), W5 (girl with glasses/portra), W5 (boy with braces/pt images), W7 (Smiling boy/Jasper Cole), W12 (Confident boy/PeopleImages), W43 (Girl infront of blackboard/Weekend Images Inc.), W47 (School girl/Compassionate Eye Foundation); Oxford University Press pp.14 (girl with scarf/digital vision), 17 (boy against tree/suzanne tucker), 17 (girl smiling/michaeljung), 32 (brown envelope/shutterstock), 41 (clipboard/shutterstock), 43 (smiling teen boy/Carolin Voelker), 46 (japanese girl/aflo/corbis), 46 (teen boy/hello lovely/corbis), 49 (smiling boy/shutterstock), 72 (boy with headphones/sverre haugland/corbis), 72 (smiling girl/westend61 GmbH), 75 (family meal/gareth boden), 76 (american flag/yui), 80 (ice cream/viktor1), 80 (chocolate/alamy), 89 (smiling girl outside/westend61), 100 (tie/gareth boden), 103 (racing/getty), 104 (fabric rolls/shutterstock), 110 (world/shutterstock), 111 (spaghetti bolognese/shutterstock), 111 (beef medallions/shutterstock), 111 (pen/shutterstock), 111 (notebook/shutterstock), 116 (colourful hands/shutterstock), 116 (digital background/shutterstock), 118, 119, 120, 121 (stickers/ivector), 118, 119, 120, 121 (retro background/gorbash varvara), W12 (smiling girl/alamy), W23 (happy girl/gareth boden); Shutterstock pp.5 (birthday cakes/bonezboyz), 12 (flags/dikobraziy), 13 (big ben/lunamarina), 14 (friends sunset/dmitry molchanov), 14 (boy sitting on bench/africa studio), 15 (african american woman/pixelheadphoto digitalskillet), 15 (business woman/ldprod), 15 (emma stone/chelsea lauren), 15 (baby boy/africa studio), 16 (brother and sister/dragon images), 16 (teen with backpack/pixel-shot), 18 (dance vector/razym), 18 (teens dancing/africa studio), 18 (abstract background/audy39), 19 (skating couple/pressmaster), 19 (isaac hernandez, ballet dancer/ap photos/dario lopez-mills), 19 (maddie ziegler/startraks), 22 (senior couple/monkey business images), 22 (mixed race couple/andy dean photography), 22 (young children/phase4studios), 22 (hispanic couple/pixelheadphoto digitalskillet), 23 (girls playing soccer/fotostic), 24 (party background/gkrphoto), 24 (teenage girl/monkey business images), 24 (teen boy in park/africa studio), 25 (mardi gras parade/gts productions), 25 (new year fireworks/mroz), 25 (Macy's Thanksgiving/a katz), 27 (ed sheeran/brandon nagy), 28 (friends laughing/monkey business images), 28 (abstract background/elesey), 29 (boston red sox/brandon vincent), 32 (magazine/zeber), 32 (blank book/esb professional), 32 (toy cat/mr yanukit), 32 (patterend background/julia remonino), 32 (holiday photos/jakkapan), 38 (NYC/ventdusud), 39 (young woman/studioloco), 39 (teen boy/africa studio), 39 (buckingham palace/daliu), 39 (the white house/vacclav), 39 (burj al arab/romrodphoto), 39 (santiago/jose l stephens), 41 (brazilian house/ronaldo almeida), 41 (talking in hallway/brocreative), 42 (bedroom/photographee.eu), 42 (young girl/denis kuvaev), 42 (girlfriend friendship/rawpixel.com), 42 (shells/elena schweitzer), 42 (Smiling boy/Torgado), 42 (boomerang/richard peterson), 42 (bed/luisa leal photography), 48 (2 cent piece/mark_kostich), 48 (50 cent piece/somchai som), 48 (foreign currency/chrupka), 48 (us coins/vladimir wrangel), 48 (one dollar/nimon), 49 (shop assistant/dmitry kalinovsky), 49 (price tag/cameramannz), 49 (watch/olga popova), 49 (camera/taelove7), 49 (cap/food travel stockforlife), 51 (boy with dog/gladskikh tatiana), 51 (girl gaming/alena ozerova), 51 (mountain biking/travelview), 52 (asian woman/studiobythesea), 52 (teen boy/digital media pro), 52 (cooking sausages/oleg mikhaylov), 52 (volleyball/monkey business images), 53 (boy using laptop/monkey business images), 56 (laptop/zentilia), 56 (sports equipment/mike flippo), 56 (skateboard/homeart), 56 (bean bag/creativesunday), 56 (Games console/Ballball14), 56 (dorm room/radiokafka), 56 (pool table/hurst photo), 56 (bookshelf/paikong), 56 (projector screen/igorxiii), 56 (projector/sbko), 57 (skateboard icon/vectroisland), 57 (Laptop icon/Rauf Aliyev), 57 (book icon/davooda), 57 (camera icon/notbad), 57 (sunglasses vector/mirgunova), 57 (bicycle vector/ihorzigor), 62 (infographics/avian), 62 (Cinema tickets/Chinch), 62 (nintendo switch/wachiwit), 62 (apple and crisps/sarah2), 62 (High school student/Monkey business images), 62 (mixed race teen boy/monkey business images), 63 (girl on phone/pepsco studio), 63 (ice cream/virtu studio), 63 (camping/asukanda), 63 (pizza/africa studio), 63 (student on phone/ajr_photo), 65 (volleyball/andrey yurlov), 65 (fanned book/unuchko vernokia), 65 (breakdancing/chaoss), 65 (girl gaming/gorodenkoff), 65 (photographer/prostock-studio), 66 (school background/evgeny karandaev), 66 (school hallway/monkey business images), 66 (cafeteria/africa studio), 67 (happy boy/michaeljung), 72 (food background/stockcreations), 73 (girl with healthy food/rasulov), 75 (apple and milk/slosync), 75 (milk and cookies/alexkich), 75 (toast and coffee/tomophafan), 75 (breakfast/josef mohyla), 76 (peanut butter and jelly/baibaz), 76 (beef jerky/hong vo), 76 (grits and shrimp/africa studio), 76 (s'mores/olga miltsova), 77 (empanadas/noirchocolate), 79 (smiling friends/sergey novikov), 80 (vanilla pudding/new africa), 80 (roast chicken/maraze), 80 (lemon/jag_cz), 80 (ham/gita kulinitch studio), 80 (tuna/manolyto), 80 (oranges/markus mainka), 80 (peaches/beats1), 80 (fresh mint/luliia timofeeva), 86 (stadium/oleksii sidorov), 87 (sports vector/macrovector), 87 (soccer player/gino santa maria), 87 (social people/qvasimodo art), 88 (no swimming/alexey pushkin), 88 (karate suit/eatcute), 88 (runner/studio martin), 88 (bouncing ball/willeecole photography), 88 (hand up/m1shanya), 88 (aviator sunglasses/blan-k), 89 (smiling boy/africa studio), 89 (sports bag with equipment/djtaylor), 90 (Dancers/Africa studio), 90 (san francisco/sheila fitzgerald), 90 (cake/kath watson), 90 (balloons/jakkapan), 91 (smiling boy/samuel borges photography), 96 (shop assistant/monkey business images), 96 (woman shopping/odua images), 96 (clothes shop/fiphoto), 100 (stripe background/artefficient), 100 (male students/monkey business images), 100 (school cafeteria/lightfield studios), 100 (japanese students/kpg_payless), 101 (students leaving school/monkey business images), 102 (woman in ski outfit/max topchii), 102 (cyclists/jacek chabraszewski), 102 (sportsman/stockfour), 105 (man silhouette/anna rassadnikova), 106 (zayn malik/jstone), 106 (meghan markle/kathy hutchins), 106 (alicia vikander/kathy hutchins), 106 (sean paul/s_bukley), 106 (keanu reeves/s_bukley), 106 (blue and green background/leigh prather), 107 (the radford family/ken mckay/ITV), 107 (baby bottle/eatcute), 107 (bed/mary long), 107 (bread/elegant solution), 107 (pram/oleksandr derevianko), 107 (minibus/zhenyakot), 107 (shoes/okhristy), 107 (pasta/sunflowerr), 108 (yellow home/karamysh), 108 (japanese home/interoir blender 3d), 109 (marbles/luca pape), 109 (plastic spring/seika chujo), 109 (chess/will thomas), 110 (teen students/speedkingz), 110 (3 female students/creativa images), 111 (al mahara burj al arab resturant/dmitry birin), 112 (nilton santos stadium/donatas dabravolskas), 113 (thrift shop sign/rusty426), 114 (grandfather and grandson/dobo kristian), 114 (grandmother and grandson/photobac), 115 (volcano/budkov denis), 116 (hi-prosthetic arm/acreative), 116 (3d printer/enmyo), 117 (emiliano di cavalcanti/keystone pictures usa), 117 (Mario de Andrade 1916/historic collection), 117 (São Paulo Art Biennal, Pavilhão Ciccillo Matarazzo/gabriel pozzi), 117 (NYC modern art museum/anton_ivanov), 120 (peas/krishnat chavan), 120 (carrots/ansty), 120 (glass of water/nokhooknoi), 120 (salad/skalapendra), 120 (tin of tuna/pogorelova olga), 120 (soda can/altagracia art), 120 (cheese/alfmaler), 120 (eggs/makc), W4 (Ken Watanabe/Denis Makarenko), W4 (Melendi/Beatriz Zambrana), W4 (Gael Garcia/Ovidiu Hrubaru), W4 (Chris hemsworth/dfree), W4 (Katarina Johnson Thompson/Hayoung Jeon), W4 (Gisele/Marcelo Sayao), W5 (4 young teens/Monkey Business Images), W6 (african american girl/syda productions), W11 (Happy students with flag/Lightfield studios), W11 (Sydney Opera House/Adny Copeland), W11 (cats/ysbrand cosijn), W11 (Family/Monkey Business Images), W11 (Puppy/JStaley401), W13 (Zendaya Coleman/John Salangsang), W13 (Ross Lynch/Kathy Hutchins), W17 (House/Artazum), W18 (Abacus/Aris Suwanmalee), W18 (Bathroom icons/13ree.design), W18 (House icons/13ree.design), W19 (Luxury home/Breadmaker), W19 (Dorm room/Elnur), W19 (Hostel reception/Vereshchagin Dmitry), W22 (Rat/photolinc), W22 (Guitar/AlexMaster), W22 (Skateboard/fotoslaz), W22 (Puppy/oksana2010), W22 (Camera/taelove7), W22 (Maths/m.jrn), W23 (Phone/ptystockphoto), W23 (guitar/gelpi), W25 (Backpack/Perla Berant Wilder), W31 (Teen girl in bedroom/Pressmaster), W31 (Girl on phone/takayuki), W31 (Skateboarding/Josep Suria), W35 (Chocolate cake/Lesya Dolyuk), W37 (Market/Lungkit), W37 (Family/Syda Productions), W40 (Pile of balls/Lightspring), W42 (karate/fs stock), W43 (Playing piano/Marian Fil), W43 (Soccer/Monkey Business Images), W49 (Central Park/Songquan Deng).